RAV

"This story is compelling, intriguing and inspirational. The author takes us on her personal journey as she experiences life's challenges and triumphs. This book will resonate with the struggles of today's youth; and serve as a testimonial that no matter what we face in life, God's providence will lead us to our divine destiny. I highly recommend it. Once you pick it up, it is hard to put down; what a great read." ~ **Lori A. Keels**

"At a time when the moral fabric of our generation is eroding and young women no longer have virtuous role models, Candra Ward gives us an example of what a redeemed life looks like. In this powerful and captivating memoir, you will be inspired and you will laugh but mostly you will be grateful to know that God uses broken vessels whose hearts are towards Him to become mentors to the lost young girls of the world." ~ **Tracey Ward**

"Candra Ward's life is a light in the darkness that compels you to follow her journey and encourages you to continue your own. This book is an encouragement to the young and a reminder to the old and will stay in your mind long after you put it down. Her candidness is a gentle reminder that compels you to look into your own life and be freed by the testimony within ... this book needs to be rewarded." ~ **Angela McFadden**

"It's the secrets, emotions, and experiences we all had growing up. Riveting, colorful, honest, and identifiable Candra Wards coming of age story is an instant page turner. You feel her uncertainty, pain, and fear all while rooting for the moment she finds her strength and listens to the voice within. "I am so proud of her for doing this! God bless! ~ **Lauren Kingcade**

RAVE-REVIEWS

In My Mind

Candra Ward

COPYRIGHT NOTICE

No part of this book may be reproduced in any form without permission in writing from the author or publisher, except for the inclusion of brief quotations in a review.

In My Mind

© Copyright 2012 by Candra Ward

'Relax Your Mind' Publishing

All Rights Reserved Worldwide.

13-Digit ISBN: 978-1481087704

10-Digit ISBN: 1481087703

Library of Congress Control No. 2012935853

Cover Design by: Danielle Pettiford

Editor: Sological Underpennings

CONTACT THE AUTHOR

For more information about Candra Ward and *In My Mind*; individual orders; discounts for bulk-quantity purchases; audio and DVD products; information on speaking/seminars; booking the author to speak at your next event; or other reason; please contact the author online at:

www.CandraWard.com

Dedication

To my mother, Sharon Justice.
(The strongest woman I know and love.)

To all those who suffer in silence.

Acknowledgment

Amir, my son, you are a great man that God has made; continue to trust Him; I love you. Mom thanks for always being there, I love you. Grand mom you are a great and strong woman, I love you. McKee my brother, thank you for serving our country and being an awesome brother, I love you. Mario, my love, thank you for sticking it out with me and loving me for me, I love you. Dad thank you for being there when every phone call was made, I love you. Vinny thank you for being the best little sister, I love you. Gilbert Coleman thank you for being my spiritual father and leading me in the right direction, I love you. Deborah Coleman thank you for being my friend and second mom and accepting me for me, I love you. Pat Betters thank you for tremendously helping me in my journey, you are a great woman, I love you. To my aunts and uncle, Candra, Chrissy, Clark, thanks for being there when I needed you, I love you. To the gang, my niece and nephews; Jael, Jair, Tre, McKee, I enjoyed watching you grow, I love you. Tracey Ward you hold a special place in my heart, I love you. To the other crew, my cousins; Amber, Briana, Anton, Anya, I always enjoyed our Christmas Eve's together, I love you. Michelle Albright, thank you for loving me and Amir and keeping us a part of the family, I love you. My god-sisters Helena, Sparkle, and Maleka, I had fun growing up with you guys, I love you. Angela McFadden I truly appreciate your friendship, you have been there for me through thick and thin, I love you. Anitria Odum, you have been an awesome and true friend, thanks for listening to every word, I love you. To the rest of my cousins, sisters, nieces, nephews, brother, and Brenda Fain, thank you for our every moment together, I love you. All of my mentees throughout the years, you are amazing, you are great, you are a blessing and I believe in you, I love you. And last but not least, if it was not for you guys, I would not have been able to fulfill my dreams properly: my clients. You have been a true blessing to my life by supporting me through the good and bad times, I love you.

Introduction

Achieving fulfillment is a natural human desire. Numerous people wander around aimlessly trying to figure out why they feel so empty inside. Some try to fill their lives with people, relationships, money, possessions, drinking, drugs, status, partying, sex, and activities that are not good for them, while others try to be fulfilled by religion, church attendance, Easter Sunday, New Year's resolutions, going to the altar every week, having a ministry title, and praying the longest prayers.

None of those things bring ultimate fulfillment. Our souls seek and enjoy temporary pleasures, while our spirits are longing for something much deeper.

Many people don't actually know what they are looking for. It can be very frustrating at times because they want to know their meaning and purpose in life instead of just existing. Not knowing that could be enough to cause someone to go into a deep depression or even contemplate suicide.

Fulfillment is the energy of life. It is what makes people smile and feel alive. According to research, you are physically, mentally, and emotionally healthier when you are fulfilled.

In my years I have come across many women who look great on the outside but lack tremendously on the inside. The female gender has many hats to wear. We have to keep going and be the

IN MY MIND

strength of the house no matter what. We get the kids off to school while checking our bank accounts to make sure we have enough money to pay a few bills so the lights can stay on – all while we are suffering inside.

May I please share with you that everything you go through is not in vain? You are being watched and caressed from above. Trust me when I tell you that low self-esteem, insecurity, fear, inferiority, depression, confusion, and rejection will cease once you become fulfilled.

Come and take a little journey with me as I share my life's ups and downs with you. As you read, make sure your heart is open and your mind is clear. See you in freedom!

Prologue

Sitting here on the side of my bed
All kinds of thoughts running through my head
Hoping and praying they will subside
If not, I know how to run and hide
From all of the stress, strain, hurt and worry
Why does everything have to be in a hurry?
I cannot understand these responsibilities, heartaches,
and pressures of life
Whenever I turn around there is always strife.
Between love, work, and personal affairs
It really doesn't matter because no one cares
All I ask for is respect, honesty, and love,

IN MY MIND

They don't know how to give it so I'll get it from above

Oh God! Please deliver me from these feelings

of hurt and pain

What in the world is happening, am I going insane?

Hands on my head, head on my knees,

Screaming inside, please! Please!

Anxiety and anguish pouring from my soul,

Hoping something would fill this open hole

Oh how badly I want something and it seems so far away

All I want is to be held and know that everything is okay Please

help me to understand your perfect way

And keep me from my folly, so I don't stray

When is there ever going to be time for myself?

Somehow I continue to be put on a shelf

I think I'm blessed; well at least that's what they say,

I don't have a choice but to hustle from day to day

That's how it seems to regularly work with me,

While the illusions are portraying "blessings not for free"

There was a time when joy abided and anger subsided,

Happiness was abound, and sadness not found

PROLOGUE

Love awakened, but quickly shaken

Situations tried stealing my peace,

Bleeding, scars, no release,

Tension was building a security wall,

That didn't last; it was destined to fall

He loves me too much to allow me to stay that way,

All He asks is that I worship and pray,

I definitely will have those ups and downs,

I will grow from them, as crazy as it sounds

My life's maturity level is based on trials and tribulations,

After overcoming a few I got the revelation

Now I'm on the road to great success,

I praise God for the setbacks, downfalls, and mess

My character in Him will be stronger than ever,

Remember one thing; never say never.

Contents

Dedication

Acknowledgment

Introduction

Prologue

1: Risky ... *1*

2: Unprotected ... *27*

3: Distorted ... *39*

4: Preparations ... *51*

5: Faith ... *61*

6: Guarded ... *77*

7: Attainable ... *83*

8: Self Esteem ... *97*

9: Prayerful ... *103*

10: Enjoyment ... *113*

11: Challenging ... *139*

12: Protected ... *151*

13: Swayed ... *161*

14: Heartbroken ... *171*

15: Family ... *177*

16: Loved ... *187*

17: Conviction ... *197*

18: Together ... *205*

19: Journey ... *215*

20: Freedom ... *225*

Words Of Encouragement

Personal Prayer To God

Scriptures For Life

About The Author

Book Club Guide

1

Risky

"I gotta get this abortion! It's my only option. I cannot have this baby, let alone have two children." My girlfriend Nikki on the other line just listened to me as I declared woe in her ear. She stayed on the phone until I got myself together. Before we hung up my decision was settled, along with her agreement.

I spent a day contemplating how I was going to get the money to have it done. I heard it cost about three hundred dollars, and I needed that in my hands quickly, before I made the appointment. I didn't want to lie to my parents but I couldn't come to grips with telling them the truth. So in desperation I called my dad and told him I needed money for books. I told him we were getting new textbooks in school and I needed it by Monday of the following week. When he asked me how much, I said one hundred and fifty dollars. I already had the rest of the money saved up from doing hair.

The next morning I called Planned Parenthood to make an appointment. As soon as the receptionist picked up the phone, I paused for a moment; fear gripped me. After her second hello, I finally opened my mouth and asked if I could schedule an appointment. She started going through a series of questions. First, she asked me how many weeks I was, and what was my age. I told her that I was sixteen and I did not know how far along I was. She told me to come in on Friday at eight thirty in the morning, and not to eat or drink anything before I arrived. She also informed me that it would be wise to have someone accompany me; I would be drowsy after the procedure.

The shocking part to me was it being strictly confidential. My parents didn't have to know, even though I was underage. I hung up the phone feeling somewhat frightened. I never had anything seriously done to my body before other than giving birth to my son. Reality then hit me: I could actually die from this unnatural procedure. There would be a life forcefully sucked out of me against its will. But I had to do it.

Friday seemed like it took forever to come. I got up that morning, took my shower, got dressed and started getting my son Amir together, who was five months old at the time. I bathed, fed, and dressed him, and we were out the door on our way to the babysitter's house. Once we got there and he was situated, I kissed him and headed out for the bus. The bus was sitting right on the corner, making it perfect to arrive at the abortion clinic on time. I arrived just one minute shy of eight thirty. Nikki was standing outside the building waiting for me. Walking to the front door of the bus seemed like the longest walk I ever experienced. The doors opened, I got off, smiled at Nikki, then we entered the building. There was a lady with a stern disposition sitting at the front desk, and about a half dozen teen girls sitting in the waiting room. Some were waiting to be seen, and some were there for support, like my friend.

"Candra Ward" the lady at the front desk yelled out loud enough for everyone outside to hear. "Come over please." I got up with a little hesitation and wandered my way over to the desk. She asked me to sign a few papers then have a seat and wait for my name to be called. About thirty minutes later she called me and told me to follow her as she started walking up a flight of stairs that resembled the house of horrors because it was dark and the stairs seemed to be never ending. She instructed me to take my clothes off, put one of those backwards capes on, and lie down on the cold table. My eyes were closed at first, but upon opening them, I looked up and saw

CHAPTER 1 – RISKY

pictures of unborn babies. Immediately my mind began to rehearse all of the things that could possibly go wrong.

The doctor knocked on the door and asked if it was okay if he came in. I answered "yes" with a shy pitch to my voice. He came in, introduced himself and asked if he could do a quick examination to determine how far along I was. When he finished he sat on his stool and asked me a few questions. He asked if I have been pregnant before, and if yes, do I have any children. I told him yes to both, and informed him of my son. Then he asked me when my last menstrual cycle was. After that, he asked me an array of questions about STDs, drinking, smoking, and family history. He then told me to put my feet in the stirrups and just relax.

As I laid there and stared at those pictures on the ceiling, I tried to convince myself that I was doing the right thing. Once the doctor finished jotting things on his notepad, he turned to me and told me that I was four to five weeks pregnant. He asked me if I still wanted to go forth with the procedure, and my response was "yes." He then explained two different types of anesthetics that were available to me. One was local, where I would be awake, but in and out of grogginess and feel no pain. The other method would put me to sleep and I would awaken shortly after the procedure was done. I chose the local because I didn't want to take any chances.

In the midst of my fear and anxiety I couldn't help but wonder what the sex of the fetus was, and what it would look like. My wondering was not impressive enough to make me want to keep it. All of my selfish thinking and fear prohibited me from seeing anything else.

"Candra, you will feel a little pressure," the doctor said, after swabbing my arm and thigh with alcohol. I gritted my teeth and held my lips together with my eyes closed while the needles were going in. The medicine started working about three minutes later. I started to feel a little silly and out of it, but still coherent. Once the bottom half of my body started getting numb, two nurses rolled in a big machine. They put on gloves and started to pass instruments to each other.

IN MY MIND

I could slightly see and hear some of the things that were going on, but I was so out of it that even if I wanted to change my mind, it would have been difficult because I couldn't lift my head or mutter a word. The medicine had me very lethargic. All of a sudden I heard a loud blasting noise that sounded like a vacuum cleaner, but on super charge. Then I heard suction and sucking noises from the machine. It felt abnormal just knowing those noises came from a life passing through me.

"Okay Candra, you can get up now and put your clothes on, a nurse will be back in to get you." I laid there for a minute trying to get myself together. Then I staggered up off the table to get dressed. After I got my last sock on, the nurse came in and carried my sneakers for me while we walked to another room; there I was given graham crackers and apple juice. They wanted me to have something on my stomach before I left so my body could recharge from the trauma and also for the nausea. I sat there for at least a half hour for safety precautions. After sitting for a while Nikki came in and helped me up and told me to come. It was about one o' clock in the afternoon by now. I had just enough time to pick my son up from the babysitter's early, and also kill some time downtown before I had to be home from school without any questions being asked.

When I got home I was so exhausted. I got the baby a bottle and plopped right down on the bed. I had to make up something to explain my debilitated state. I told my mother I wasn't feeling well and I needed to lie down. I was so drained that night that my mom took the baby for me, and cared for him so I could rest.

Waking up was a bit painful. My entire insides were hurting. I had a headache from the medicine and was extremely fatigued.

It hurt to even throw my legs down off of the bed. In spite of my pain I got up, got myself and the baby together and headed out the door on my way to school. After I dropped him off at the sitter's I hopped on the train. All I kept rehearsing in my head was "what if my mom found out?" I quickly blocked that thought out by saying "I got this, I got everything under control!" My stop was coming up next. I grabbed my bag and jumped up, trying not to get caught in the mad morning rush of people getting off and crashing against

CHAPTER 1 – RISKY

the ones trying to get on. Once I made it off I started walking fast because I hated to be late. I had a clean record of being on time and I didn't want to mess that up. My school catered to pregnant girls and girls who had already given birth. My mother found it after learning that I was pregnant with Amir. She felt that my other high school was too far and she didn't want me traveling that distance while being pregnant. Also once I had the baby, I would have been dragging him out too early, so she kept us close. Philadelphia is huge and it took me one and a half hours to get to the old school by bus and train combined. My new school only took thirty minutes to get to by train.

The maternity school consisted of girls who were from the ages of twelve to nineteen years old. One girl was thirteen, pregnant with twins and she already had a baby. Some girls there were pregnant for the first time, and some had been pregnant multiple times. A few of them were scared to death and some couldn't wait to give birth. They thought that having a baby would make them and their boyfriends closer. Some, like me, just wanted to finish school.

Living on the edge was what I did, it was who I was – so I thought. I can go all the way back starting from the age of twelve at 5' 10" in height, and wearing a size eleven and a half shoe. I was very self-conscious of my height. I hated being tall with big flat feet. I would get teased by family, friends, and classmates, and that haunted me. Because I had severe flat arches, I had to get specially made orthotics to fit in my shoes so they wouldn't continue to turn over on the sides. Every time my mom would take me shoe shopping I would try on shoes that were too small and tell her they fit just so my feet could look smaller.

I was very quiet and shy at times. I hated for people to look directly at me because it made me uncomfortable. But then I had my moments where I was silly, loud, and loved to have fun. This was around the age where interest in boys started to discretely creep into my life. Before that I was into writing poems, plays, and creating my own customized books on construction paper, along with reading anything I could get my hands on. I also got enjoyment from dancing, so I would get my friends from my neighborhood and put together a dance group and make up routines- of course I was the leader. We had some serious ones down pat, especially when it came to songs from the singing group DeBarge, and old school Hip Hop.

My favorite thing that I enjoyed out of all of my other interests that I did almost every day for hours at a time was doing my hair-it put me at peace when I did it. I loved my mind being challenged and being creative. I would go to school with a different hairstyle every day. That is how I started gaining clients at such a young age because people would see my hair and want me to do theirs. I inherited a lot of my talents from my mom, except the hairstyling. She couldn't even plait or put ponytails in but she could write a mean play, poem or anything you needed her to do when it came to putting anything literary together.

In addition to that I had my dolls that I adored, especially Crystal who I named after one of my favorite aunts. She was the size of a four or five month old baby. I received her as a Christmas gift one year from my mom and she never left my side. I enjoyed having someone to depend on me. I would dress her up and wrap her in receiving blankets every time we would go out. She was who I talked to most of the time when I was home because my brother McKee was away at school and my mom and stepfather would come home from work and either be tired or had to do something concerning church.

I loved those times when my mom finally settled in and got her munchies to go sit on the front porch or go to her bedroom to watch T.V. because I would go and plop down right there and watch the shows with her. My mom did the best she could to keep me busy with certain activities. She had me in dance classes at Philadanco Dance Company, and I would sometimes be involved in little fashion shows here and there either with my school or church. I would also hang out with her and her friends when they went to the malls and out on day trips on the weekends. I lacked a little social stimulation by being the only child with adults all of the time because most of her friends did not have children. If they did, the kids were much older than me. I never really had a problem being by myself, but it

CHAPTER 1 – RISKY

did become pretty lonely at times. There were some weekends that I spent at some of my classmates' houses, but during the week was very boring.

I had a lot of time to myself which allowed my mind to wander. I remember one day I was standing in front of the mirror looking at myself and made the decision to become rebellious. There was no real strenuous thought involved, just action. As I was staring at myself all I could think was "I am tired of being talked at and not talked to." At that time my stepfather had been in my life since I was three years old. He could be very stern and anal at times which made me extremely on edge, especially when it came to touching things. He was the type of man that loved his gadgets. Every week he came in the house with something new. He didn't want anyone near his possessions especially me. He would call me clumsy Annie because he said that I broke everything that I touched. So I lived on egg shells most of the time.

My stepfather was a hardworking man who made sure that my mother, brother and I were taken care of and had a roof over our heads. He made a pretty good living as a carpenter and a business man. He could create something by just looking at it. He actually built up the house we lived in. It was a condemned house that the city owned and they practically gave it to him for free. It had just about burned down years prior from a horrible fire. It was missing most of its inside steps, half of its roof, all of its piping, and was trashed by squatters with graffiti inside and out on every wall available. He transformed all of that into a beautiful home for us to live in. Whatever he put his hands to he did it well because he was so meticulous.

He was also very strict and his tone could be aggressive at times. I was never allowed to have a key to the house; he seemed to question every move I made and I felt like I couldn't do anything right. He would ask "why did you ring the doorbell like that?" or "why did you put the fork down like that?" His demeanor and personality hardened me over the years causing me to create a brick wall within myself which became a continual defense that I used in most relationships and interactions with people. As I was growing

IN MY MIND

up, this wall manifested as rebellion. That rebellion was a path that led straight to destructive patterns and behaviors: broken virginity, hooking school, lying, and being sneaky. In my mind it seemed normal and actually felt okay after a while. It was fun, adventurous, and an escape. My conscience was seared as I learned how to master putting disappointments and pain aside; I became numb to certain emotions.

The rebellion really began to come out one night when one of my girlfriends from my aunt Regina's neighborhood came over and spent the night at my house. We were in my kitchen at twelve o' clock in the morning, sneaking and playing on the phone. She knew about this dating service called The Party Line, where you could call in and listen to prompts from different guys. You could push number one if you wanted someone age eighteen to twenty one, or number two to get someone twenty two to twenty five and so on. Of course my girlfriend and I pushed number one and started listening to recorded messages from guys describing themselves and sharing their interests. We picked two of them, got their numbers and called. I ended up talking to both but only met up with one the following week. I would hang out at my aunt's house quite a bit which was a ten minute walk around the corner from my house. Because she thought I was over my girlfriend's house, she didn't check on me for hours so I went to visit the guy for the first time. My girlfriend went along with me. Once we got there he told me he was seventeen, not eighteen like he said on The Party Line. I didn't tell him that I was only twelve. Although he had a real calm demeanor, there was something different about him that I could not put my finger on. My girlfriend and I stayed over his house for about an hour. While we were leaving he told me to call him. I was not allowed to give my number out to boys; therefore I had to do the contacting. I called him later on that day and he wanted to see me again. I then planned another trip over his house about four days later, but this time alone. This was my first time ever hooking school. This was totally out of character for me because I was always the good girl. This time, that was not the case, I truly went against the grain. It only took that one time of hooking and it became a

CHAPTER 1 – RISKY

repeated offense. I spaced my hooking out so I could still keep up my grades. It became easier, and I got wiser. I figured out how to catch the call from my school's machine reporting that I was absent. They would normally call around six or seven at night when they thought that parents should be home from work. I would hang out around the kitchen where the phone was and watch T.V. As soon as I heard the phone begin to even whimper a ring I jumped up, picked the phone up before anyone else could get to it, and exclaimed that it was a wrong number.

The first day I visited him alone was the day that changed my life. All I could think to myself after I left his house was, facing my mother, knowing that I just had sex for the first time and hoping she didn't notice that I was shaking from fear and discomfort.

It didn't take long for me to get the hang of skipping school. I was so enamored by the self-proclaimed freedom. After about a year of seeing that guy, it broke off. Right after that, there was someone new. I was thirteen and a little more experienced by now. There was more hooking and more sex that took place. This new guy was fifteen and we were so-called "in love" until I found out he had a baby. I didn't know about his child until we were six months into the relationship. I met him through my cousins which were not the best influence. I didn't have any family members or siblings my age, so my mom would let me visit them frequently, and sometimes spend weekends over their house. I don't believe she knew much of what was going on in that household. She believed it was a safe environment and that I would be taken care of. Little did she know there was some of everything going on there. They were not blood related to me. They were my brother's relatives on his father's side of the family but they accepted me as one of them anyway which made us pretty close. I had a very tight bond with one of them who was a little older than me. He was like a big brother; always looking out for me. He was the good guy who never smoked or drank; he was just plain old lazy and trouble free. My other cousin who was close to my age was a little fast with the guys, and always getting into trouble. She was a very smart and pretty girl, just always into something. I remember when we were ten years old, she would take her mother's cigarettes and go into the bathroom and smoke until a few years later when her mom allowed her to smoke with her. Her mother's motto was "I rather she smokes with me, than behind my back." There was always some sort of chaos which I was never a part of: I just watched. I remember a time being over there and everyone disappeared. I went upstairs, opened the back bedroom door, and there was everyone sitting around a small table with a white substance on it. It was my cousin, one of my aunts and two of her friends. I kindly shut the door and went downstairs and waited until my mom picked me up. I didn't tell my mother because I didn't want to stop going over there. Even though I didn't participate in everything that went on, I still had fun in the neighborhood. I made friends and still enjoyed hanging out with everyone. I allowed the freedom and liberty that I experienced to blind me from the dangerous surroundings I was in while being there.

Good morals kept spiraling. People that met me for the first time and talked with me had no clue of my lifestyle. I outwardly carried myself very mannerly. I didn't even know how to use curse words correctly.

I did have a little temper but it really didn't start to flare or get out of control until I met this new guy that lived in my aunt's neighborhood. He was the cutie of the block: dark chocolate, bow legged, white teeth, wavy hair, and dimples. All the girls were falling over him and he picked me, wow! He was a roughneck with a soft side. There was also a dark side that came along. Within those five months we had sex twice, and in conjunction with that was verbal and physical abuse. I ended that quickly. I found out that he was sleeping with a lot of other girls in the neighborhood. That information was told to me by a guy who lived in the area who was quite a bit older than me; he was in his twenties and was just trying to get in my pants. I was so naive and hurt from what I heard that I ended up at his house and had sex with him.

It seemed like I had a lot of freedom at home, but not really. In my mom's eyes she thought I was being supervised thoroughly by whom she left me with. What she didn't know was me and my friends knew how to challenge the system of obedience. My friend

CHAPTER 1 – RISKY

Nikki and I were really close. I enjoyed hanging out at her house because she had a big family and they were really fun when they all got together. I enjoyed her friendship because we balanced each other out. She knew how to get me to reason when I needed it and I knew how to get her to do the same. We could look at something and both know what we were thinking and bust out laughing. She was shorter than me with a very fair complexion and beautiful dark curly hair that I used as practice when I wanted to try a new style. We were best friends since seventh grade. One day we were at her house and we decided to go to the movies. I didn't have any sexy clothes to wear, so she let me borrow a pair of jeans and a long sleeve belly shirt. After we got dressed, we were on our way out the door, and her mother told us to be back by nine thirty. As we were walking to catch the train, all kinds of cars with older men and young guys were stopping and beeping at us. We were enjoying every bit of the attention. After we got onto the train, we missed our stop, so we got off at the next one. As we were walking towards the movie theatre, there was a group of guys that stopped us, asked us our names, and wanted our phone numbers. One of the guys who seemed to be between the ages of nineteen and twenty one - the leader of the group - chose me and said he liked dark skinned girls because they were his thing. One of the other guys chose Nikki, and we all exchanged phone numbers. Both she and I got distracted from going to see our movie, and accepted their offer to go to the arcade, take some pictures, and play a couple of games. While I was playing Ms. Pacman, this guy bumped into me and walked off. I felt my back pocket for my twenty dollar bill and realized it was gone. I informed the guy that I just met, that my money was stolen. He went looking for the guy, found him, got in his face, and demanded that I get my money back. The guy kept lying until he was about to get hit, and finally he pulled money out of his pocket, which was only ten dollars. The guy that was interested in me gave me ten dollars of his own money so I would have my entire twenty dollars back. I instantly thought "wow, he's really into me."

Because we missed our movie, and spent a great amount of time in the arcade, we decided to head back to Nikki's house. While we were walking, the guy tried to kiss me and I moved. Then he gave me a shirt that he stole out of the mall. I knew right then that I was way out of character. I never took or received any stolen property before, but because I was caught up in the attention and his protectiveness of me back at the arcade, I took it. He told me that he got his young boys to steal clothes, glasses, jewelry and sneakers. I knew I was making a big mistake when I took the shirt, but it gave me a rush.

The guys rode all the way with us to my girlfriend Nikki's stop so we could get there safely. They got off the train, walked us halfway, and then turned back around and left.

We were going to sneak out that night around two o'clock in the morning, but a divine intervention overtook Nikki. She said she had a feeling that something bad was going to happen if we went out so we stayed in and went to sleep instead. The next morning we got up and got dressed because my mom and stepfather were coming to pick us up for church. When we made it to church we were supposed to go to Sunday school, but we snuck right out and went to McDonald's across the street. That's where a lot of the church kids hung out when their parents thought they were in Sunday school. We had a routine. We knew how to blend back into the crowd once church let out. We would have 'lookouts' to check to see if church let out early, by watching for the doors to open. I believed in God, but there was just a hold over me that I couldn't seem to shake. I had no cares or fear of consequences and I never gave danger or obedience second thought.

We dropped Nikki off at her house after church. Once we got home, my stepfather started dinner, and I went to my room, shut the door, and lay across my bed while I waited. As soon as dinner was ready I was called downstairs to eat. Even though there was always tension between my stepfather and I, we still came together to eat dinner at the table every night which I appreciated. I may have been quiet most of the times and didn't say much-but I was there. After we ate, I washed the dishes and went back upstairs to lie down. About an hour later my phone rang. I had my own phone in my room by now, and paid my own bill from the money I made doing hair. I picked the phone up and it was the guy I met when

CHAPTER 1 – RISKY

Nikki and I were downtown, about to go the movies. We talked for twenty minutes, and then he told me to call him back around 12:30 in the morning. I was not allowed to be on the phone after 11:00 pm, so I was going to sneak out and go around the corner and use the payphone in front of the neighborhood bar. I didn't have a good feeling about it, so I figured that I would just wait until the next day to talk to him.

The next morning I asked my mom if I could go around the corner to my aunt Regina's house. While I was there I used her phone to call the guy back from the night before. He told me where he lived and asked if I could come over. I didn't want to go alone so I took my two god-sisters with me. One was a year younger than me and her sister was ten months old. His house was about a 30 minute walk from my aunt's house. The oldest god sister and I took turns pushing the stroller so we could get there and get back. Once we arrived at his house, he asked us to come in for a minute while he finished getting dressed. We went in and sat on the couch. I wasn't sure who else lived there but it hardly had any furniture in it which made it kind of empty and it was really quiet. It looked as though he lived there alone but I knew someone else may have lived there with him because it had different pictures and objects lying around as if they belonged to a grandmother or something. He asked me to come upstairs before my god-sisters and I left because he wanted to show me a pair of glasses and some clothes he had. I was a little hesitant but I went anyway. As soon as I got upstairs he started flirting with me then shut his bedroom door and begged me for sex. I told him no and he called himself being gentle but he had a firm grip on me. I didn't want to make any noise because I saw he had a gun in his pants pocket. My god-sisters were downstairs waiting for me, and I did not want to frighten them. I also wanted them to stay safe, so I went along with what he wanted me to do. While he was taking my pants off against my will he was trying to be very nice in the process like nothing was wrong. I resisted him but then he took his gun out of his pants pocket and laid it on the nightstand next to the bed. He stood up, put protection on and laid back down, then forced himself on me in a gentle way, still talking sweetly in my ear.

IN MY MIND

He didn't even care that my menstrual was on. After he was done, he helped me up, rubbed my face and gave me a pair of glasses. I had tears in my eyes, and was so disgusted that I wanted to throw up. I took the glasses because I was scared not to. I didn't want to cause any rift; I just wanted to leave peacefully. I got my clothes on and went downstairs very disturbed, but I did not want to alarm or scare my god-sisters so I kept my composure. We walked back to my aunt's house very quietly. I never told anyone about it because I was too afraid. First of all I wasn't supposed to be there, and secondly, I didn't know what he would do.

I started dodging his phone calls after that. He didn't know where I lived but he knew this lady that I associated with. She was in her late twenties and she lived around the corner from my aunt Regina's house, and had four kids. She liked hanging out with people much younger than her because she had the mentality of a teenager. He communicated through her to get to me. Every time he would call her and leave a message, she would come and tell me. She got tired of relaying messages, so she stopped answering his calls. Then one day he showed up unannounced at her door looking for me. He wanted the glasses back that he gave me. And he wanted them back in person. He did not want me to leave them with her because he knew her boyfriend, and he knew that he would steal them. I couldn't take my chances of them getting stolen; then he really would come looking for me. His main concern was his two hundred dollar glasses, and my main concern was getting them to him so he could leave me alone. I didn't know how else to get them to him but through her. Somehow, he got the main number to my house and my stepfather picked up. He told him in this nice calm voice that I had his glasses and he was just trying to get them back. My stepfather didn't know the severity of the situation, so without concern he just told me to give them back. He thought it was just a boy at school or something. So I ended up calling the guy and telling him to meet me around the woman's house that we both knew, and I would give them to him personally. Because I did not want to see his face, I hurried around to her house and gave her the glasses, telling her to hide them from her boyfriend, and give

CHAPTER 1 – RISKY

them to the guy when he comes. When he got to her house a couple of hours later; he retrieved the glasses. After that whole ordeal was done, days later he tried calling me a few times. He would also leave messages with her to tell me how sorry he was, and to ask if we could talk. Of course that was never entertained. After a few weeks of him stalking me, it was finally over. About five months after that, I saw him at the mall but he didn't see me. I was there with my mother and saw him walking out of a store. I walked the opposite direction hoping and praying that he wouldn't notice me.

About a month later I got involved with this other guy named Rico who was five years older than me. I actually met him before "the stalker" situation. We had eyes for each other but it was nothing serious. He started coming around, sitting with me on my aunt's steps, walking me halfway home, but never asked or pressured me for sex. Then out of nowhere he disappeared for a while, at least for quite a few months. I didn't see or hear anything from him the entire time. He started to slip out of my mind, but I would still think about him every now and then.

School was starting in a few days and I couldn't believe I would be in high school. I was really excited. My mother sent me to a pre-high school summer program beforehand so I could get acquainted with the school and some of the teachers. I also received a three hundred and fifty dollar stipend for completing the program. I ended up meeting really good people and we all became very close. We would get together and go downtown sometimes after our day was over from the program. There was a guy who hung out with us, and he was the only male in our group. He wanted to be a girl extremely bad. I felt sorry for him because he would get teased viciously. He wore everything but skirts. He would curl his hair in loose curls, and put on makeup. He ended up dropping out of the program, and we never saw him again.

During and after the program I did calm down for a while. Guys were not on my mind as much anymore. I even forgot about the guy Rico that suddenly disappeared. I really started to become focused, and was enjoying my new friends. I did well for a while but the captain of the football team started giving me the eye. He was a

IN MY MIND

senior and he was fine! He was tall with a caramel complexion, curly hair, big broad shoulders, and had his mack game right. He had that swag where he didn't have to say much to a girl, somehow her feet would just magically whisk across the room over to him. So when he started flirting with me, I responded. My friends and I stayed after school for some of the football games, and I would wait to talk with him afterwards. Then our flirting turned into the exchange of phone numbers. We talked every day for about a month, but after that everything came to a halt.

This particular day my girlfriend Lisa and I wanted to go downtown to a festival that was given once a year. We left her house, hopped on the train, and started on our way. I had on a pair of brand new 14 carat gold swirl earrings that I purchased with the money I saved from allowance and doing hair. Back in those days we would take one off when we walked the streets or rode the trains so a thief wouldn't get tempted; unfortunately I forgot. About ten minutes into our train ride, a guy came up from behind and snatched my earrings out of my ear and walked off the train. I was so distraught because I never got robbed before, so I didn't want to go to the festival anymore. Lisa understood, so we ended up getting off of the train and turning around to go home. While we were waiting for the train to come, my pager went off, and it was the captain of the football team. My mood suddenly lifted, and I found a payphone on the platform and called him back. He wanted to know if we could ride to his neighborhood to see him since we were already out. I asked Lisa and she was cool with it. So we got back on the train and rode to the north part of the city. When we reached his stop, he was standing there waiting for us. We got off and walked with him back to his house. When we walked into the house it looked liked he had a large family because there were a lot of people just sitting around. We followed him into the kitchen and he offered both of us something to drink. We then started laughing and joking around, and a few moments later he asked me to come to the basement steps because he wanted to ask me something. I didn't think nothing of it because there were so many people around that nothing crazy even crossed my mind. When we got on the staircase he shut the

CHAPTER 1 – RISKY

door and asked me for a kiss. I figured 'no problem we have been talking on the phone for a month, I could do that.' Then in the midst of us kissing he pulled his penis out. I was so agitated by it, because I didn't go there for that, I honestly went just to see him. So I came back upstairs and told Lisa I was ready to go. Then my woes about my stolen earrings came back. I asked him to walk us back to the train because by this time it was dark outside. That's when the drama began. On our way to the train, two girls were screaming at the top of their lungs. They were a block behind us. Lisa and I had no idea that they were screaming at him until they got a little closer. His face looked like he saw a ghost. It ended up being his girlfriend that I knew nothing about. It didn't help that we were not in the best part of town. She started walking towards us with a forty ounce bottle of beer in her hand in aiming position. She threw it at him and started cussing and fussing. The other girl that was with her looked like a man; she was just as big as him. She had to be at least six foot two and two hundred thirty pounds of all muscle with a cigarette behind her ear. They looked like grown women. Lisa and I were scared, but we didn't show it, we just kept walking our steady pace and left him. His girlfriend started crying hysterically asking him why was he doing this to her. They called us quite a few choice words but that didn't bother me, I was trying to get home safely. We couldn't tell if they had weapons or not. We got on the train, sat down and let out a big sigh of relief. Right before the doors was about to close, guessing who got on? His girlfriend and her manly friend. They asked us which one of us was with him. I told them it was me. Then out of nowhere she said to me, "Watch out for dogs like him. You didn't know; I'm not upset with you," I was stunned! I expected a totally different outcome.

When I got back to school I saw him and he didn't even speak to me. He acted as if nothing ever happened. As a matter of fact, he tried to flip it on me like I disgusted him when he saw me. It didn't matter anyway; I was glad that I didn't get caught up in his drama. He was quickly tossed out of my memory bank.

Every day after school I had to go to my aunt Regina's house, since my stepfather didn't allow me to have a key to the house. I was the only ninth grader going to a babysitter. One day after school I was sitting on my aunt's steps waiting for my mom to pick me up, and the guy Rico that disappeared a while back, reappeared. He came over, gave me this big bear hug, and looked happy to see me. I pushed him back and asked him where he had been. He said that it was a long story. He then explained that he had to go into hiding for a while because he got into some trouble. He said that he needed to be out of sight for some time until everything died down. Then he proceeded with, "I thought about you the whole time I was gone." We sat on the steps for a while and talked, and in the midst of our conversation I just randomly started telling him about the time when my mother and I were coming home from the mall and about to turn the corner to our street, and we got caught in the middle of crossfire. I told him that we had to duck down in the car because there was about fifteen or twenty guys running down the street shooting by the schoolyard. He looked at me and said, "I was there." My mouth dropped because he looked so innocent and well-mannered along with his outspoken and jokester personality. With me knowing all of that, it still didn't turn me off. There was something different about him.

Time went on and we were spending more and more time together. This wasn't the same like all the rest; we didn't have sex right away. He seemed to really just be into me. He broke his neck to see me every chance he could get. I loved it because I was into him just the same. He was eighteen, and at the time I was only fourteen in the ninth grade. I was attracted to his wit. He was fine with a sense of humor, daring, bold and very smart.

After we started spending a lot of time together, I found out that he sold drugs. It wasn't big time drug dealer money, but it was enough to eat and survive. Thoughtfulness was a part of his character, I received gifts often. Whether they were new, used, or hot from a drug addict, I still felt like he thought of me.

Things started getting dangerous again; I fell back into my old patterns. I would sneak out to see him. He lived five blocks from my house. The first time I snuck out my girlfriend Lisa was with me. She was the type of girl who was a very loyal friend - she was a good girl.

CHAPTER 1 – RISKY

She had very long hair to the middle of her back and she had big deep dimples. She also came from a big family which I enjoyed being around. We left around two thirty in the morning. I couldn't lock the door because I wasn't allowed to have keys to the house, so I had to leave it unlocked. It wasn't like we lived in the best area either. So I closed the door really tight, while my mother and stepfather were in the bed. There were drug addicts out walking around looking like zombies and drug dealers working their corners in hiding. I had no fear of them because half of them knew Rico anyway. He was known almost everywhere he went. He was the type of person that made his presence known because of his personality. The long streets we had to walk were kind of creepy because of the silence of the night, and it felt like things and people were staring at us. But being young, I felt invincible. When we got to his house he had his cousin there to meet Lisa. As we walked in, they were on the front porch getting their supply together for the next day. They were eating Chinese food while listening to music like it was the afternoon. When they were done, Rico and I went into the living room, while his cousin and Lisa stayed on the porch. No sex happened at all between us. Just a lot of passion marks. Time flew by and Lisa and I didn't leave until five thirty in the morning. Rico and his cousin walked us home just to make sure we were safe. I was scared to death because it wasn't dark outside anymore; it was dusk. When I opened the door, Lisa and I tiptoed in the house. I heard someone come out of the bathroom, so we stood frozen, holding our breath. We stood there for about ten minutes giving whoever that was, time to fall back asleep. Then we tiptoed upstairs one at a time and got in the bed. I felt like I was a bad influence on my friends at times. It seemed like I was the one who always made the plans. I was a leader in my own right, but it wasn't being used correctly. Sometimes I used my leadership skills for all the wrong reasons.

 I started getting bolder and I snuck out by myself for the first time without any friends along. Rico, who was now my official boyfriend, had no idea that I was coming one night. When I reached his street, he was outside working. I got a little upset because he couldn't stop, so he asked somebody to fill in for him. We spent a little time together again with no sex, which I appreciated. After a couple of hours I needed to leave so he walked me home. When I got to my door and opened it, I heard someone coming. I ran for the basement steps as lightly as I could on my tip toes, and hid behind the washer and dryer. I stayed there for fifteen minutes hoping and praying they didn't hear me. My stepfather came downstairs to the kitchen for a glass of water. When I heard him go back upstairs, I knew the coast was clear. I remembered washing clothes earlier that day, and had a pair of pajamas in the dryer. I took my clothes off, put them in the dryer, transferred into the pajamas, and went upstairs and got in the bed. While lying there, I let out a sigh of relief, "another night of not getting caught."

I had to leave my house at six o clock in the morning every day in order to get to school by seven thirty. Of course it was still dark, so my mom walked me halfway to the bus stop. This particular morning she gave me a hug; I got on the bus, and didn't bother to take a seat because I was getting off three stops later. Rico was waiting for me on the corner; we planned everything on the phone the night before.

We walked back to his house and that's when it happened; we had sex for the first time. After that it was on a regular basis. It got to a point where I hooked or left school early or went in late at least twice a week. All we did was eat, sleep, and have sex; it became routine. We slept the majority of the day away because he would be up all night. I just blended myself in to his life. We were never there alone; someone was always home between his siblings. His mother was normally at work. But the days she did stay home she would comment about us laying around but never made a big fuss because she liked me and so did his siblings. I was like part of the family. Slowly my conviction of missing so many days of school diminished. I just worked extra hard when I did go, so I wouldn't fail. I still made sure I was home in time to catch the school calls.

For the most part Rico and I got along, but there was one day we had an argument about him not being able to be found, and not returning my pages for a whole night and day, and I stopped speaking to him.

CHAPTER 1 – RISKY

The next morning I got up, got dressed, grabbed some breakfast, and headed out the door. As soon as I hit my bottom step, I heard "psssp, psssp." I looked around and saw him hiding behind the tree across the street from my house. He was hiding because he knew that my mother would either walk me outside or look out the window while I walked to the bus stop. When he noticed she was nowhere around, he followed me and tried to make up by acting silly and trying to make me laugh. I played "hard to get" for a while but gave in; I went straight to his house, and missed another day of school. The whole day at his house, I started having concerns about him hiding behind the tree, but I just shook it off.

There was another incident one night after we had an argument and I broke up with him. Around eleven o'clock that evening he climbed up to my neighbor's roof because it was lower than ours. He stood on the edge of it and tried to open my window with an umbrella. That was his second attempt after I wouldn't answer to the pebbles he threw right before. The break up was over me hearing about him cheating with a girl in the neighborhood, and possibly having a daughter by her. I felt like I needed to move on, especially if it was true; so I did for a moment.

There was a guy who would flirt with me every time I saw him on the train on my way to school. It was the end of the line where kids all over the city would get off to catch their buses. Of course I felt important because out of all of my friends he pointed me out. I did find out that he attended a behavioral school but I didn't mind. He had a caramel complexion, hazel eyes and curly hair, and he smoked his cigarette just right. One morning we exchanged phone numbers. He and I talked on the phone for about a week and then set up a date to hang out at his uncle's condo. I took one of my girlfriends with me just in case anything went wrong. I didn't want to be by myself because I just met him. So my girlfriend and I hooked school and went to meet him. When we got there he had breakfast waiting for us. We were there for most of the day just watching television and joking around. I tried to play cool and asked him for one of his cigarettes. He left us for a minute so he could use the bathroom. Once he left, I hurried to light it up. I didn't know what the heck I was doing. The only experience I had with trying to smoke was at my grandmother's house, when she would leave those long brown butts lying around in the ashtrays. So, while I was in the bathroom, I put the cigarette in my mouth, turned the stove on and bent down to light it. Let's just say that afterwards I had crispy eyelashes and a half of a bang left. After my lashes and hair caught on fire, my girlfriend was trying to pat it out. The whole kitchen smelled like burnt hair. When he came out of the bathroom, we played it cool like nothing ever happened. I visited him a few times alone after that, but it was short lived.

Shortly after that I ended up taking Rico back and we were back to normal. He was so convincing that he did not cheat and have a baby that I reasoned with myself and squashed the anger I had with him. My habits picked right back up where they left off. There wasn't a day that went by where we did not see each other. He lived directly around the corner from my aunt Regina's house so it was easy access for me. All I had to do was drop my bags off and walk around the corner. I knew what time to be back and I would check in from time to time.

Within a short span of time other areas of my life started to get messy, and for others turn violent. A friend of mine from my church had a thick gold herringbone chain on, so I complimented her on it, and she asked me if I wanted to borrow it. After I asked her if she was sure, she said yes. I put it on along with the gold rope chain that I was already wearing. I also had on a new pair of twenty four karat gold swirl earrings that I bought with my allowance I saved. So one day on the way home from school I was sitting on the train with my book bag on my lap and my back facing the doors. This guy came up behind me and snatched both earrings and just the herringbone chain. It totally slipped my mind to take one earring off and to hide the chains in my shirt. He must have been eyeing me my whole ride. It all happened so quickly that I didn't have time to react. I felt so violated to the point I was ready to cry. When I reached home I called my girlfriend and told her what happened. She wasn't upset, but did sound a little worried. After I asked her what was wrong, she told me that the chain was given to her by her boyfriend, and he

CHAPTER 1 – RISKY

was a big time drug dealer around the neighborhood. She knew that he would be upset if he found out. That chain was worth about four hundred dollars. So I told her as soon as I got some money I would replace it before he found out. But it was too late, two days later her and her boyfriend got into an argument and he asked her for the chain back, and she didn't have it. She tried explaining to him what happened, but he didn't believe her. He accused her of giving it to another guy or selling it. He was so furious he just left her house. She didn't hear from him for a couple of days. She thought he just needed time to cool down, but little did she know something was waiting for her. One day on her way home from school, she went to pick her daughter up from daycare and got jumped by three guys, one girl, and the girl's mother. Her head was split open with a baseball bat, along with her getting kicked and punched on the ground. She ended up getting sent to the hospital for a couple of days with a concussion and other injuries. Her boyfriend had set her up over the chain.

When I found out about it, I felt responsible, even though the chain was taken out of my control. I had to do something. I couldn't bear the fact of knowing that she was sent to the hospital over a chain that I was wearing. I felt the need to retaliate on her behalf, so I gathered up six people. Three of them were friends from school and two of them were my cousins, and the last one was one of my best friends from school named Sheila. The four of us left school early to meet the other three downtown. Once we all met up, we walked to the neighborhood where the people that beat my girlfriend up lived. We were mainly looking for the girl and her mother because they were the only real lead we had. We had hammers, ice picks and box cutters. We walked around for hours looking for them and came across nothing. We also asked people in the neighborhood if they knew or had seen them, but nothing came about so we left.

The next day while we were in school, the cops came and raided Sheila's locker looking for one of the box cutters we had the day before. She had pulled it out of her book bag that morning on the train to defend her sister. Some guy slapped her sister in the face and was about to start hitting her, so Sheila started fighting him and then took the box cutter out. Students that were on the train that morning were watching and when they got to school they started spreading the news and also told the teachers. So the school called the police. Sheila was arrested and sent to a disciplinary school.

The kids that told on her were the same ones that had their own little private clique. There were five of them. They were really cool at one time and I used to talk to them, but they turned on me and started hanging with this big brawny girl who had a very dominant personality and was a bully. A lot of people were scared of her because she towered over them and weighed more than almost all of them, and was very muscular. She intimidated everyone but me, and she did not like that. They did everything she told them to do. Once she entered the train it was hail to the queen. It burned her up when I did not become her groupie. It frustrated her to no end when she couldn't find anything to ruffle my feathers with. So one morning, she got on the train and stood by the door and did not sit down. After we started moving, she pulled a huge piece of chocolate cake with a ton of thick icing on it out of her bag. Then she asked one of the girls in a loud voice so everyone could hear including the other passengers, what they thought would happen if she smashed the cake in my face. They then dared her out of fear, looking at me as if to say 'I'm sorry.' So I sat there and didn't say anything because there were six of them and one of me, and I didn't want to fuel a fire unnecessarily. I thought she was just talking to hear herself but she actually took the cake and reached over the chair across an old lady that was sitting next to me and smashed it right in my face. It got all in my hair and on my clothes. When I looked up, she was gone. She and the other girls were running through the train cars. When the next stop came, I got off and so did the little old lady that was sitting next to me. She got off and started wiping the icing off of me and giving me tissues to do the same. I went all the way back home, because I knew that I could not go to school like that. I ended up going to my boyfriend's house and staying there all day.

When I got to school the next day I heard she was bragging about what she did to me, so I purposely walked by her locker, gave her a harsh look, stared directly into her eyes for a moment and with

CHAPTER 1 - RISKY

a rigid voice said, "good morning" while walking by slowly. It really took her by surprise. She could not understand why I wasn't scared to walk by her and speak to her. After that day she tried to befriend me, but I kindly dismissed her.

2
Unprotected

I turned fifteen over the summer after ninth grade. I worked in my first hair salon downtown as a shampoo assistant every Saturday, and a couple of days during the week. Working there afforded me to make good money and to also hone my skills and learn more about hair.

I worked for a few stylists there, but had one main boss. He was really cool, but very high strung. I never understood why he would race around the salon the way he did. I later found out he was snorting cocaine every morning before he came to work. Nevertheless, I appreciated the fact that he paid me very well. Once I got paid I would save and not waste my money frivolously.

During the same time I was working at the salon, Rico and I were still going strong. We still had our ups and downs, but remained consistent. Even if I felt he was cheating, I foolishly believed that it was ok because I was his main girl. I had a key to his family's house and could come and go as I pleased, so that gave me comfort. I was also able to bring my friends over anytime I wanted to. My girlfriends would date his cousins and friends, so we had a tight circle. Our circle was so tight, that one night it became dangerous. Three of my friends and I were over Rico's house one night when Rico's friend told my girlfriend

IN MY MIND

Sheila who he was interested in, to come to his fight party and bring the rest of us. Rico and I wanted to spend a little time alone so we didn't go. He and I stayed at his house while my girlfriends went to the party. An hour had passed and I paged Sheila, but she didn't call me back. I waited a little while and paged her again, and still no response. By this time I started to get a little worried so Rico and I were about to walk around there to check on them. Before we could get down the steps, my girlfriends came running around the corner out of breath, looking petrified. My heart started pumping rapidly, wondering what was wrong, and why they looked so troubled. While they were trying to catch their breath, they started talking over each other and trying to tell us what happened. One of them said they almost got arrested. She said when they got there everything was fine. People were sitting around laughing, eating, and socializing. They walked through the living room to get to the basement where most of the people were, and sat down, grabbed a couple of chips off of the table, and got a drink out of the cooler. After about ten minutes they heard a lot of ruckus going on upstairs above them. They heard people being slammed down on the floor, so they ran and hid behind tables and speakers. All of a sudden they felt the vibration of heavy boots stomping down the basement steps. She said it sounded like ten voices yelling "Police!" As soon as the police got downstairs they started pushing people on the ground. They were putting their boots on people's backs to hold them down while cuffing them. My girlfriends were cuffed for at least an hour before they let them go. Their faces were on the hard, cold cement basement floor the entire time. The police started ripping down the ceiling tile and putting holes in the walls, looking for drugs. They found drugs on some people, but not my girlfriends, so they let them go.

When my friends finished telling us the story, we all went inside Rico's house and he ordered us food from the store. After they calmed down and got themselves together, he then treated us to the movies. That week was very traumatic and I felt

CHAPTER 2 – UNPROTECTED

responsible once again. I know that they were just unfortunate events and my friends had minds of their own, but I always felt like I escaped the dangers that my friends were involved in even though I was an influence in some cases.

The very next week after all of the chaos, Sheila spent the night over my house so we could go to school together in the morning. When we woke up, we got ourselves together and left. A guy from my neighborhood who I dated one month before I met Rico walked with us to the bus stop because we were all going to school the same way. While we were waiting for the bus, Rico popped up out of nowhere, and confronted us. He had this look in his eyes that I never saw before; it was a look of controlled rage, with a slight touch of hurt. He thought the guy was with me because he was waiting there with us. The bus came and the guy got on and left us standing there. I became frozen with a little fear, so Sheila and I did not get on. Rico started talking to me in a demeaning tone, saying he wanted all of his things back that he had ever given to me: sneakers, clothes, teddy bears, etc. I started yelling back at him. Before I could get another word out, he hit me in my back. He swung around Sheila because she was standing in between us at the time, and hit me in the middle of my back. Her natural reflexes kicked in and she hit him back for me. We started walking back to my house so I could give him his things. We got into the house and of course my mother and stepfather were gone off to work by now. I was not allowed to have a key to the house, so I snuck and had one made at the hardware store on the avenue, weeks prior. We went upstairs to my bedroom and I got a large trash bag, putting in everything he wanted back. I did it quietly because I didn't want anything to flare up again. Then he turned around and hit me again, and this time I hit him back. Of course Sheila jumped in again, and punched him, and he tried to punch her back but he missed. We got caught up in a pretzel position and started rolling and tussling around on the bed trying to fight. Somehow we stopped fighting, and he took the bag and left. I cried out of frustration and devastation. Sheila comforted me, and then we left and went to school late.

As the day went on I started to break down. I wanted to talk to Rico and explain that the guy at the bus stop and I had nothing going on. My strength was diminishing, and I was getting weak.

Before I even thought about picking up the phone, he called. When I answered, he already started to apologize about what happened earlier that morning. He wanted to return my things back to me, and because I was already in a vulnerable state, I gave in and accepted his apology. Later on I had planned to sneak out and meet him, but I didn't, it just didn't feel right. From the first time Rico hit me, he instantly placed a gripping fear in me. I was tossed back and forth by my emotions.

I needed to get away for a moment, so I took one of my girlfriends up on her offer. She wanted me to come over her house for the weekend. I asked my mom and she said it was okay. She knew the family because we all went to the same church. She knew I would be going to church with them on Sunday so she didn't mind. I practically lived at this house; I was over there almost every weekend, outside of being with my own family and other friends.

Her parents were pretty strict and very much into living right for God. Her mother didn't play. There were six children and each had their own responsibilities and accountability for being a good steward over their lives. Ironically, every single one went astray, some worse than others. Their house was the hangout house. Everyone in the neighborhood would come and sit on the porch, or come in and get a glass of juice or something. They were well known and liked.

But my friend had a few issues. She was sweet and intelligent but became buck wild. She ran away for two months, and was staying with some friends in the projects. God always spoke to her, especially in visions. They would play in her mind while she was awake. There was one time when she was sitting on her bed and was in and out of sleep when she saw a vision of the whole

CHAPTER 2 – UNPROTECTED

sky turning grey. Strong winds were blowing and the front door of her house blew open. It was empty outside, no people, cars, buses, or animals, just vacant. Then she came to herself, a little shaken. Right after that she heard God speak to her. He told her to tell people to get themselves together so they would not be left behind. She had another thing happen that was a little different – she was lying in her bed asleep, and woke up suddenly and tried to move but couldn't. All she could move were her eyes. There was a strong gust of wind that came rushing into her bedroom, and the arms of her coat which was hanging on her closet door started swaying back and forth. Then out of nowhere these little white faces were surrounding her and telling her to come with them. She kept trying to say no but mumbled because she couldn't speak; no sound was coming out of her mouth. Then finally she was able to blurt out "The blood of Jesus" and they left. She then jumped up and started praying.

After church that Sunday, I got my bags out of her parents' car and went home with my mother and stepfather. I was a little quiet when I got in the car because I had a bad headache. I knew it was from the previous night because we were drinking and I got drunk for the first time. My girlfriend and I went around the corner from her house to this little hole in the wall. It was a bar as well as a club because it had a dance floor. They let me in because I looked older than fifteen. They didn't card me at all. I had no idea of what to order so my girlfriend's friend ordered me three drinks back to back. All I remembered was floating back to my girlfriend's house. My head was pounding badly; all I could do was pass out on the bed.

The next day there was no school because of a mandatory teachers' meeting. Because I was not allowed to stay home when no one was there, I had to go around the corner to my aunt's house. If I wasn't with Rico, the majority of my time was spent sitting on my aunt's steps with my friends and my god-sister all day long laughing at the guys in the cars riding by flirting with us, and also watching drug transactions being done.

IN MY MIND

There would be all types of people involved in the transactions: hardworking, middleclass, grandfathers, grandmothers, young mothers, and young guys. It was very sad to see people strung out looking vulnerable and desperate because they needed their next hit. There were women selling their babies' diapers and food just to get high. I saw people come up foaming at the mouth with bulging eyes and doing some crazy things. Their bodies were enslaved to those drugs.

The weekend finally came and I was off punishment for having a nasty attitude. I asked if I could go over my girlfriend Sheila's house. She was really a good girl when it came to guys; she just had a short temper and would fight if she had to. People would call us the twin towers because we were both tall and were always together. I loved going over her house because she had a lot of brothers and sisters and her mother could cook. They always had seafood on Fridays. The unfortunate thing for her that I felt sorry for was the fact that she had to take care of her siblings as though they were her own. She would always babysit and couldn't do too much. Her siblings were very appreciative of her because she had such a nurturing spirit. That night my mother dropped me off at her house and we went out. She was allowed to stay out late as long as she came home. We were going to Rico's house to meet up with him and his cousin. She had been dating his cousin for some time. When we got there we all decided to go to a motel. She didn't normally do things like that, but she went along anyway. When we got to the motel it was a motel strictly for sex. You were only allowed a room if you were a couple and you had to book it by the hour. She and I were a little skeptical and embarrassed because everyone knew what people went there for. Even though I felt grown and unstoppable, I also felt like the little girl that I was.

Once we got inside, it felt a little creepy. It was very dark and dreary; the rooms had dark red curtains with matching comforters and phony satin sheets. The bathroom was hideous and you heard everything that the people in the next room were

CHAPTER 2 – UNPROTECTED

doing. I was extremely uncomfortable, but blocked it out of my mind because I was with Rico. He and his cousin paid for three hours. After our time was up, motel staff came and knocked on our door to let us know we had to go. While we were walking back to the train Rico and I got into an argument over nothing and started yelling at each other like wild banshees. Sheila was laughing at us because we looked and sounded silly. I said a few choice cuss words that would only come out when we argued. Sheila and I got on the train and rode to her stop. When we got off we started walking toward her house, on a long, dark street. There were drug dealers and drug addicts all scattered around. We took off all of our jewelry, because we didn't want to get stuck up like she did two weeks prior. She was held up at gunpoint from behind, and told to take off her earrings. They took her earrings, pager, and the money she had in her pocket.

Three weeks went by and it was almost summertime. It was the month of June 1991 and my menstrual did not come when it was supposed to. I wasn't scared. I was actually happy. We had been trying for a while. Both Rico and I wanted a baby. I had my reasons, he had his. I wanted my own personal companion. I wanted someone to love, and also someone who depended on me. As foolish as that sounded, it was real. I went to the store to get a pregnancy test, and hid it in my book bag to take it home. While everyone was asleep, I got the test out of my bag and took it to the bathroom. I followed the directions and waited for the results. It read POSITIVE with a bright pink plus sign that appeared on the top. I walked back to my room, put the test back in my book bag, got back in the bed, and started daydreaming about what it would be like to be a mother.

School let out early the next day, and I went straight to the free clinic. I needed to get checked out to see how many weeks I was and what I needed to do. While I sat there twiddling my thumbs, one of the nurses called me back to the room. She took my vital signs and handed me a cup and asked me to use the restroom. She then handed me a drape to put on, told me to

IN MY MIND

get undressed and to have a seat on the table. A few minutes later the doctor knocked on the door and waited for my response to come in. He introduced himself and said, "So Ms. Ward, I hear you might be pregnant." He proceeded with telling me that he had my urine sample and was about to do a pregnancy test, just to be sure. He took a long stick out, dipped it in the cup, and laid it on a napkin. While waiting for the results, he asked me questions about my last menstrual. After I answered, he turned around, picked up the stick, and said it was positive. He told me to lie down on the table and prop my feet up in the stirrups. After he did his examination, he said that I was about six weeks. He told me to get dressed, and the nurse would be in with a pack of prenatal vitamins and would take me to the front desk to make a follow up appointment. When I left the office, I called Rico to tell him, and he was excited. I walked straight to my aunt Regina's house to tell my oldest god-sister that my other god-sister and I looked up to. She seemed to have it all; friends, guys, and a fun and active life. After my excitement faded, reality set in and I was petrified, because I didn't know how I was going to tell my mom. She didn't even know I was having sex. My god-sister walked me home and I was a ball of nerves; I couldn't even walk straight.

We got to the house and rang the doorbell. My stepfather opened the door and we walked in a little quiet and nervous. My mom was upstairs and my god-sister called her to come downstairs. She told my mom that we had something to tell her, so both her and my stepfather sat down. The room was so silent you could hear a pin drop. Then my god-sister spoke up and said, "Cee is pregnant, and she is six weeks." My mom was quiet for a while with no expression on her face. Then she asked me in a soft subtle voice, "What do you want to do?" I told her I wanted to keep it. Then she came over and gave me a hug. I felt a little scared, but at the same time I felt comforted. It kind of confused me, because I thought she was going to go off, but instead her response was gentle.

CHAPTER 2 – UNPROTECTED

After the big announcement, the house was quiet for the rest of the night. I went to my room, my mom and stepfather went to their room, and all doors were shut. I lay on my bed staring at the ceiling. My mind was racing. I had all kinds of questions ranging from what is it like being a mother, to what it would be, a girl or a boy. Who would they look like, Rico or me? Would they be big or small? Would they have a lot of hair? I drifted off to sleep while pondering the future.

My tenth grade school year was almost over. That's when my mother found the maternity school for me. I knew this whole ordeal was tough on her because sometimes I would see her sitting around looking sad. I'm sure she wanted something different for me, and she had to face all of the ridicule for having such a young teenage daughter, especially from the church congregants. But she didn't allow it to show.

Over the summer I kept my prenatal appointments. I was extremely interested in my pregnancy and my fetus. I bought a lot of books on childbirth. I wanted to learn the process after conception, and what happens during the different trimesters. I spent most of my time reading. I became more fluent in my knowledge about what was going on inside of me.

The first day of the maternity school started, and I remembered my mom and I walking towards the doors. I got a little apprehensive and nervous, but was in anticipation at the same time. The nervousness came from me not knowing anyone, and the anticipation came from getting ready to invite change. Once we got inside, my mother signed a few papers, and walked with me to my classroom to meet my teachers. I stayed in one room most of the day. The set up was not like regular school. I was still enrolled in my main school; they would send my weekly assignments and homework for me to complete. We did our work at our own pace. The teachers were there to monitor and help us with our assignments when necessary. All ages and grades were mixed together but we worked individually. They gave us snacks throughout the day, along with our lunch break. We were also allowed to take a quick nap every now and then if needed, so we could recharge from any fatigue that the pregnancy initiated. Some people would have looked at this program as a babysitter, or a place where teenage pregnancy was congratulated. It was actually very structured with rules and restrictions. They also gave detentions and expulsions just like any other school.

I was very happy to see someone I knew. She came from my previous school, and we became very close. Both of us were five months pregnant, having boys and our due dates were three days apart. We had a lot in common. We would hang out after school sometimes and get things for the babies. We also got together on some weekends, to do the same things nonpregnant teens did, like going to the movies, and shopping. I felt sorry for her because her mother was very mean and hard on her. She never just talked to her, she would talk at her. Every time I went over there, all they ever did was argue. She would always say that when she had her baby, she was going to be the best mother she could possibly be.

One thing I promised myself and my baby was that, I was going to be the best teenage mom, ever. All of my risky behavior stopped: I stopped drinking, I stopped smoking, and I started eating healthy. I ate a lot of fruits and vegetables, stopped drinking sodas, and cut out all of the unhealthy snacking. My pregnancy was pretty close to perfect. I had minimal morning sickness, and only vomited once. Everywhere I went, I made sure I walked. Once I walked from my house into town at eight months. That was about a three hour walk. I wanted to make sure the baby and I stayed healthy.

Being in church with a lot of judgmental people was a little difficult for my mother, because she really got scrutinized for having a pregnant teenager. Some parents even told their children not to hang around me. They had no idea that their children were running the same race I was. That really didn't matter to me. All that mattered was that I had a healthy baby. It could have taken a toll on us if we let it but my mom was strong and mature about

CHAPTER 2 – UNPROTECTED

it. I on the other hand, had a charm about me that dismissed any wrong treatment. I knew how to handle the ignorance that was displayed by putting on false humility while they made a fool of themselves by their rude actions and gestures.

I really missed my brother McKee being there for my pregnancy. He joined the Marines not too long after high school so he was away most of the time. He was seven years older than me and we were very close growing up. I remember us playing little games we made up. There was this one game called boo-boo where we lied down on our backs and put the bottom of our feet together and circled our legs around like we were riding a bicycle. We would do that sometimes until dinner was ready. Those times lasted until he went away to private school. My mom wanted him to have a better opportunity, and education. The only children that were allowed to go were those kids whose parents died, or were not in their lives. His father died at the age of twenty one when my brother was only three, and left my mom to be a widow at such a young age. My mother knew that the school was the best thing for him at that time, even though she would miss him being at home every day.

Because my brother didn't have a father, and I didn't see my father much because he lived in California at the time, it was basically just the three of us: my mom, my brother, and me. Then my stepfather came into the picture. I was three, and my brother was ten. My stepfather was a jack of all trades. Outside of him being a carpenter and a business man, he made sure he lived a full life. He had been a bus driver, truck driver, accountant, police officer, chef, real-estate agent, military man, photographer - you name it, he's done it. He was also heavy on sporting ventures like hunting, fishing, boating, riding motorcycles (he had three), and traveling. We were always on the road doing something. I remembered us taking trips to my brother's school every couple of months, and on holidays, if he didn't come home. It was about a two and a half hour drive in our big red van. That van was known everywhere. It was one of a kind, mainly because of the

IN MY MIND

large mural on the side of it which was its signature around town. It had a bed in the back, with a sink and refrigerator. All of our road trips were taken in that van; that was our second home.

I was excited every time I knew we were going to visit my brother. Once we got there he would be waiting in anticipation for us. The campus was absolutely beautiful. I loved the smell of the fresh flowers and grass. Everything was well manicured. The trees were full and evenly planted with colorful and bright flowers placed strategically. I loved the sense of nature. I would stand there and imagine myself just rolling down the hill with a sundress on and a big flowery brimmed hat. We would make a full day out of our visit with lunch and dinner included before we left to go home. I felt sad every time we had to leave because I did not want to say goodbye. I looked at my brother like he was my hero. He was handsome and intelligent, and had a mind of his own. I never really fully understood why I couldn't see him as often as I would have liked, but I was glad when I did. I always said when I grew up I wanted my husband to be just like him. Every time we pulled off he wanted to come along, but deep down inside he knew it was the best for him to stay.

3
Distorted

Push! Push! Push! "Okay!" I exclaimed as I scooted down on the hospital bed with no feeling in my legs. My lower body was numb from the epidural that was used to ease the pain of the contractions. I was only allowed to have two people in the room with me during delivery, so my mother and Rico were there. My mother held my legs along with the doctor, while Rico stood to the side. He had enough for that night. He almost fainted earlier when they stuck the long skinny epidural needle up my spine. The delivery room was very nice, and also pretty big. It had a sofa and a huge television which displayed reruns of the Cosby show during my labor. It kept me focused while I pushed until my medicine ran out a few times. I had to call for the anesthesiologists at least three times to give me more. Once the drugs kicked in, labor was a breeze.

After extensive pushing I started to get a little exhausted. I kept asking for ice every twenty minutes because my mouth was getting extremely dry, and I felt dehydrated. After that last hard push the doctor said he saw the head. I had reached my limit of pushing, so the baby stopped moving. I needed a little help, so the doctor had a plunger-like object he used to suction the baby's head and pull him down. Then he got a pair of forceps that looked like salad tongs, and gripped the sides of the head and maneuvered him out. Then he said to Rico, "Here is your healthy baby boy!" He said it with such excitement as if this was his first delivery. He probably was in amazement because he remembered that just sixteen years earlier he delivered me. My mom sought him out to be my obstetrician

IN MY MIND

because she felt safe with him.

The doctor passed Rico the scissors to cut the umbilical cord, and said 'Congratulations! Dad, he looks just like you." After he cut the cord the nurses wiped Amir off, wrapped him up in a blanket, and laid him on my chest. They had to tap him a couple of times because he wouldn't cry. He came out very quiet, looking around with these big saucer eyes. When they laid him on my chest, I was in awe. I couldn't believe it, I was officially a mother. Joy overwhelmed my heart.

Rico and my mom left when I started getting tired and needed rest. After I took a nap, the nurse brought Amir back into my room so I could feed him and bond with him. His testing was complete, so he stayed in the room with me for the rest of the night. He was a 100% healthy baby boy, with no abnormalities. I named him Amir because I really liked the name, which meant Ruler. He weighed 7 pounds and 14 ounces and looked as if he was body building inside of me because of his muscular appearance. I was in shock because it didn't seem real. I thought it was a big dream, but every time I looked at him, reality was setting in. I stared at him until I drifted off to sleep.

My four week maternity leave was up and I had to get back to school. My mother had a baby sitter already lined up, but Rico wanted to keep him, so a couple of mornings I took Amir over his house before I went to school. Everything was good until I started to notice that the same amount of bottles and diapers I put in the bag were still there when I picked him up. That meant he had the same diaper on from that morning. The last straw was when Rico's sister came downstairs and found Amir on the cold hard basement floor. He had fallen off the bed, and cried for at least half an hour. Rico didn't hear him because he was asleep. When I dropped Amir off those few times, Rico would be wide awake and assuring me that he had everything under control. I couldn't take any more chances so I used the babysitter my mother had for me in the beginning. She was a very nice lady, and was actually one of my babysitters when I was younger. My mother worked about ten

CHAPTER 3 – DISTORTED

minutes from her house, so she would drop Amir off for me in the mornings, and I would pick him up after school.

There were very few occasions when I needed Rico to watch Amir because my mom or I was not able to get him to the sitter. This one particular time was when he was five months old, Rico watched him while I went to school. After I got out of school, and got to his house, I went upstairs to his mother's room where he and Amir were, opened the door, and Amir was on the bed, propped up on some pillows nice and neat, while Rico was cutting up drugs and bagging them right next to him. I was furious! All I could think was 'what if Amir sneezed or something and the dust flew in the air and got in his nose or mouth?' I went off. I grabbed Amir off the bed, got his things and tried to leave, but Rico started blocking the doorway. He was trying to explain something but I was so upset I didn't want to hear anything. I just wanted to go home. I finally got out of the door and started walking. I didn't bother getting the baby's stroller, I just wanted to leave. A block and a half away, Rico came yelling and cursing. He had a rage in his eyes that sparked fear in me instantly. When he finally caught up to me his shoulders were square, eyes red, and he was panting heavily. In a stern voice, he kept asking me repeatedly why I left. When I didn't answer him, he pushed me really hard and I lost my balance a little, with Amir in my arms. I braced myself and started walking home, away from him. Tears were rolling down my face while I held Amir really tight. I was hoping he wouldn't follow me, and he didn't. He went the other way. He later tried get in touch with me, but I ignored his calls for a couple of days.

After days passed, one evening I sat on my porch and stared out the window. Confusion and disappointment arose inside of me, and I was hurting to the core of my existence. It was so bad I couldn't even eat. I was wondering what to do, leave Rico or stay. 'Leave' kept coming to the forefront of my mind, but then the question kept popping up "How?" "How do I leave?" I didn't know. "If I left, would he kill me?"

As the night progressed, my phone rang. When I finally

decided to pick up, it was Rico. He started acting silly and making jokes, so he could warm me up to accept his apology. He pleaded with me to forgive him, and he told me that he didn't know what got into him. He said he was sorry and would not do it again. I gave him a hard time at first, but I eventually gave in. I expressed my frustrations and disappointments to him. He listened without saying a word. When his heart was soft it was really soft, but when his other person came out, he was unrecognizable. After I forgave him we were lovey-dovey again.

Lack of trust and other turn-offs started to slowly surface. Going through the motions with Rico really took a toll on me; I was getting very weary. He was the sweetest, most personable, and caring person when substance abuse and other women weren't involved. But when that other side came out he was very unappealing and not pleasant.

In my weariness I started distancing myself. Every time he would kiss me or get close I felt like vomiting; I had these horrible nauseating feelings of disgust. By this time I was too afraid of him, so I felt like I had to stick it out, be silent, and live in torture.

I believed in generational curses. I knew that his abusive behavior was passed down from his father and what he experienced when he was growing up. His father left him when he was young. Even though he never talked about it, I knew it played a big part in his dysfunction. Some people can function well with that missing parent, and some can't. Unfortunately he could not, and the streets took him in. He was pretty much a leader and really didn't follow people. Because he had a stubborn mind of his own, and did what he wanted to do, his leadership abilities were compromised and used in the wrong way.

I needed an escape. He and I were falling away from each other. He did his thing, and I wanted to do mine but was too afraid of any repercussions. To switch up my scenery, I started hanging out with a girl that I knew from childhood. The one main thing we had in common was, our sons were the same age, only days apart. She was the type of girl that kind of raised herself. She didn't go

CHAPTER 3 – DISTORTED

to school, and she smoked a lot of weed daily, along with being a chain cigarette smoker. Her heart was made of gold, but she buried her pain in getting high and being with men. We hung out at her boyfriend's house quite a bit. I would play hooky and have Amir with me sometimes. Her boyfriend and his brother shared a house together in the northern part of the city. I believe someone else lived there, but we never saw them. It was evident that the brothers didn't work because they were always home. I did not know at first, but they sold drugs out of that house. Someone was always coming up to the porch looking crazy. It wasn't the safest part of town, but that didn't matter. It was my escape for a little while. Her boyfriend's brother and I started seeing each other for a short time. It numbed the pain of everything I was going through with Rico. The four of us would smoke weed together. I made sure on those days the baby was not with me. I started to limit my time with them when things got too crazy. My friend's boyfriend would beat up on her, because her son wasn't his. Every time he looked at him he would get angry with her. I couldn't bear to keep seeing her bruised up all the time, and still going back to him. I was dealing with enough on my own trying to figure out how I was going to get out of my situation, so I had to back off.

Things were getting extremely dangerous between Rico and me by this time. One day at his house, we were arguing, and we ended up in a scuffle. During the scuffle my ankle was twisted. His mother and sister heard all of the commotion and ran downstairs to see what was going on. His mother came and stood in between us and shielded me. He left and went to the basement and came back up with his gun in his hand by his side. He was just trying to scare me, because he never drew it. His mother told me to walk home while she kept him in the house to calm him down. There was no doubt by now that I definitely wanted out but I still did not know how to make that happen because of my crippling fear of him. The only way I thought I knew how to end it was by getting involved with someone else.

There was a guy from New York that would come and visit his

cousin every other weekend. His cousin lived on my aunt Regina's street and my girlfriend was involved with him, so I would go over there to hang out with her. My heart raced every time I walked up those steps, or came out of that house. I knew if Rico saw me or found out, he would go off. Well, I was right. This one night my girlfriend and I were coming out of the house and Rico was standing right there on the sidewalk. Someone from the neighborhood told him that I was in the house with the guy from New York. As soon as I walked down the steps, he came towards me looking enraged, and the next thing I knew, I was holding my mouth because my two front teeth were loose and my mouth was bleeding. He had punched me in the face before I could even blink. Then the guy from New York tried to take up for me, and stepped to him. Before he could even open up his mouth, Rico pulled him by his shirt and dragged him down the steps like a rag doll. He threw him on the ground and started beating him profusely. Some people who were standing around watching him had to try and pull him off. I then ran to my aunt's house a few doors down and called my mom and stepfather. Then after I hung up, I called my dad, and Rico's mother. My aunt ran in the kitchen and called the police. By the time she hung the phone up with them, Rico left the scene and was nowhere to be found. By this time the streets were filled with people. My dad must have gotten there about seven minutes later, and started asking around in the crowd if they saw which way Rico went. Adrenaline kicked in and he jumped in his car and drove around scouring the neighborhood for at least a half hour. I was scared because someone in the crowd said that Rico had left to get a gun, and I assumed that my father was out there defenseless. He was old school; he just had his fists, and was ready to use them. I also knew that if those two ran into each other there would definitely be violence, especially because Rico was super drunk at the time, and would not be able to reason.

    My mom and stepfather pulled up and got out of the car. By this time there were still no police, and Rico showed up on the scene again. My mom and stepfather were trying to say something

CHAPTER 3 – DISTORTED

to him and he started getting smart with them. This took them by surprise because he never did that before. He always presented himself with the utmost respect, especially with my mother. Out of nowhere Rico's mother came around the corner yelling his name. He was sort of listening to her, but not. It was a struggle, but she did get him to leave. As soon as they left, my dad came driving around the corner looking pissed because he couldn't find him. When the cops finally arrived thirty five minutes later, they took a report from me. The next day I went downtown to get a restraining order and it was so crowded that they turned a bunch of us away and told us to come back the following day. I never went back.

After everything died down, I went back with him; fear had me so captive. What was constant in the forefront of my mind was, 'if I stay with him Amir and I will be safe.' Every time I was with him, it was torture. The sad part about it was, I saw this nice person on the inside crying for help. But the monster of substance abuse had the dominant power. When he was sober everyone fell in love with him. But when he was influenced, that brought out the ugly, which gave him a short temper, and helped to keep the doors of prison revolving for him. Unfortunately, I spent a lot of time hooking school to go and see him in those prisons. It really had become mundane. I had a fake ID so I would get through even being underage during school times. I hated being patted down and having to take all of my jewelry off. But when I was determined to do something I made it happen regardless of the cost.

My heart was very hard after a while, and nothing mattered anymore. I contemplated for a while, but finally just decided that I was going to leave Rico. I had the attitude that 'if he kills me, he just kills me.' At least it would feel better than living like this everyday. I called him over my house, so I could tell him. When he arrived, we sat outside on my steps, and I told him I wanted out, and I didn't want to be involved with him anymore. I braced myself but surprisingly, I got the opposite reaction of what I expected. Instead of him getting enraged, he looked very hurt. His eyes became really glassy, and he was silent. After about a minute, I guess he thought

IN MY MIND

about it, and his pride kicked in. He said in a real low but sad tone, "Okay, no problem, I'll just start another family." By this time I was so numb that I didn't even care. His response was actually a relief. Once he left, that was it. I didn't hear from him for a couple of weeks.

A few months later, I found out that he really did have another family on the way. A girl on my aunt Regina's block was pregnant by him, and she was a few months shy of delivery. However, ever since he left I felt a burden lift off of me that was unexplainable. He tried from time to time to get back with me, but all I could think about was the fear and pain I endured. There wasn't even a second thought. I didn't allow his handsome presence and charming personality to sway my decision.

There did come a time when we actually became civil at one point for our son's sake. We were able to communicate a little better than before. A while later things started to change. His visits to Amir started fading. It seemed like he felt like, if he couldn't have me then he wouldn't have his son. I knew deep down in his heart, he loved Amir, he just did not know how to show it. He popped up every now and then, but it would be at inconvenient times. Sometimes he would just show up out of the blue and want to take him right then, after weeks and months of disappearing. I let him take Amir about three times until I discovered him on a corner with a crowd of guys late at night where they sold drugs. I kindly walked over and asked him politely if I could have the baby. I explained that I did not want him on the corner like that. He gave Amir to me without a fuss, and that was the last I heard from him for a very long while.

I had some time to regroup, and gain my dignity, but I started to slip back into some old patterns. One night, Nikki and I hung out with these guys from another neighborhood. We were smoking weed, getting high, ended up falling asleep, and not waking up until the next morning. We had every intention of going home that night, but we were so high that we didn't think of priorities first. We were actually supposed to go back to her house that evening.

CHAPTER 3 – DISTORTED

My mother was giving me a break from the baby and allowing me to spend the night out. Because I fell asleep, I didn't hear my pager when my mom kept calling it. So she called Nikki's mom to see if I was there, and her mom said, "No, I thought they were at your house." After that Nikki's mother started paging her. Because she also fell asleep, she didn't hear her pager either. When we woke up around six o'clock that morning and realized where we were, and how many missed pages we had, we panicked. I was too afraid to call my mom back, so I just went straight back to Nikki's house with her. Her mom was yelling as soon as we got in the door. I knew that I had it coming much worse. I called my mom back and she said, "Come home now" in a tone that was very disturbing, so I asked Nikki to come along with me so I wouldn't be alone. When we got to the door my mother told me to go back to Nikki's house and don't come back. She had Amir in her arms at the time and told me that I couldn't take him with me, and then slammed the door in my face. That only lasted a day; I never allowed that to happen again.

One morning towards the last week of senior year, I was waiting for the bus. While standing there, a guy pulled up at the red light. He rolled his window down and said 'hello.' I didn't have Amir with me this time because there was only a half day of school. Normally I would have had him with me so he could go to the daycare that the school provided. I attended this high school only for senior year, because my time was up at the maternity school. My mom picked this one for me because of the daycare, and the fact that it was only twenty minutes from my house. After the guy spoke to me, I spoke back very nonchalantly. I didn't want to be bothered with any guys at that time. I was trying to clear my mind and my system out, and just focus on Amir and myself. He kept trying to talk and I kept brushing him off. He finally pulled off, and I was relieved. Two minutes later, he came back. He was very persistent in a flattering type of way. He asked me for my phone number, and I told him to give me his first. He kept trying to offer me a ride to school, but I told him I was okay, and I didn't need a ride. He actually pulled over to the side and started talking more in

IN MY MIND

a gentle but flirtatious way. The bus never came and I was running late, so I let him convince me, and I got in his car. After that day, we were inseparable. He picked me up from school the rest of that week until my last day. I met his parents right away, and after some time he met my mine. We really hit it off. He loved Amir just as much as he loved me. His family also took Amir in like he was one of their own. He was a very family oriented guy with great character. I loved being around him and his family because they had a tight bond. They were very close knit. I was addicted to the feeling I had when I was around them.

We did everything together. I went to all of his family functions. He took me places with him that I never knew existed. He opened my eyes up to so many new things. He loved to drive, so we were always going somewhere. There was never a dull moment. When we started becoming intimate, it was a little awkward because he didn't have his own home, and neither did I. Unfortunately we became very creative with finding ways to have sex, and would put ourselves in some dangerous situations. We would park in stranger's driveways or parking spots in quiet neighborhoods in the evenings. We also went to parks, and found our own space. It all seemed fun and exciting until the warning signs caught up with me. There was one incident where we had been drinking and I got too drunk, and we were at the park on the hood of his car with half of our clothes off. Twenty minutes later, a bright light was shining in our faces. It was the police. They were out there because there had been a string of rapes, kidnappings, and robberies in that park. There were a group of young gang members that were committing these crimes, and they only targeted couples in their cars. The park was known as lover's lane, and it was known for making out. The gang members would take the guy out of the car, tie him up, and put him in the trunk. They would then take the girl into the woods, blind fold her, and make her perform all kinds of sexual acts. The police officer told me to put my pants on and get back in the car. Then he made my boyfriend get in the back of the police car just to do checks, to make sure he was not one of the gang members.

CHAPTER 3 – DISTORTED

I was scared to death, which sobered me up real quick. I thought they were going to take him, and I also didn't know how I would be getting home. Of course I didn't want my mother to find out, so I became very paranoid. Then the cops let him go and told me to be more careful. They told him to have more respect for me, to not have me out there like that and take me to a hotel instead. After that he started taking me to hotels.

My drinking habits started increasing with him. In our travels, we visited a lot of bars. Because I looked mature for my age, and had a phony ID, it was no problem for me to get in. I could consume a lot of alcohol without feeling instant effects. My tolerance level was very high. That was dangerous for me because if I didn't feel anything right away, I kept drinking and it would hit me hard later on. One night when my mom thought I spent the night at Nikki's house, I was at a very expensive hotel with my boyfriend. He brought a fifth of E&J brandy along with him. The only thing that I remembered was sitting in a bathtub full of hot water and bubbles, and almost drinking the whole fifth by myself. Then when I got out of the tub, the room was spinning and I vomited. I plopped down on the bed and reached for the phone to call my mother and check on Amir. He was actually with Nikki, but I was so out of it, I forgot who he was with. I stopped in mid-dialing because my boyfriend begged me not to call; he was so scared. First of all he didn't want my mother to know where we were, and secondly I was in his care and he allowed me to get that way. When I woke up the next morning, I didn't remember anything. He told me I did some crazy things, and then passed out asleep.

There was also another incident that happened when I was with him. I had to be carried out of a bar, to the car. We used to frequent this sports bar because it was the happening place to be. I got a hold of too many drinks and had no control. I hated that feeling of being out of control, but I continued to put myself in that predicament. I would end up saying "God if you get me out of this, I won't do it again." But the temptation seemed to keep presenting itself, and I kept on indulging.

IN MY MIND

I found myself spiraling again to the edge of consciousness. In my mind, I would sometimes conceive my actions as normal. But deep down, I knew something was wrong. Being blind was leading me to self-destruction. Living in the moment cost me a lot. The crazy thing about it was I didn't feel like a teenager. I felt like an adult living an adult life. The feeling was weird. I had no fear. I felt like nothing would ever happen to me, and by the grace of God, it didn't.

4
Preparations

After I graduated high school I really didn't have the desire to attend college. I just wanted to go to cosmetology school. Being a hairstylist was one of my many skills that I excelled in. My love for it was discovered at the age of three when I would go to my grandmother's house during the week, while my mom worked. I would gather up all of her combs and brushes and stick them in my Osh Kosh B'Gosh overall pockets and forget they were there. By the time my mother and I got home, my grandmother would call and ask her if she could please bring her combs and brushes when we came back the following day. The combs and brushes intrigued me so much that I didn't really play with toys too often. During the entire day at my grandmother's house, if I wasn't reading a book, I would be sitting on the back of my pop-pop's sofa chair and twisting his hair, while he read the paper, hummed, and smoked his cigars. I had globs of Vaseline smeared everywhere in his head and face. He just sat there and allowed me to do it. The only break he had was when I stopped for lunch and dinner.

Cosmetology school was starting in just a few days, and I was ready. I had a month and a half after graduation to kick back and relax until I started. This was a big accomplishment for me, especially being a young mother who was not a high-school dropout. I kept a personal determination that I was going to be something great one day, even after all of my mess. When I was in that mess, I looked ahead of me, and saw a bright future; I just didn't know how to attain it. I had some friends that didn't make it. I tried to talk to them and tell them that they could do it too. Some listened and some didn't. I knew that some of them weren't as fortunate to discover their natural determination as early as I did with the help of my caring family. I would tell them to look at their children and let that be their motivating factor.

It was my first day. There was nothing but business on the floor. Students were standing at their stations blow drying and curling clients, while teachers were walking around, being pulled each direction and attending to the needs that were visible. They had grade books and combs in their hands ready to assist if necessary. Clients were sitting in the waiting area reading magazines and waiting to be seen, and the receptionists were on the phones booking appointments. A student who was about to graduate showed me to my classroom. I felt a sense of excitement because this was my passion. I loved making people look and feel their best. After some time, I finished my theory classes and was able to work on the floor with the clients. I learned quite a bit of terminology and techniques, but I already knew a lot. There were four of us who everyone came to for help. Even some of our teachers needed our help occasionally.

A few of us became really close. We went to lunch together every day. We would either go to the deli next to the school or to the mall across the street. The only thing I didn't involve myself in was the shopping. I was saving money to buy a car. I didn't even spend money on lunch, I used food stamps. While they were buying clothes, sneakers, and jewelry, I was wearing run down shoes with holes in the bottom. I finally saved up enough money to buy a car. I bought it from the father of one of my girlfriends. He owned a used car garage and he would buy cars, fix them up and sell them. His cars were very reputable, and known to last. I called him and asked if he had anything in my price range, and he told me to come down and look at a Nissan Sentra. Even though it was eight years old, I trusted him. When I got there it was a rusty color but the inside was clean. I told him I didn't like the color and I wanted

CHAPTER 4 – PREPARATIONS

it painted black. After the car was finished and inspected, he sold it to me for seventeen hundred dollars. I didn't have a license yet, nor did I have great driving skills, but I needed a car for my baby and me. I was determined to get one because I didn't want to be dependent on anyone for rides. When I finally did get my license, I drove to school wearing my run down sneakers, but I had a full tank of gas. There were some haters amongst my friends, but that didn't bother me; I was doing what I had to do to move forward.

Graduation was soon approaching and I wanted to stop doing hair in the house and work in a salon. I started calling around for open positions. One salon called back and told me to come in and bring a model. After I finished styling my model, they were so impressed with my work that they hired me on the spot. I worked with my temporary license until the test date came for me to take the state boards.

A month went by at the salon and I had enough saved up for a down payment on a one bedroom apartment that was available. The apartment building belonged to my mother's best friend's brother. My mom's friend, whom I called my aunt, lived right across the hall from the vacant apartment, so it was a good move. I didn't have any credit yet, but the landlord knew my mother, so he gave the apartment to me in good faith. The rent was three hundred dollars a month, and I knew I could handle that, along with day care and other expenses.

I set a pretty good foundation at that salon. I worked there for a year. After that, I left and started working at another salon, which was known as one of the best in town. It was very popular and I enjoyed the atmosphere. After a month of being there, I sold my car to one my best friends, and bought a brand new car off the lot. Because I didn't have much credit, my grandmother co-signed for me; I greatly appreciated her for that. I never wanted a man bragging that he got things for me. I didn't want to become a helpless girl who couldn't do for herself. If men offered me things like rent or car payments, I turned them down. I wanted them to know that it didn't go down like that.

IN MY MIND

By now my boyfriend and I weren't doing so well, our relationship was very rocky. When he would drink, things started getting physical. I knew I couldn't go through that again, so my feelings for him started to change. One night we were at a Halloween party at a hotel, and everyone there had a few too many drinks. Out of no where we started arguing intensely over nothing important enough to remember. In a quick flash, he snatched me by my hair and pulled me down on the bed. At that point, I shut down. I shut off everything, every emotion, and every feeling, just like I did with my son's father. That day was the turning point of our relationship. I knew that there would be no recovering. So I moved on. I knew if I stayed it would go totally down hill. It did hurt, because my son and I were so close to his family. That was one thing I didn't want to leave, or lose. I knew I had to pull myself apart from them emotionally for a while, so we could possibly remain close in the future.

    I wanted to get off of assistance from the state, because I didn't want to feel needy. I had a goal. So I got a job at a bank, processing checks from eleven in the evening to seven in the morning. I also started working at a new salon because it was closer to my home. It was rough doing both jobs because when I got off from the bank in the morning, I would go to my mom's house and get my son dressed and fed for school. She watched him for me while I worked. After I took him to school, I would go home and sleep until it was time for me to pick him up. My schedule was different on Thursday, Friday, and Saturday because those were the days I had to work at the salon. On those days, after I took him in, I would go straight there. By the time I needed to pick him up, I was already done working. I would bring him home and feed him, and my aunt that lived across the hall from me would sometimes watch him for a couple of hours, so I could try and fit a nap in. At times my sleep was lacking so I tried to make up for it in the bathroom stalls at my bank job. I would tell my co-workers to come and get me in fifteen minutes. One day one of my co-workers forgot, and my supervisor was looking for me. By the time I got back

CHAPTER 4 – PREPARATIONS

to my desk, I had been written up. Throughout the weeks more write ups were coming because I was incurring numerous errors. My work was coming back incorrect and out of order, because I was so tired. My supervisor asked me if I wanted to take a short leave of absence while I got myself together. I took the leave; but never went back. Before I left that job, I met a guy who was ten years older than me. It was hard to tell at first because he looked and acted younger than his age. He was thirty, and I was twenty. He was fine, smooth, and funny. He gave me so much attention that it was ridiculous. Out of all the women at the job, he made it known that he was interested in me. He had the gift of gab, and was very outspoken, and intelligent. We would hang out, especially on those days when I didn't have to work at the salon. I would get my son, get him situated, take him to school, and then go straight to the guy's house. We sometimes had breakfast and went to the gym afterwards. Then we would go back to his house, have sex, and sleep for the rest of the day until it was time to pick my son up from school.

He was a challenge to be with because he was much older but a little immature at the same time. Other than that, we had sons that were close in age. We would take them almost everywhere we went. He did most of the driving, but the problem was, his so called car that we were driving in, was an ex-girlfriend's car that he still had casual relations with. I knew nothing about her until she popped up in a conversation by accident one day. They saw each other at least once or twice a week because of her job. Because she worked many hours, she left her car with him. I never liked coming in second nor did I like sharing, and would have normally left, but my soul was already tied up. I was never the type to be with anyone else's man because to me, that was the bottom of the barrel. However, my state of mind at that time allowed me to stay. A year was fast approaching with him and I was no longer interested in sex at all. One time I was over his house and I did not want to have sex, but he pinned my arms and legs down on the bed with his body. He called himself playing around but I didn't think it was funny. He

IN MY MIND

laughed and started saying things like "What would you do if I hit you?" When I became free, I ran out of there and didn't look back. A couple days went by, and he kept calling. I finally answered the phone and he was apologizing and sweet talking. By this time I was turned off completely and any emotions for him were dead. I didn't let him know right away. I was strategic in my actions. I continued to act like everything was okay. We talked on the phone for about a week, but I avoided seeing him. His dominating personality and aggressive behavior along with the fear from my past that began creeping in caused me to strategically drop away. He got the hint and started backing off.

 I didn't want to see another guy for a minute. I just wanted to hang out with my friends. My girls and I had planned to go out one night. I hadn't been out in a while, so we were going to leave after I finished with all of my clients. I had an apartment full of people waiting to get their hair done that day. There was one new client that I serviced and she kept talking about God. She was talking loud enough so everyone could hear. For some reason I was the only one paying attention. I had my booty shorts on, my hair done, and I was ready to go out once I finished working. But for some strange reason, my heart started opening up and the hardness I was carrying became soft. The whole time, everyone in my apartment was so tuned into the television and conversing with each other, that they didn't hear a word she was saying; I was the only one really listening.

 I still went out that night and enjoyed myself with my girls, but something was missing. I was having fun but it seemed a little different. It was almost as if I had to force myself to party. When I got home that night, the client that kept talking to me about God was on my mind, along with everything else she was saying. It was definitely not anything that I haven't heard before, from growing up in church. As I sat on the edge of my bed thinking about everything and pondering what I already knew how to do but wasn't doing, I felt a little sorrowful. After mentally trying to sort it all out, I started to weep. I had to finish packing, because I

CHAPTER 4 – PREPARATIONS

was leaving for Bermuda the next morning, so I got up, wiped my face, and put my sorrow and tears to the side. My god-sister and her friends planned the trip and I was a tag along. I was the youngest one in the group, but I knew how to hang. There were six of us and we stayed for a week. I was able to join them because the money I made from doing hair afforded me to go. While on the plane thoughts of God kept coming to my mind. But once we landed, all of them erased and went right out the window; it was party time. We stayed at a house that belonged to the mother of one of the girls in our party. She was actually from the island and her family still resided there. We did something different every day. The island was beautiful, but also had a lot of opportunity to get into trouble. One night we went to a club and I got overly intoxicated by a drink that one of the islanders made. I had no recollection of how I made it back to my bed that night. The very next night, we went to a beach party where they did nothing, but smoke marijuana and get lifted. After getting all of the contact in the air, everybody was in relax mode. As my god-sister and her friends and I were sitting on the sand, four guys came over and tried to talk to us. Because everyone was in a flirty mood, we accepted their advances. The guy that was talking to me gave me his address and asked if I could come and see him before I left. I said to myself, 'what the heck, I am on vacation.' I already had in my mind that I wasn't going to do what some of the girls did. Two of them went off with guys and stayed with them for a couple of days. I was on the edge at times, but not that daring. The girl's mother who we were staying with had to go to her friend's house the next day. It was right down the road from where the guy I met lived. So I asked her for a ride to his house. She actually took me and picked me up. When we got there I made sure he saw her car. I also made sure he knew that she was picking me up in an hour, so he wouldn't get any ideas. While sitting on his couch he lit up a joint. He then started to put his hands down my shirt and I didn't stop him. As he tried to go farther, I ended it, jumped up, buttoned my shirt, and waited by the door for my ride. He had a confused look on his face wondering why I wanted to leave so soon. I gave him a look that said, "thanks but no thanks, I'm out of here." I am so thankful that he was not a crazy person that became aggressive and held me against my will out of frustration. My friend's mother actually came back in exactly one hour. I knew I would never see him again, but I told him I would check him out later. He held me to that because somehow the day before we left to go back home, he spotted me in a tourist van in town, and ran alongside it yelling my name. All I could do was turn my head and act like I didn't see him. I enjoyed the trip, but I wanted to get home to see my son. When I was sitting in the plane on the way back home, God's thoughts met back up with me.

The following week my god sister and I ended up visiting my client's church. The service was touching. It reminded me of that same feeling I had when I was younger. I was really close to God. I used to talk to him all of the time, and he would talk back to my heart. Towards the end of the service, the preacher made an altar call, and I felt like I just floated down the aisle towards the altar; I didn't even remember standing up. When I got home I told my mom all about what happened with me accepting God back into my life. She was so happy for me. She knew she had planted the seed and someone else watered it. She was definitely a God fearing and praying woman. I visited the church about three times but I realized that I was looking for something a little different, so I ended up at a church that was a perfect fit for me.

The older guy that I strategically moved away from started calling me again. He would call and ask me if I could sleep with him. I told him no, and he acted like I never responded. He was very persistent. I told him that I didn't want to sleep with him anymore, and that I was a new person inside. Then he asked if I could just wean my way off of sex gradually. And again I told him no. He asked why I was stopping cold turkey, and what had gotten into me. I told him that I gave my life to Christ and I didn't want to disappoint him anymore. He then got off of the sex issue and started asking me questions about what made me take that step, and why didn't I pick his religion, which was Islam. He even came

CHAPTER 4 – PREPARATIONS

out of his mouth and said that he would go to church with me. I couldn't trust that. He was nothing but a distraction because he was trying to smooth talk me and seemingly inquire about my faith as if he was interested or something so I cut the conversation short and hung the phone up.

About two weeks went by with him trying to reach me on and off, by leaving messages. I would not answer the phone. At that time I started becoming closer with the client who led me back to God. She would call and check up on me daily, and sometimes come by. Our bond was quickly tightening. She loved to cook so she would have my son and I come over and eat dinner with her and her family. She was a very outspoken woman, and she loved God. Wherever she was, she talked about him. She would always befriend someone and tell them about Jesus. She was very radical, and also a person who came from the streets and didn't play any games. If she really cared for you, and you were getting messed with, her warrior side came out. I knew firsthand! One night my phone rang and I picked it up without checking my caller ID, and it was the ex. I thought he had given up because he hadn't called in a couple of weeks. It was a Friday night around eleven, and he was outside my apartment. He was on his way to the club and wanted me to come out and see his outfit. He loved to dress and show off his clothes. I guess he thought that I was actually going to bite the bait. It was nerve-racking because he would not leave, and every time I hung up, he kept calling back. I started to panic, so instead of thinking to call the cops, whom I knew always took forever any way, I called my client, her husband, and my dad. When they heard the fear in my voice, it was no question that they would be there in a matter of ten minutes. I have no idea how they got there that fast but they did. When my client and her husband pulled up, they jumped out of the car with pajamas on, carrying a baseball bat. When I came down to open the door, they had him pinned up against the wall, with the bat raised just in case they needed to use it. Then my dad showed up. He jumped out of the car without even shutting his door and ran up the steps, skipping at least three at a time. Then he came and cornered the guy on the other side. My dad asked me calmly if I wanted the guy to leave me alone. My answer wasn't coming out fast enough, because I actually felt sorry for him. He looked like a little baby standing there, scared to death. I was surprised, because he was more muscular than my dad, my client, and her husband. Then my dad asked me again and I said yes. My dad told him to leave quickly before he broke his legs. After that was over, the nosy neighbors went back inside. I had the most peaceful sleep ever. The following week I kept getting calls from AIDS clinics on my pager. I was not worried. He wasn't doing anything but trying to scare me. By this time the fear and control was over.

When I finally had a chance to sit back and observe the last few months of my life after all the chaos, it was a joyous and refreshing time, but also a time of isolation. My friends that I would club with started leaving me whenever they would go out. I couldn't understand at first, and would be hurt. I felt lonely and rejected. Then it got to a point where they just disappeared totally for a while. Little did I know, it was supposed to happen that way. God had intended for all distractions to be out of my life for a time, until I became stronger in Him. I stopped having the desire for alcohol, cigarettes, and marijuana. Then the sexual desires decreased. When I realized that all of that happened in synchronized order, I knew that it was all a set up by God. All of my crutches were stripped from me, so I had nothing else to depend on. My spirit was being worked on so I could be able to receive. I had been put in an isolated state from everything and everybody. It was as if danger was right ahead, and a roadblock was put in place. Everything came to a halt. It felt like I was in the twilight zone. All of the fast life ceased and I had to take a look at myself. The only thing I had left was God, and my son. That was the beginning of my journey in discovering who I was. I knew it would take years although I didn't know how long it would take. There would definitely be some roller coaster rides mixed in.

5
Faith

Life was really changing for the better. I was able to think more clearly and see a better way of living. Although stumbling blocks were always present, I stayed focused on what I wanted out of life. All of my clients, friends, and family noticed my visible change. They would compliment me on a natural glow I carried. I would constantly hear "there is something different about you, you look so pretty." I told them about new things that were happening with me and how God was changing me. There was one client that I talked with on a regular basis. She was a member of a gym that wasn't too far from a salon that I worked in. She was an avid fitness buff and encouraged me to come by and check it out. I ended up joining and would go almost every morning before work. It sometimes felt awkward because the members of the gym were predominantly men. After some time, I became comfortable because we all got to know each other. It was a close and personal atmosphere. There was this one guy who started training me at no charge. He would give me workout regimens and eating charts to follow. I really started to see a big difference with my body, and I was happy with the results. We became really cool, and would talk on occasion. I drove him to his home sometimes because he didn't have a car. While driving him home we would talk about God and the Bible. He had so many questions, but I could only give him what I knew at the time. Surprisingly I knew quite more than I expected. I guess I paid more attention than I thought when I was younger and attended Sunday school.

He had a son that he cherished close to his heart and would have him every weekend. We would take our boys to Chuck E. Cheese and to the park on some of those weekends. After hanging out a bit, our feelings for each other began to grow even though we tried to keep them under the rug. I didn't want any distractions; I wanted to stay on the right path. After a bit of trying, I gave in, but I found out for the first time that God could keep me even when I was weak. One day he came over my apartment to watch a movie and hang out. It got kind of late, and we both ended up dozing off, and not waking up until one o clock in the morning. When we woke up he just started kissing me, and things got heated after that. By that time I was in another zone, but my conscience was battling with me to bring me back. I wanted to do it but I didn't want to do it. Foreplay was now taking place from my living room couch to the bedroom. My mind was saying no, but my flesh was saying yes. Once we made it to the bed, before anything could go any further, it all ended. He was not able to stand at attention, and was frustrated because he couldn't understand why. Instantly I understood. That was my way of escape, through God. I jumped up, put my clothes on, and took him home. That was the end of that. We talked periodically, but eventually we drifted apart.

Camaraderie was important to me but not enough to lose focus at work. The stress mounted when I was trying to stay humble at a salon where I worked. It was extremely challenging because a couple of the girls had their own personal issues with me. One of the girls spent most of her day thinking of things to do and say to me that she thought would tick me off. She was trying to rub me the wrong way because of her own insecurities. Her troubled spirit couldn't take the fact that I was at peace. That didn't bother me, and I surely didn't care, I was there to make my clients happy, and make my money. One day she came up to me and gave me a phone number to a salon where she knew the owner. "This is a Christian salon,

CHAPTER 5 – FAITH

and I think you might like it," she said. She didn't even realize the favor that she was doing for me. She thought she was getting rid of me, but she actually pushed me toward a greater space and time. I took the number and held on to it for a day or two, and then called. When I arrived for my interview I received such a warm welcome. I talked to the owner and he was very nice. I showed him some of my work and immediately he asked me when I could start.

While working there I started to blossom. I was getting groomed by a group of people who genuinely cared about me and my well-being. Everyone who worked there belonged to the same church. I was the only one who went somewhere different. I felt uncomfortable at first because all they would ever talk about was how their church services were, and how they hung out together afterwards. Unconsciously it seemed like no one would ask me about my church and services, or what I did for the weekend. One of my coworkers took notice and made sure she asked me about my happenings, and actually went to church with me a few times. I had been at my church for almost a year and found it to be planting good seeds and keeping me grounded; but something was missing.

One day as I was sitting in my chair waiting for my next client, my coworker's pastor and his wife entered the salon. The pastor would get his hair cut by the owner. While he was sitting there waiting for his turn, I walked by him to go out the door and get something out of my car. He said to me "you're searching for something and you're not settled." The weird thing about that was, I was at a standstill at my church, and that whole week I was trying to understand why. I was at a point where I felt like my learning had come to a halt and that my time was up. I felt like I was placed at the church for that year in order to get balanced. It was a good place for me while I was in the crawling position, and I was now ready for the next stage. I pondered what my coworker's pastor said to me in the salon that day, and then decided to visit their church. I actually enjoyed it, I felt like I was coming out of stagnation. Over the next few months, my heart was toiling, and I felt like a cheater, but I knew I had to do what was best for Amir and me. After visiting this church for a while, I ended up joining. I didn't do the traditional walk down the aisle to the altar, because I suffered with extreme shyness when it came to being in front of people. So after service was over, I went into a room in the back of the church where all of the new congregants were. They were giving their information to the ministry leaders so they could be put into the church's directory.

I grew tremendously in a short span of time. The messages that were being delivered across the pulpit helped me to move to the next dimensions of my life. I also encountered some really great people who became very special to me. I stayed pretty busy and on the move, which was good for me at that time because it allowed me to focus on what was ahead of me and not become sidetracked with any distractions. I still knew that I had a long road ahead, but at least I got a jump start on my path.

Part of my path was women. That included young ladies, as well as my peers. My particular preferences were troubled, unfortunate, and pregnant teenagers. For some reason, it seemed like the younger girls were drawn to me. They seemed to be really intrigued with me, wherever I went. I never knew why, but later on someone told me that I carried a certain aura about myself. I really enjoyed making the young ladies happy, especially the unfortunate ones. There was one little girl that I absolutely adored. She lived next door to me. I would take her everywhere with me, amusement parks, church, shopping, restaurants. She never really left the neighborhood before, and I wanted to give her that chance. It brightened my heart, because after a couple years, I saw a big change in her. She became more feminine, open-minded, and aware of her surroundings. Unfortunately, when I moved, I lost contact with her. Every time I would try and call her mother no one would answer. Then her phone became disconnected. One day I stopped by her house, and they had moved. I guess it was my assignment to be a catalyst for her at that time.

My peers held a special place in my heart as well. I knew that many of them experienced some of the same things I did and even worse. There was this young lady that used to come by the shop with

CHAPTER 5 – FAITH

black eyes. She was a pretty girl, and had two children by a man that was at least fifteen years older than her. She lived with him for five years. She had no relationship with her family, and relied on him. In her mind, she had the best of everything. He gave her diamonds, furs, cars, and a house. She was a constant reminder; although things may look good on the outside, nothing could compare with those things that were corrupt internally. Her strength showed in the streets, but when it came to that man, all power and control were gone. Her man had kids scattered all around the city. There were times when she would come into the shop crying so hard that I had to take her and calm her down. I also remember this one particular time when he stomped her on the ground to the point where she was bleeding and couldn't see out of one of her eyes. He put her out of her own house and she had to stay with a friend. As mischievous as we all were, I believe the people I surrounded myself with really helped me. I am certain my past allowed me to be able to help destitute women and girls. Because of this I was able to have compassion and be understanding of their issues.

Although I stayed busy and fellowshipped with my new friends, my desire for male companionship was still there. I didn't want a relationship. I just wanted someone other than women to hang out with all of the time. But of course when a male entered the picture, it ended up being the opposite; I always seemed to hang out with just one person at a time. This created familiarity, and bonding. There was a guy I started spending time with who belonged to my church. We would hang out with some of the same people. We grew into a relationship pretty fast, but it wasn't a healthy one. It started off okay, but after a while, we got caught up in non-intercourse activities that were not appropriate, and I would feel bad afterwards. I remembered my mother telling me not to get serious because it was my first Christian relationship, and I was still growing. The relationship shortly ended, and it hurt for a quick second. Because I was so cold to the hurt of relationships at this point, it actually shocked me that I allowed this one to touch a nerve. What I discovered within myself was I allowed God to enter my heart and

I was now able to feel; my heart was softening up.

During my times of blindness God always held my hand and forgave me. Amazingly, I still shunned Him with negative thoughts. I would feel condemned, thinking He was going to punish me severely every time I made a wrong move. I had not yet learned how to accept His love. I saw Him through the distorted view that had become all too familiar throughout the years. I compared Him with man. I was used to being reminded when I did something wrong, but not congratulated when I did something right. It kind of became factual in my mind that as human beings we were supposed to make each other feel bad about something we did until we got the point, through silence or harsh discipline. In spite of that, he loved me anyway.

One day I came to work with a thousand dollars in an envelope. I went to the bank before I got there that morning. After I made the withdrawal, I had fifteen dollars left in my account. When I walked in the door, the assistant pastor of my church was sitting in the chair getting his hair cut. I reached into my pocketbook and took the envelope out and handed it to him. I asked him if he could give it to my pastor as soon as he got back to the church. I felt so relieved when I let the money go. The day before, I felt led to sow that amount into my church. Then that same night I had a dream that implied that I gave the money and then my car blew up. It wasn't a fearful dream, but puzzling. I guess the assistant pastor gave my pastor the money right away because he called the salon the next morning and thanked me with great appreciation. He then said to me, "Cee, you don't know what you have done for yourself. I want you to read Genesis 26 every chance you get because it is for you." Right before he hung up he said, "Thank you baby, you are a strong and special young lady." I felt so giddy inside after I hung up because I never had a man speak into my life in a positive and strong manner like that before. I had such a great feeling of joy that day.

During those next few weeks after I gave the money, business dried up almost instantly. Things seemed like they got slow out of nowhere. All of a sudden, my car which I was still paying for started

CHAPTER 5 – FAITH

acting crazy. Of course the warranty was now expired. The car was costing me too much money to maintain. It was still practically brand new but it was in the shop every three weeks for something different. I had to call the manufacturer and fight with them for another warranty, for free. Rent and bills were piling up. The thousand dollars I gave to my pastor and my church was the last of my savings. I was a little anxious but yet at peace because I knew what I felt about giving the money was not from me; it was from God.

The following week was still slow for me at work. My pastor came by to get his haircut, and while waiting his turn, I went and sat next to him. I started to express how weary I was getting because of my finances, and the state of my clientele. I let him know how it was affecting me. He gave me some advice and suggested I should make this my last two weeks at the salon and do it from home for a while. I took his advice and talked to my boss. By the end of those two weeks, I was gone. Two days hadn't even passed before my phone was ringing off the hook for appointments. I was so ecstatic, I couldn't believe it. By the end of the four day work week at home I made back what I gave to the church and more. I paid all of my bills and had an overflow to put in the bank. I knew it wasn't fortune or luck; it was my Heavenly Father who kept His word about how He would supply all my needs according to His riches in glory.

One week after that great blessing, my car broke down again. I had to get a rental for two weeks while the car was in the shop and while the dispute was going on regarding the warranty. I needed something to get around in because Amir and I practically lived in our car because we were on the go so much. The rental was candy apple red, and sporty. It had a nice smooth ride, and was pretty spacious inside. My car dealer paid for it; they didn't want any more hassle out of me, especially after I wrote a letter to the head of the company concerning my issues. After two weeks I finally got my car back, and my warranty was approved. But for some reason I was not excited. That car had given me such a headache that I didn't care anymore. I knew it would have still been an inconvenience, and I just didn't want to be bothered. It was from the first batch of models that were made, and all the kinks were probably not ironed out.

I didn't know what to do, so I called my pastor's wife's sister, Mrs. Pat from my church. I really looked up to her as a mentor. She was a very wise and practical woman. She was straight and to the point with everything. She sugar coated nothing, and that's how I preferred it. I expressed my car dilemma with her. She told me to trust God and go get another car. She said to pray and ask God to send me the right car salesman. I didn't exactly know what I wanted, I just wanted something reliable.

The next day I grabbed one of my girlfriends and asked her to go with me. I drove around and ended up at a dealership about twenty five minutes from my house. I took Mrs. Pat's advice and did exactly what she told me to do. I asked God to show me the salesperson who was supposed to service me. One salesman walked up to me and introduced himself and asked if I needed help, and before I could say anything he got a call on the loud speaker, and excused himself. We were standing there waiting for him to come back, and another salesman just popped up out of nowhere. He introduced himself and asked if we needed any help. I instantly knew that he was the one that was supposed to help me. From there, my girlfriend and I went with him and looked around the lot. I fell in love with the higher model cars, but after we did a few numbers, the prices were not in my range. He then asked me to come with him, and said, "I have a great car for you, and I think it would be perfect, and more affordable." Then he said, "Actually this car is in more demand, and it's prettier than what you looked at earlier." So we followed him around the corner and guess what was sitting in the middle of the show room floor - the same exact candy apple red car I had as a rental, but this one was more appealing because it was shinier, had nice rims, plush insides, was brand new, and had my favorite thing of all- a clear and very loud radio with extremely good bass. I loved listening to good, loud, clear music while I drove- it was therapeutic. I just started laughing because I already knew it was mine. After we did the numbers, I traded my car in with money

CHAPTER 5 – FAITH

still owed on it, and no money to put down. Before I knew it, all the papers were signed, and I rode off the lot with the car in time to pick up my son from school. I thanked God all the way home. My faith started to grow even more; I knew God loved me. Not because He gave me something, but because I started understanding His process of faith in my life.

I was twenty two by now, and ready to move out of the neighborhood where we lived. I wanted to go somewhere peaceful, and I wanted Amir to grow up in a better environment. It was also time for him to have his own bedroom. We were outgrowing our one bedroom apartment, and my kitchen and living room were becoming too small for my clientele. I was also ready to open up a salon and own my own home. I started driving around to different parts of the city that I knew were better neighborhoods and I saw a few nice properties. There were storefronts and side entry basements, but I wasn't too fond of the streets they were on. When I did come across a few decent streets, the traffic flow wasn't good for business. I finally ended up asking my girlfriend for her realtor's phone number. I called him to set up an appointment to meet. Once we met, he ran my credit, and checked my finances to see what I could afford. Then we went on our search to see what was best suitable for me. I saw quite a few interesting things but only one caught my eye. It was everything that I was looking for: a great neighborhood and well-manicured corner property, with a side entrance to the basement. It also had three bedrooms, a nice size kitchen and bath, and hardwood and carpeted floors.

It was very cute, and I got excited. The next day I made an offer, and the owner accepted. A problem occurred when I went over to the house one day just to check and see why the owner hadn't returned the realtor's calls or mine. Much to my surprise, I found out she didn't sign the sale agreement and ended up selling it to someone who had all cash. I was in shock for a moment and had to regroup. My disappointment only lasted for a very short moment. After that ordeal I still wanted to move, but not within the city anymore. My whole mental state had changed. I decided to venture

IN MY MIND

out of my comfort zone, leave Pennsylvania and go to a new state.

One morning I woke up and drove to the Seven Eleven to grab a real estate and rental guide. I went to the park and sat in my car to look through it. My desired areas were Delaware and New Jersey, which both seemed to offer good things. I changed my mind from buying to renting because I didn't want to be stuck in one place, just in case I didn't like it. I came across a complex in New Jersey that had really nice townhomes. The prices seemed okay for what they were offering. I called and made an appointment to come in and tour the development, and fill out an application. The next day I asked a girlfriend to ride over with me because I didn't want to get lost by myself. When we got there, the complex was pretty nice. The landscaping was perfect. It had three playgrounds, a large basketball court, and an Olympic-size swimming pool. After I got to the office and filled out the application, the lady behind the desk said there was a six to nine month waiting list. I got a little discouraged because I was ready to move right away. I didn't think of everything else as far as Amir's schooling and my work, not to mention the time it would take to switch everything over. I went home a little disheartened because I fell in love with the place. All I could hear were birds chirping in my head, and the peace and quiet. I wanted to experience that right away. I wanted Amir to be able to go outside without me and play safely.

A week had passed, and the townhomes were still on my mind. My phone rang and it was the rental office. The woman that took my application had excitement in her voice while she informed me that I was the most eligible person on the waiting list, and that there was only one townhouse available. She said if I was ready, I could move in, and it would be available in two weeks. My mouth fell open with disbelief which was quickly replaced with happiness. She told me in order for the townhouse to be held, I had to come in and put a deposit down as soon as possible. I told her I would be there first thing in the morning. I had just enough saved up in the bank for the deposit. I found out that unit was supposed to go to a gentleman that week. He had put a deposit down, but the

CHAPTER 5 – FAITH

apartment building that he was moving from would not allow him to break his lease. The funny part about it was, two days before the office called me I was riding through a suburban area in my city, and just happened to ride past a street with the same name as the complex in New Jersey. It startled me, because I rode past that street many times before and never noticed its name. All I could think was God was showing me things to come.

The next morning, I quickly drove to the complex to give them my deposit. I had to pay one month's rent and security, which totaled twelve hundred dollars. My rent came out to be six hundred dollars per month. That was three hundred dollars more than what I was already paying at my apartment. Those numbers didn't scare me because I had such peace about it. I knew I would be taken care of. I gave my landlord three weeks' notice, and paid extra for such a short notification. While I was at my apartment for those two weeks packing, the townhouse was getting painted, cleaned, and ready for Amir and me to move in. I got one of the best views in the entire complex. My bedroom overlooked the pool which was set up like a resort area. It had lounge chairs and tables with umbrellas over them. The flowers and trees surrounding it gave it a Caribbean feel. I also had a big tree by my window, where the singing birds sat on the branches and made melodies every morning. It had two bathrooms and a laundry room upstairs. I appreciated every amenity; it just made life a little simpler compared to my one bedroom apartment where I had to walk to the Laundromat and drive to a place for Amir to play outside because we lived on a four lane street with a lot of traffic.

Because I was moving to a new area and another state, and couldn't do my clients' hair at the apartment anymore, I had to find somewhere else to service them close by. There was a new salon that opened up, not too far from the old apartment. I wanted to make sure that my clients weren't being too inconvenienced. But after working there for two weeks I couldn't do it anymore because it was a hassle. Some clients were happy for me because of my new beginnings, but some were very disappointed and actually upset with me. The commute back and forth and having to pick Amir up and continually bring him to the shop along with me and not being able to be close to our home after I got off of work was very tedious. The fortunate thing that did come out of it was that I had a couple of faithful clients that did follow me to New Jersey. They would either drive the forty minutes across the bridge, or catch the train, so I did have some consistent money flowing. I got my keys to the townhouse and started going back and forth across the bridge every day bringing boxes and bags. It took about four days to get everything moved and settled. My brother on my father's side, my father, and my boyfriend at the time helped me on the last day to move the big stuff. My brother had a Sanford and Son truck so they loaded everything on, and took it over.

After making my decision to leave the shop in Philly I drove across the street from my complex on my day off, to a barbershop with a hair salon in the back of it. I asked the owner if he was looking for any help, told him where I was from, and that I was licensed. Before I could finish my introduction he said, "yes" in an anxious voice. He proceeded to tell me that he had one stylist but she just got up and left a week prior and never came back. She had a large clientele. He also said that she left a pile of her client's names and numbers in the drawer. Then he asked if I had to build my clientele from scratch. I told him yes, but it wouldn't be a problem. He then stated "Well, you can pick up where she left off because her clients have been coming in frantic, trying to find her." I asked him when I could start, and he replied, "as soon as possible." I played it cool until I got in my car, then I just lost it. I cried, because God showed Himself faithful once again. Once I got myself together, I drove around to the neighborhood school and registered Amir. After about a week and a half, everything was settled.

I was the only woman working amidst six barbers. It was good that the salon was a separate section, but the women still had to walk through the barbershop in order to get to the back where I was. At least they did not have to get serviced in front of the men. Everyone was extremely nice, and got along with each other. My

CHAPTER 5 - FAITH

clientele started to grow tremendously in a matter of weeks. A few of my clients and I became really good friends. Some of them actually lived in my complex. They too had children, which allowed my son to gain friends. My mind transformed with a whole new way of thinking. The atmosphere and surroundings were an entirely different outlook for us. It was amazing to know that just across the bridge was a whole new world.

A year had passed and it was about time for me to depart the salon. Things were getting a little haywire because the boss wanted to change his policies. He noticed that my clientele was growing fast, and felt as though he wasn't profiting the way he thought he should have. He told me that starting the following week I had to rent out the back of the shop for three hundred and fifty dollars per week instead of a percentage. He also said I had to purchase my own supplies, and had no choice in the matter. His manner and tone was very direct. That would have been fourteen hundred dollars per month including supplies for a small one- sink two-chair room in the back of a barbershop. I thought to myself, "He must have lost his mind." There was no way I was going to pay that; I could have owned my own salon for that amount of money. He must have thought I was stupid or something. When I did not agree, he told me to give him all of my clients' information, because they were his and not mine. In a nutshell he was basically saying if I chose not to work there, fine! But wherever I go I would have to start from scratch, so he thought. When I rebutted, he said he was keeping my pay.

We ended up getting into a heated argument, he bucked at me and I bucked back. We were standing there toe to toe, close enough to feel the mist of his saliva on my face. Two barbers were still in the shop cleaning up, watching everything and shaking their heads. Even though it looked as if he was about to hit me neither one stepped in to help. I guess they didn't want to lose their jobs. I ended up calling one of my friends from Philly and told him to come to the shop. In the midst of his travel, I called him back and told him to turn around and not to come. I decided to diffuse it myself. I went home, got all of my clients' information, went back to the shop, and gave it to him so I could get my money. Little did he know I always kept copies of my clients' information. Once he was satisfied, he gave me my money, I left and that was it! For the rest of that evening, I called as many clients as I could and told them what happened. I started making appointments for them to come to my home. God had a purpose for everything. It was meant for me to work there to gain ground, but not to stay.

I did hair at home for a while, sometimes at five o clock in the morning. I worked a lot; my life was extremely busy. The only days I had off were Tuesdays and Sundays. Tuesdays were strictly for taking care of personal business in the morning, and kicking back relaxing, whether it be by the pool reading my Bible, walking the track, or going to see a movie. I got all of that done before it was time to pick Amir up from school. One of those Tuesdays I would go to the market and buy groceries for the month. I would then cook enough meats and vegetable to last for about three weeks, and freeze them. It was something my grandmother taught me, so we could eat healthy, save time, and save money. Every Tuesday evening Amir and I would have date night. We either caught a movie or went out to eat. Tuesdays were kids eat free night, so after he finished his homework and I finished my chores, we would go. We both looked forward to it. That was our quality time together. Sundays were strictly for church. I would get us up early so we could be on time because we still went to church in Philly. That was the only thing that kept me going and the only thing that kept Amir in the loop with people and direction besides school.

Amir struggled a bit with not having Rico around, especially when he saw other children with their fathers. We heard from and saw Rico maybe once every couple of years. I always stayed informed of his whereabouts through one of his sisters. She and I were pretty close. She would invite us to some of their family functions. She was the type of person that believed in family, and was a stickler on keeping people together. I loved and admired her for that. If it wasn't for her, Amir wouldn't have had any type of connection with

CHAPTER 5 – FAITH

that side of his family, even though it was still very limited.

I couldn't recall the last time I had spoken with Rico prior to the family reunion that his sister invited Amir and me to. By that time I heard he had five other children. His last two children were boys, and he was still with their mother. He didn't bring her to the reunion at first because he knew Amir and I would be there. Amir was so excited to see him, he couldn't wait, I could tell by his countenance. The park that the reunion was held in was okay, but it had a walking path I didn't care for. It had abandoned cars, broken glass, tires, and trash all over the place. Rico wanted to take him on a walk in it but I didn't feel comfortable, so I said that I didn't think it was a good idea. He instantly got mad, stormed off, got in his car, and sped away. Amir really didn't have any expression on face during that time. He just looked away and ran off to continue playing with the other children at the reunion. I was baffled because I didn't say anything out of the way; I even had a peaceful tone in my voice, and had a good reason for my decision.

After he pulled off, I just sat on a blanket that was laid out on the ground, while Amir ran around and played with the other kids. Rico came back about forty five minutes later with his newborn son and girlfriend. Some of his family at the reunion pre-warned me that she was supposed to be super tough. What did I care, I was there for my son. She got out of the car holding the baby with an attitude written all over her face. She started walking really fast towards the area where Rico's mom and his sisters and I were. Then in a loud voice she started saying "hey everybody, look at the baby, he's here." She kept repeating herself, so everyone would know they arrived. I guess Amir's father brought her there to make me jealous. It made him even angrier because I reacted in an opposite manner. When she got close enough to where she could hear me, I asked her if I could hold the baby. It must have startled the both of them, because he just walked away. She was hesitant at first, but gave the baby to me any way. I guess I caught her by surprise, and threw their whole game plan out the window.

While I goo-gooed and played with the baby, she got up and

made herself a plate. When she came back we started talking. During our conversation she began to open up. She started by telling me that she heard so much about me and Amir. She said she saw him once when Rico brought him by the house one year. I listened, and I expressed to her how God was taking care of us. Then she started tearing up and saying how she needed to go back to church, and then continued by discussing certain things that went on in her and Rico's relationship. I felt really bad for her, so I encouraged her and gave her words of hope. In the midst of her receiving them, Rico came over and broke the bonding up. Her whole tone changed when he strolled up, and she left the same way she came in. After they walked off, all I could do was thank God that it wasn't me.

It was very unfortunate that every time Amir saw Rico, it was only for a moment. Then after that he would not hear from him again for a couple of years, unless it was by accident or through a family member. The last time he saw him, I was driving down the street, and Amir spotted him, and said, "there's my dad" so I pulled over. Rico came to the car and took a bundle of money with fifties, twenties, and tens out of his pocket, pulled one dollar bill out of the stack and gave it to Amir, along with the bag of chips that he had in his hand. The interesting part of it all was that I never asked him for child support. Some people thought that I was making an unwise decision by not making Rico responsible, but I guess I had a lot of pride in that area. I didn't want him doing anything if it wasn't from his heart. I wasn't interested in obligatory giving. Amir and I were well taken care of. I may have struggled financially at times but it was a peaceful struggle, and I knew that I did not owe anyone, or have anything held over my head. I would rather he spent time with him over money any day.

6
Guarded

Amir's first grade year was over by now at the school he was attending. His school was okay, but I wanted something a little better. It was an average neighborhood school that three of the neighboring townships shared. I needed something more personal and diverse for him so I searched out one of the better private schools in the area. I applied and they accepted him because of his high test scores and grades. He was an intelligent child, the only problem he had was his mouth. He was a talker and that would get him in trouble quite often. Another habit he struggled with was falling asleep in class, even if he did go to bed on time the night before. I think I engrained that in him subconsciously because whenever we were in church I would make him lie across my lap and go to sleep. He was very active at times, and I was a newcomer and needed to pay attention as much as I could. I knew the routine I set for him was for my convenience, but it ended up spilling over into his everyday life.

Whenever he was somewhere he didn't want to be, he could make himself fall asleep, even if he wasn't tired.

I felt bad because the pastor would say "all of you parents out there should not allow your children to sleep in church because that shows a lack of respect for God, and it forms bad habits." Of course I felt horrible and would try and wake him up, but he was an extremely hard sleeper and a cranky person when his sleep was interrupted, so I would miss most of the service. One thing my pastor did that made me feel a little better was give me a look that said, "it's okay I understand."

Amir had one main buddy in our development that he hung out with. This boy was two years older than him and had a little more experience. His mother and I became pretty good friends, and she would watch Amir for me. I loved going over her house because she was the best baker I knew. She would bake whenever she was in deep thought or was going through something. All of her pastries were gourmet. I gained so much weight by being her taste tester every time she made a new batch. She took her hobby and made it a side business and did well. I admired her wit. She was an intelligent woman but let too many things get in her way. She graduated from the top business school in the country with honors, and managed to do that being a single mother while her son's father was in prison. Her decisions weren't always wise and she paid for them in the long run, but in the end she came out great. Her son provided such great inspiration with his smile. I think God painted it permanently on his face when he was born. I enjoyed having him around because he was always so cheerful, and he and Amir were good company for each other. Unfortunately there did come a time when separation had to come between them. His family had a few personal issues that needed to be attended to, and he had to move away for a while.

Not too long after that, Amir befriended another boy who lived in the development. His mother and I also became really close. She was three years older than me and her son was four years younger than Amir. We all bonded pretty well. She was like a sister to me even though she acted like a grandmother. She had such a nurturing spirit about her. She would cook for her and her son but share her food with Amir and me all of the time. In return, I did her hair, so everything was good. I appreciated the fact that she watched Amir for me every Saturday while I worked. He was fed very well when he was in her care. God made sure we were surrounded with what we needed.

There were two other special people in my life, my pastor and

CHAPTER 6 – GUARDED

his wife. It just so happened when I moved to New Jersey, they lived only about seven minutes away from me. We weren't even aware, until one day Mrs. Pat told us. That's when my pastor's wife and I grew a strong bond. She made me feel comfortable in whatever state I was in. She would take me out shopping with her and teach me how she bargained for her family, and saved money, along with showing me little things like hanging pictures on the wall correctly, and changing my dishcloths regularly. She took me under her wing and poured into me. She also enjoyed my company because I was her shopping buddy during the day when everyone else was at work. And boy, did she know how to shop!

I appreciated all of my newfound New Jersey friends. They loved on me no matter what. They knew how to read right through me and didn't mind taking the time to cultivate some things within me because I could be very closed off at times. I knew it came from my past, dealing with things that I wasn't emotionally delivered from yet like blaming myself for bad relationships and some friendships that were lost. I always had an overwhelming belief that I chased people away. I struggled for years over my best friend Nikki because of the loss of our friendship. She and I were together through a lot of things and then she decided to move out of town to another state and start a new life so we lost touch. I tried contacting her for years but it just didn't happen. I would actually feel sorrow at times because I walked with a spirit of rejection. She was the only person out of all of my friends that I felt I could be my full self with.

In addition, the lack of outwardly affection from men in my life played a big part as well, because I longed for that most of the time. Most of the men I had known throughout my life whether in my family, my neighborhood or my romantic life were very aggressive, although some had their tender moments. It was the tender moments that I longed for but they never seemed to last. I had been in a relationship with so many men who were abusive, possessive or controlling in some way that I wondered if there was any man who could simply love me without adding any of that other stuff to it.

The lack of intimate bonding between my mother, father and

I also definitely played a part in my loneliness. There was some distance because of personality conflicts as well as the distractions of life that came between us. My mother loved me unconditionally and I loved her the same way, but we did not know how to share our emotions with each other in a way where we both could understand one another clearly. She would be frustrated with me because I was so obstinate at times and thought I knew everything. I was frustrated because I was always searching for her approval and understanding.

My father loved me as well but there was always a sense of distance between us. Our contact with each other wasn't what it should have been. I think the enemy enjoyed every moment of it. He was proud of himself for thinking that he had separated yet another family emotionally and spiritually. How I related to those closest to me was reflected in how I reacted to other people. My exterior was warm until affection and intimacy presented itself. I would throw up a wall that said, "back up about ten feet, you're getting too close. We can laugh and smile together without all of that mushy stuff." At the same time my internal being would scream out, "Hello! Hello! I'm in here, Hug me! I am loveable. I am not really who you see, I just don't know how to show it. I don't know how to get out!"

That behavior affected some of my relationships because some people did not understand what I was feeling. I would sometimes come off cold to them and they would back away. I did have a warm demeanor most of the time but unfortunately the cold side took the dominate role. People did not view me as being a mean spirited person, but I was so guarded that they felt like they did not have the time or the strength to try and break through. As bad as I wanted to be loveable and be loved, I just did not know how to express it. There was this one woman in church that noticed my lack of physical affection and taught me how to hug. Every time she saw me she gave me a big bear hug. Afterwards she would tell me to stop hugging with one arm. She would call me the one armed bandit. She told me to use both arms and squeeze, and to stop doing the Miss America pageant hug. It took me a while, but practice made perfect. It really felt good, but my emotions were still secretly distant. The fear that

CHAPTER 6 – GUARDED

I retained in that area came from different rejections over the years. My heart was hiding and that was not good at all. I learned how to stand tall and be strong, yet be absent of emotion. Sometimes in the midst of private moments, my emotions would burst forth; no one saw my tears but God.

I tried not to let anyone see me cry because I didn't want to be known as a cry baby and a weakling. After I finished crying, I would get food and that would settle me. It was my comfort and it became a crutch. I got tired of living a peephole life, where I could see out, but no one could see in. I had a "prove it to me" attitude at times. Some of my perceptions were distorted because I didn't understand how this thing called "give and take" worked. I thought if someone really wanted to know me, they would read between the lines and dig to find out. I felt that if they didn't force their way into my life, then they didn't care. It took me a long time to learn that everyone didn't have the grace to do that. People would just assume that I didn't want to be bothered and would move on. Only a few had the grace to help chisel some of my rough places.

The problem that did occur when I let people in was that I loved too hard. I loved so hard that I became possessive and protective. The thoughts of people not staying long remained in the forefront of my mind. I felt like I needed to enjoy the moment with them because they would be gone later. I had some really serious battles going on in my mind.

Sometimes I distanced myself intentionally from people when I thought they saw right through me. I gave no eye contact and had little speech. After that, I just knew that they would not want to engage in conversation with me again, so to avoid any further perceived rejection, I distanced myself even more before they had a chance to make that decision on their own. The only thing that kept some people coming back and not leaving was they had the grace to see my loving and caring heart through the hardness I portrayed.

There was a lesson I did learn from this type of behavior. I learned it working in a nursing home doing hair for the residents. It taught me that the behavior I exhibited could spill over into my old age if I didn't allow God to soften my heart. Age isn't always a sign of maturity and wisdom. I knew that I could be stifled by not opening my heart. I knew wisdom and experience was always in front of me, but it was my choice to make it into something good. I learned this from the elderly women that I serviced at the home. Some of them were so cute and adorable, while others were feisty and hellions. A few had already checked out mentally, while others were in their right mind. But there was one thing they did have in common- they all had limited visitors or none at all. I felt bad because I could feel their loneliness. The assistant nurses would bring down two ladies at a time. I would try and pick their brains to get any wisdom I could while doing their hair. Some would share, and others would hold back because of their distrust, and bitterness. They seemed to never have obtained peace in their spirits. There was one little old lady who was alive and well. She was one hundred and two years old, and she looked just like the little old maid on the playing cards. She had beautiful white hair, with these little beady eyes, and thick round glasses. She was just as cute as she wanted to be. I loved when it was her turn to come down, because she had this spunk about her that just tickled me. She was in her right mind, and would always talk about getting a boyfriend. I enjoyed how she talked positively about living life to its fullest, and by her temperament she did that. She was okay with not getting any visitors because she was at peace with herself. She had outlived all of her family and friends.

On the flip side the nurse would bring one lady down who did nothing but speak negatively. She complained about everything including how many pills she had to take, and how horrible life was. I felt so bad for some of them, because I could see the pain in their blank stares. I also felt bad because of their horrible living conditions. The aids that cared for them were only working for a check. They had no concern about their well being at all. The facility was not strict on cleanliness because the ladies were brought down to me smelling like urine, and sometimes waste. I tried to bear it as long as I could, but after I complained a few times and saw no progress, I had to go. Overall, that experience was definitely an eye opener for me.

7
Attainable

I wasn't even interested in looking for another salon. After the mishap I had with the owner from the last one, I was a little skeptical about working for someone else. Therefore I continued working out of my house. I knew how to hustle and stay afloat. But the clean-up of hair and lack of personal space for Amir and I started to become a bit much, so I changed my mind about working from home. One day, a client told me she had a friend who was opening up a salon with her husband. She told me they were looking for a stylist as soon as possible. They were new to the industry, and needed someone to give it a jumpstart. So while she was sitting in my chair, she called her friend and told her about me, and then passed me the phone. We introduced ourselves and set up a time to meet the next day. Because it was about two townships away from my home, I was excited and looked forward to meeting new people and gaining more clients.

As I drove to my interview, the scenery was beautiful. I took the back roads, so I didn't have to deal with the heavy traffic. When I pulled up, no one was there. I waited in my car and scoped out the place and its surroundings, to see if it was suitable for me. It looked okay, and appeared to be in a great location. There was a gas station right across the street and two restaurants next door. The rest of the area was a lot of open land,

and a few housing developments. It was very peaceful and quiet, and that's what I liked. A car finally pulled up and parked. A woman got out and came over to me. She had a big smile and asked me if I had been waiting long. We greeted each other, she opened the door with her key and we went inside. When we got inside I was very happy to see that everything was brand new, including shampoo bowls, styling chairs, stations, and supplies. As she was giving me a tour of the building, I was surprised to see a huge barbershop in the front. We came in through the side door and I didn't see it at first. None of the barbers were there because it was an off day for everyone.

We finally sat down and discussed business. She explained to me that she and her husband wanted to start a salon together and that she was still in cosmetology school. She needed the shop to be managed until she got out of school every day. She told me that the barbers had a large clientele, and a lot of their wives were waiting for a stylist to arrive. I got excited inside, because that meant opportunities for more business. Before we left, we went over the rules and came to a mutual payment agreement. I expressed my concerns as well as listened to hers.

We clicked instantly, and I felt it would be a good journey.

It was my first day at the salon, and I had to walk through the front entrance where the barbershop was located because the side door was locked. The place was filled with men. There were about seven barbers, and it was packed with clients. I confidently said hello while nervously walking to the back where the salon was.

I started unpacking my equipment and products quietly because I was the new kid on the block. Right before I finished, a couple of guys came back to introduce themselves. It was like a candy store. I didn't want to get a cavity so I kept it moving with a friendly hello. As time went on, a few of them tried their best to get a good game rolling, but I kept it strictly business. I think I was a mystery to them because I didn't budge to any of their advances. A couple of them were really cool, and we

CHAPTER 7 – ATTAINABLE

became pretty close. They would come back to the salon area when they weren't busy, and tell me about their love lives and financial moves. Others were the opposite, especially one of the guys who tried to hit on me and didn't succeed. He got his ego shattered, and tried to flip the script on me. He started acting cocky towards me and would come in the back some mornings and not speak. When he did speak, he was very sarcastic and exaggerated his greetings. He made comments such as "hey pastor" or "holy roller." He got that from watching me read my Bible in the car during my lunch breaks, or when the salon was slow.

As time went on my clientele really grew. There was another girl working there with me, but she and I really didn't mix. She was very condescending at times, and would send off little vibes here and there, which allowed me to know that she was not too pleased with me and my consistent work ethics. She ganged up with some of the guys up front, and then started to bash my name, which was okay with me. They didn't know that they were right up my alley; I actually got a kick out of it.

One year later the salon did so well that my boss and her husband decided to get their own building. The new building was an old dental office which her husband transformed into a salon in a matter of weeks. Amir's school was only about eight minutes away. It was one of the better private schools in the area. The location was perfect because I was able to pick him up from school and bring him back to work with me. Most of the time he just wanted to sit in the car because he was tired of coming to the salon. I felt horrible because I had no one to watch him in that area. I would turn down hundreds of dollars a week in the salon just so I could get him home. I had to do hair in the house quite a bit because I couldn't stay late in the salon. There was a sense of tension there because I chose to leave and take my son home to feed him and do homework, instead of making the extra money. I guess what was not understood was that his well-being came first. It was sad because it came down to being a bit of a conflict and misunderstanding, about me leaving so early and doing my own clients that I generated from my previous salon at home, so I left. I guess they felt like I was taking from the salon but in actuality, they had husbands and family who kept their children while they were working, so they did not have to worry about much. My boss and I got into a heated argument so I gathered my things and left, jumped in my car, pulled off quickly, went to the park to cool off, then went home and started calling my clients that I had on the books for that day to come to my home. I also called back a salon owner that heard about me and was interested in me working for her. She had been trying to get me to come to her salon for weeks but I kept declining because I wanted to stay put at the salon where I was and be stable for my clients. After talking with the salon owner, I went in to meet with her, her husband and the staff, and I instantly fell right in. It felt like a family. I was so grateful for the provision that God was allowing. His grace was definitely sufficient for me. My boss had quite a few children, some teenagers and some Amir's age. Amir would spend time over their house and play games with the kids or sometimes get in the pool when I had to work late. My boss and her husband would also make sure he ate something if I was really busy. They truly looked out for us. Nevertheless I was very grateful for the time I spent at the salon prior but it just didn't work out too well.

Life was difficult at times because I never really seemed to fit in. No matter how hard I tried, it just did not seem to happen. After experiencing rejection throughout my life, the spirit of loneliness would creep in. That feeling was so strong at times; it felt like I was losing my mind. I would cry out to God so hard for comfort and peace. Sometimes trying to fit in would become such an obstacle. I would go into a situation already expecting to be pushed out. My perceptions were really taking a hold over me. I realized this behavior wasn't good because it was causing my own reality. So I started putting my perceptions,

CHAPTER 7 – ATTAINABLE

expectations, and fears behind me and started going into situations naked. I stripped my mind of all false accusations; yet still got pushed out. I felt like I couldn't win. This really confused me, and I didn't know what to do, so I spent a lot of time alone. But who was I kidding; deep down inside I wanted to belong. Perhaps God would not allow me, because He knew what He needed out of me.

The problem I discovered was, I was having a hard time accepting the fact that God made me a bridge for some people, and when it was time for them to depart out of my life I had a rough time; I wanted to hold on. I would be brokenhearted every time. I perceived this as rejection, when it was only each individual fulfilling their assignment in my life, whether they knew it or not.

There were also other things that were hard for me to accept; especially when it came to Amir. I had many days and nights filled with tears. I was surprised that I didn't get dehydrated. There was one particular morning when the phone rang; it was Amir's principal from middle school. He said he called because he wanted to bring a particular incident to my attention. He told me that Amir's behavior had been very unacceptable within those past few weeks, and he would like to talk to me about it. He shared with me that the teacher disciplined Amir and told him to do something, and because it wasn't very favorable to him, he got upset and threw a pencil. The principal stated that they would have to give him a detention after school, and take away a few recesses. I had very little to say. First of all, I was embarrassed; secondly I was hurt. I felt extremely helpless. Helpless because as a mother and a human being I tried my best to do what I could. I fell into a guilty pattern of 'what did I do wrong, and where am I failing.' I started to beat myself up really bad so I called my pastor's wife so I could talk with her. She had previously told me to call her anytime, and she meant that. As soon as she picked up the phone I just burst into tears. She said, "What's wrong honey?" As I whimpered I told her about the phone call from the principal and how I felt. She began to sympathize with me as well as encourage me. She pumped hope back into me. After we finished talking, she told me not to hang up because my pastor wanted to talk to me. He must have heard her concern while we were on the phone. When he got on the phone he said, "Baby it's going to be alright. Understand that you are doing a good job as a mother, but ninety five percent of Amir's issues are because of a lack of fatherhood and a male presence in his life." He informed me that he just had a lot of frustration within him, and the only way he knew how to express it was through anger. He was directly on point.

Later on that day I got myself together and went to the park after dropping Amir off at school. I spent most of my time talking to God, and listening for answers. My heart was soothed, and my anxiety was gone. That was one of those desperate moments.

I was told that Amir needed a mentor. I wanted to get one for him, but I didn't know how to go about it. There was this man in my church that the assistant pastor at that time recommended. We got a chance to meet him, and he took Amir out about three times. Everything was going smoothly. He was a cop so on one of their outings he took Amir down to the station and showed him around. The other two times they went bowling and out to eat. He brought his son along who was the same age as Amir so he would have company. Unfortunately, all of that had to come to a halt. One day I went to his house to pick Amir up. I asked him how their day was together. His response was "It was fine, just like you" in a mac daddy tone. Instantly my radar went up and I was furious. He was engaged to a woman at my church, so that was the end of that. How could he have been a good role model for my son if he was flirting with me and about to get married? I know that I probably could have had a talk with him and told him that I felt a little uncomfortable with his comment, but I was so against people cheating that I was infuriated by his actions and cut off Amir's time with him

CHAPTER 7 – ATTAINABLE

cold turkey. His fiancé was already looking at me kind of weird when I was at church and I did not want to be the cause of any rift between them, so I left it alone. I did not really have a talk with Amir about it; I just let it drift away. Amir didn't seem to be affected by the change.

God started showing me that He himself wanted to be Amir's full time father. Because I was on such a quest to find a male figure, I doubted God. I could remember feeling hopeless at times and questioning Him, wondering why He would allow Amir to be without his father. It hurt because I knew that one of Amir's silent desires was to have his father in his life. His actions spoke loudly, but he would not verbalize his feelings. My trust in God for that situation continued to be a struggle.

Things were looking up, and were on the move. I was so excited because I had bought my first home and was about to make settlement back in Philadelphia in just a few days. It got a little frustrating driving around for so long searching in different areas of New Jersey for places to open a business. After a while, I gained a sense of hope in knowing that it would happen in its own time. The process was not the easiest and there were a lot of ups and downs associated with it. The realtor who was selling the property I was interested in was selling it for a nephew of the deceased older couple who owned it. This realtor was stuck in the eighties. He still had a typewriter instead of a computer, and hand delivered everything instead of mailing it. After all of the waiting, I was finally in. I thanked God for allowing everything to go through and for allowing me to start a new season of life. Amir really didn't want to leave New Jersey, but I expressed to him that we had to in order to follow God's plan for our lives. I also told him that sometimes things don't seem like the greatest at that time, but it's good for us in the end. He just couldn't understand how we moved from three playgrounds and a pool to loud police sirens and crowdedness. The major thing that opened my mind to the decision to look back in Philadelphia was, my brother. He and I were on the phone one day and out of the blue, he told me that I was going to open up my first salon in Philadelphia. He had no idea that I was even looking for one. It was amazing because everything fell right into place. He called when I had spent months of searching for property, and found nothing. I took his advice and started my search. I would come across the bridge every weekend for a while and stay at my father's house with him, my sister, and my stepmom. While being there, I got up one morning, and decided to look for rent or sale signs. I already knew if I was to find something I wanted it to be near my church. In my travels I drove up this one street and saw a rent sign in the window. As I rang one of the bells, I realized there were apartments up top. An older lady came to the door with a mean look on her face, and said, "Yes" with a rigid tone. I said hello and introduced myself. I told her I was interested in looking at the place because I saw the rent sign in the window. Before I could even finish my sentence, she cut me off and blurted out "it's already taken" and shut the door. I stood there for a moment, did an about face, and walked towards my car. While I was walking, I looked across the street and saw another salon with a for sale sign in the window with a realtor's name and number on it. I wrote the number down and started to walk to my car. But while I was in motion, I decided to go and knock on the door of the house next to it. Another older woman answered the door, but this one was polite. I asked her if she knew anything about the building and who owned it. She informed me that the owners died. They were an elderly couple who ran the business for thirty five years. She said that a cousin of the husband ran a paper stand across the street on the corner, and that he would know everything about it. I thanked her, gave her a warm smile, and walked across the street to the paper stand. Pete was an older gentleman, a little rough around the edges with a mild temperament. He told me that he had keys to the place and when the stand closed at four o clock, I could come back and look at it. I told him that I would come back with my father. When four o' clock came, He met my

CHAPTER 7 – ATTAINABLE

father and me in front of the building. While he was unlocking the doors, he explained to us that he stayed there three days out of the week just to keep it occupied because of its long term vacancy, and attempted break-ins. Out of those attempts, one was successful. He told me he was in there at the time when the burglar entered. The burglar got as the far as the front vestibule, where Pete knocked him out; at least that's how he told it.

When we got inside, there were curlers, dryers, combs, and equipment lying neatly on the stations. Of course the place needed some updating because it had been sitting for years. But I saw right past that. It was painted bright pink and green, and it had the old fashioned brown bamboo blinds on the windows, with old stations and chairs. But the thing that sold me was all of the equipment. There were so many curling irons, shears, and dryers, all ready to be used. I can tell they were taken care of because they were clean and not worn. All I could think to myself was how I didn't have to buy anything. Everything I needed was all right there. When he finished showing us around, he said, "Okay follow me upstairs to the house." I asked him "What house?" He said, "Upstairs." I was shocked because from the outside, it just looked like a salon standing alone. He said it was a three bedroom house. I looked at my father and said, "Wow!" He said, "This is a blessing." I was taken back for a moment because I never heard my father say that before. Right then, I knew this was it. The best part about it was, after everything was done, and all papers were signed, my mortgage for the business and home together was a couple of hundred dollars less than the rent I paid for my town house in New Jersey. It was situated on a well-kept block, and in a decent neighborhood. More importantly it was on one of the busiest streets in the area, which was excellent for business. Only God could have set that deal in motion. It was my season; I was meant to be there at that particular time.

It was a little fearful for the first few months after moving in. Amir and I left quietness and nature with unlocked doors at night, to noise and bolted locks. That's city living. I slept downstairs on the couch close to the front door for the first six months, because anxiety gripped me for a while. Everything from the neighbors' slammed doors to trolley vibrations and police sirens, kept me on alert. I had been gone for so long that I forgot what it felt like.

After six months and finally getting settled in, I was ready for a grand opening. I needed that time to fix up the place, and also get all of my business matters in order as far as my licenses and documentation. It wasn't too hard because I was on a mission. I did everything that I was supposed to do to be legal. I made all of my appointments in City Hall, along with being on the phone many times with product distributors, contractors and sign makers. I did most of the cosmetics myself, except for laying the carpet and putting up drywall. I would get up at five-thirty every morning and start cleaning and painting. The grand opening was one week before Christmas. I was a little worried because I wasn't sure if people were going to show because of the holiday and shopping. But the outcome surpassed my worries. It was a great turnout. I said to myself, "Wow! I am truly a business owner now. No more bosses, hallelujah!"

After my grand opening, I cleaned up, counted the money, and locked the shop. I was so tired afterwards, that by the time I reached upstairs, I took a shower and got in the bed. I turned the lights off, put my hands behind my head, looked up at the ceiling, and thanked God for this wonderful day. I laid there and reminisced on what He brought me through over the last few years. It allowed me to get where I was. I pondered on how I pushed through every tear, heartache, and anxiety. It was amazing that I made it through those survival moments – as I called them, even when I had doubt.

I thought about that doubt and how God loved me through it whenever it would arise. He knew how He created me and what He put within me. It was just a matter of me totally

CHAPTER 7 – ATTAINABLE

figuring it out. There were times when I allowed a lack of faith to get the best of me, especially when it came to me trusting Him with my entire life. I knew building faith was a process in some areas but I had no idea that I was subconsciously allowing the lack of to affect me from within. I remember one morning years ago, waking up feeling a little funny. My heart was racing, and I was short of breath. It lasted all day, and started progressing later on that evening to the point where I could not sleep. It was so bad you could see my heart palpitating through my shirt. I jumped out of the bed in the middle of the night and got my clothes on. I pulled Amir out of his bed and took him to my girlfriend's house around the corner. I drove myself to the hospital because I was sure that I was having a heart attack. There was no time to wait for an ambulance. When I got there I was gasping for air. They gave me an EKG and also an ultrasound to see my heart. After all of the tests, they found nothing. They gave me something to calm my palpitations, a phone number to call first thing in the morning, and then sent me home. It was the number to Deborah Heart and Lung center. I had no insurance at the time, so later on that week I had to sign up for charity care. The very next day I called and they told me to come in. That morning I took Amir to school, and drove straight there. It took me about an hour to reach it. When the nurse called me back to the room, she took my vital signs and drew blood. Then she took an EKG and some other tests dealing with my lungs. Everything came back normal, even though my heart was still racing like a horse. After the x-rays and the ultra sound they gave me a heart monitor to wear for seventy two hours. They wanted to see if I had any serious heart rhythm problems, outside of the small murmur I already had. I had to wear it day and night, even at work. I also had to wear a mask to work because my breathing was so limited, and my lungs could not withstand the chemicals. They later told me I had an anxiety attack and prescribed medicine to slow my heart rate down. They also gave me advice on breathing techniques, so I could relax. I had no idea that I wasn't relaxed, it just snuck up on me. I guess with all the years of responsibility, and staying afloat, along with keeping everything stable, and multi-tasking, it took a toll. It came together and crashed upon me without my knowing. I guess I did not recognize it because I kept everything inside. I opted not to take the medicine prescribed. I did not like being dependent on drugs without trying natural remedies first. I did however take the nurse's advice. She told me what I could do to relax my mind and calm down the anxiety and palpitations. She said along with the breathing techniques, I should take long hot baths, and not drink any caffeine, like coffee and some teas, and not to consume large amounts of chocolate. She also said I should read a long book that I enjoyed. Well, I started doing those things, and in a matter of two weeks the anxiety fully subsided and did not come back. This was a lesson for me to trust God instead of trying to handle everything on my own and causing so much worry, stress, and anxiety. One of the awesome things that did come out of the situation besides God showing me that I wasn't trusting Him enough was the name of my salon. Even though this situation happened years prior to me starting the business, it birthed the name "Relax Your Mind" which popped in my head while I was in my healing process of settling my heart palpitations down by reading and taking it easy. I felt like that was my motto for life that I could think about whenever I felt any anxiety or stress coming on. It took time and patience to put it into practice, but I kept working at it.

My faith was tested on all levels. There were numerous hospital visits over the years. I remember one particular incident being the most frightening. Amir was outside playing baseball with one of his friends and their dad, and a ball caught him right in his eye socket at full speed. He came in a little hurt, but not crying. I checked it out and it looked okay. I gave him a Popsicle and he went back outside. Early that next morning I

CHAPTER 7 – ATTAINABLE

was doing my girlfriend's hair and I heard him screaming and yelling for me at the top of his lungs. I ran upstairs in a panic and asked him what was wrong. He kept saying "My eye, my eye, I can't see and it hurts real bad." I asked him to open it, and in the midst of him crying, I caught a glimpse of it. All I saw was red. His eye was full of blood. All of a sudden, I went into super woman mode. I don't know how in the world I grabbed his whole body off of the top bunk and threw him over my shoulder. All he had on was night clothes and no shoes. I told my girlfriend to ride with me, and sit in the back seat with him. The only thing that was going through my mind at the time was, "If we don't hurry up and get there, a blood clot or something is going to burst." That's how bad it looked. I ran every light there was. It took us about ten minutes to get there. We pulled up in front of the emergency area, and I jumped out of the car. I left the door open and my girlfriend took him in for me. While waiting for the nurses who seemed to be moving at a slow speed, I started pacing the floor back and forth praying hard. I couldn't even look at him because it made me more upset. They finally took him back and examined him. After they finished, they called an ambulance to come and get us to rush us over to Wills Eye Hospital. Because his case was so severe, they said that they didn't have any specialist there to see him, and there wasn't anything they could do. As soon as we arrived, the doctors were waiting for us at the door. They rushed him right in and straight to the back. After all of the tests and examinations, they informed me that he would not be able to go to school for four weeks. Also he wasn't allowed to run or walk for a week because of the pressure behind his eye. They couldn't do any operating; we just had to wait it out. They gave me a glass shield to keep over his eye at all times, so nothing would come near it and cause any further damage. He had to stay in the bed most of the time with his head elevated, so the pressure could go down. The doctor informed me that he had a five percent chance of developing glaucoma as he got older. The blessing that came from all of this was after his final eye exam weeks later. Everything went back to one hundred percent and the eye that was hit was actually stronger than the other one.

I knew that if God wasn't with me, and had not given me grace to endure my fear and lack of faith, I don't know what I would have done. Looking back on those times made me extremely grateful, it all taught me that I solely had to depend on God.

8
Self Esteem

Throughout my life I battled with a touch of low self esteem. Even with all of my success and accomplishments, I allowed myself to fall into traps. Relationship traps were my downfall! At the age of twenty-seven perhaps I should have been a little more mature in this area. Actually, age meant nothing. I realize that insecurities and fears have no name and no age.

A guy I started seeing quite a few months before I opened my business was a true gentleman. We were introduced by my cousin and her husband. He was different. I truly felt like a queen when I was with him at first. He opened doors, pulled out chairs, and called when I was at home to make sure I was safe. If I sneezed, he would appear with a box of tissues. He also treated his family like that, so I didn't feel like he was putting on a front. He seemed to be in my life at the right time because everything started to fall in line. I had never asked a man for anything before and with him, I didn't have to ask, he just gave when I fell short. No one had ever done that for me, so I was intrigued. There was no sex involved for him to do those things; it was strictly from the heart. He was newly saved, and had not been fellowshipping anywhere. So he started attending church with me. He would come regularly, even without me. I trusted that his heart was sincere.

I believe that we could have been great friends. After a while I started to realize that we complemented each other physically and socially, but not spiritually and emotionally

The way our relationship crumbled was very bittersweet. I saw signs of it not working early on, but I pushed them aside because I was already getting attached. I decided to ignore the signs, because I figured everybody has issues and his didn't seem that bad. I also thought "who was I to judge when I had issues of my own," and instead of walking away early, I just dealt with it. I never had anyone treat me the way he did or do the things that he did for me. I would get random gifts all of the time. He was nine years older than me so he opened my eyes to a lot of things as far as fun activities and things I liked to do. We went bike riding in parks I never knew existed in the city, and to restaurants that I never dared to try. He was also a good cook so he would cook gourmet food for Amir and I and serve us. He was not selfish when it came to external needs but very absent with emotional and mental needs. He had signs of control that reminded me of my past, but I still didn't do any thing about it. It felt like I was possessed or something and I couldn't leave. The relationship had its ups and downs and when the down times came, I would call my friends and tell them my woes and have them on the phone for hours looking for a way to feel better and possibly try and find a way to get out of the relationship. I appreciated the fact that they were there for me, but I felt like I was getting on their nerves. They stuck it out no matter how many hours I had them on the phone. After hanging up from talking with them I always felt much better. I would be filled with confidence and strength. The opposite happened whenever I was with him. My confidence and strength would dissipate. Fears made me buckle and come under subjection to dysfunction. I couldn't understand how I allowed that when I thought I was over the abuse of relationships. I hadn't let anyone run over me like that in a very long time. I knew I could walk away but it wasn't that simple. There was a stronghold from my past that I thought was gone but it wasn't. I prayed all of the time for God to give me the strength to walk away from the relationship, but I kept giving in.

CHAPTER 8 – SELF ESTEEM

People flocked to him, because of his personality and the outwardly warm heart he had. It was as if he was two people. I could tell that the good side wanted to be out all of the time, but the other side kept pulling the curtains back and peeping out. There were times when he would not speak to me, but would ride all the way across the city in my neighborhood and shovel my snow before he went to work. He would do it before I woke up. He also put salt down and wiped my car off. There were other times when my car would act up and he gave me his with a full tank of gas and took mine so I could do what I had to do, but he would never say a word to me. I knew the silent treatment by heart. It became very confusing to me at times.

He would become silent because the slightest little thing would tick him off. If I said a word or a sentence incorrectly he would get agitated. I remembered one time playing around and calling him by his last name in a flirty but playful way and he instantly switched his demeanor, got upset with me and reprimanded me to not call him that because people called his father that. There was another time when we were joking around in the car and I said a playful phrase that I always say and he instantly became furious and told me not to say that. It really became hell every day for me along with a lot of heartache and tears. Because he joined my church and we now had to fellowship together, I didn't enjoy going anymore because I had to see him each time. A lot of people assembled around him because he was also in the process of becoming an ordained deacon. I felt like I was on the outside. It really made me feel inadequate because I felt like people only saw the surface of who he was when I knew that as soon as he left out of those church doors he would ignore me and Amir, or answer me with one word answers- if he felt like answering. I remember one Sunday when church let out he was in the hallway talking to some people and I came out and he totally ignored me like I was not even there. Once we got outside I was so hurt so I called him and asked him why he ignored me like that and he said because he had to do his deaconly duties and talk to the people. I also had women from my church come to my salon to get their hair done just to ask how he and I were doing and try to befriend me to dig information out. One woman had the audacity to sit in my chair and tell me that he had been coming by to pick her up for ministry because her car was down and that they were studying a spiritual book together on the phone. One day in worship service I couldn't focus so I got out of my seat and walked three pews in front of me and tapped her on her shoulder to come and talk to me in the hallway. Once we got out there I confronted her on some things and she tried to blame the devil. After that my heart started becoming hard towards the rest of the women. Then all of the confronting began- one after the other. There were numerous incidents that took place and I had to look these women in the face every Sunday and Wednesday in church. As bad as I wanted to leave, my stubbornness and God's grace kept me. I was determined not to let anybody chase me away as long as I had breath. I would be tortured in my mind every time I went but I kept going because I was not going to look like the quitter. By now I had no fight left in me and people were definitely noticing. I felt extremely helpless over my emotions. I knew that this was not me but it felt like a thousand pound weight was tied around my neck. It seemed that every time I did gain a little strength and run four miles ahead, I would get pulled back ten miles behind. I couldn't seem to break free of my mental torture. My self-esteem was drastically shot down and my mind was being controlled.

As time went on I stayed depressed; I was always crying, never happy, and had no joy. I went through different emotions of jealousy and rejection because it seemed like everyone else got his nice, happy, jovial side, while I encountered the solid, rigid, mentally controlling, quiet side of him. Even though I allowed myself to enter into something further than what God intended for me, God still had his hand on me. I believe the devil thought to himself, "I finally got her. I am going to break her so far down that this will mess her up for the rest of her life. She will never

CHAPTER 8 – SELF ESTEEM

be able to trust men again. She will always walk in rejection, inferiority, fear, intimidation, and jealousy." I was at a point where I really struggled wildly with my identity while being with him. I allowed him to come in and out of my life whenever he felt like it. But thanks be to God, the devil was wrong. After a few years of bondage I was finally free. In the state of mind that I was in, I never thought it to be possible for me. The enemy had my mind so twisted that it took a while for it to be unraveled. I remember the exact moment I became free after two and a half years of sadness. It was one day when he called me after we had been broken up for a few months with no verbal contact at all and I was so strong. I would see him in service and it would not even move me. This would have made about the fourth time going through that with him. I had made up in my mind that I was free, but I allowed distraction to come in. Because I got so comfortable in feeling free and ignoring him, he couldn't deal with that. So I started seeing his discomfort. After weeks of trying his best to be cordial with me, I finally responded back. He was back to his playful and soft teddy bear considerate self which attracted me to him in the very beginning. I still didn't give in to any advances or flirtatious compliments from him, but they kept rolling in, so one day when he asked me if he could take me out to dinner for my birthday, I accepted. I thought about it twice because I wanted to be cautious, but because I felt strong enough and thought I could handle it, I said, "why not?" Well that day came, we went out, and he seemed so humble and regretful about the past. He really treated me like a lady, and we actually had a good time. I felt like superwoman because it felt like I had the power and upper hand now- but was I sadly mistaken. I later found out that this was a set-up from God because He needed me to be free for good. So maybe about a week later I found out that he was trying to date a girl in the church during the same time that we were dating and I heard that they had went out a few times to the movies and to eat. So I asked him about it and he lied and then I asked her and she gave me her side. Both stories were very conflicting. At that moment I was hurting terribly because they were both prominent people in the church and I had no clue the whole time, I just thought they were cool like brother and sister as they would claim, and some people were actually rooting for them to be together. At that moment that was the worst hurt that I had ever felt in my life and that is a night that I will never forget. I cried harder than ever, my heart felt like it was going to beat out of my chest, and then instantly, I jumped up off the floor wiped my tears and started laughing and shouting at the same time and declaring God's word and telling the devil off at the same time. Once I finished I felt a huge weight lift off of me and I felt so good. It was unexplainable. After that day I never looked back, not even a temptation. When he tried to figure out why I didn't want to talk it out, I didn't even explain, I just said in a really calm monotone voice that I wanted to move on. That was the last time we saw each other or even talked because he left the church that week and never came back. I had no unforgiveness or malice in my heart towards him at all. I was totally free. Once everything was over, I actually thanked the devil because he was a tool used by God to teach me some things about myself, and what I lacked within. I appreciated the burden that was lifted after my lessons were learned.

After it was all over, I had a lot to be thankful for. I had a chance to get back on top of things and get rid of mindsets and situations that I thought would never leave. Many opportunities were coming back around to me and not passing me by anymore. Because of my blindness I couldn't see the good things that were being presented to me. All I could see was struggle. I thanked God for being my strong tower.

9
Prayerful

Prison was again reality for Rico. One day I went to pick up the mail, and there was a letter from him, with the prison's address on it. We had not heard from him in years, so it was a total surprise. I decided to open it first before I gave it to Amir because it was like receiving mail from a stranger. I had to review it so I could make sure that everything was appropriate for him to handle. The letter was actually very touching. He shared that he loved him, talked about mistakes that he made in his life, and said that grown men do cry when they are hurt. He wrote things that made me think to myself, "Wow! What a change." When Amir came home, I gave him the letter to read, and after he read it, I could see the happiness on his face. He wrote him back a few days later and after Rico received the letter, he started calling the house. I never held any grudge towards him. I actually felt sorry for him. He and Amir would talk on several occasions, and so did he and I. He would try to find out how I was doing, but I kept it strictly about Amir. Not too long after that, I decided to take Amir to the prison to see him. It was a very difficult decision because I did not want him to get the wrong impression and think that it was okay to be in that setting. I spoke with my pastor about it to get wise counsel. He said to do it, because Amir needed some kind of connection. We ended up going, and had to go through the same routine they had years ago when I used to visit him. We had to strip ourselves of everything, jewelry, belts, money, candy, you name it. We then had to get patted down. We waited inside at least thirty minutes before he came down because his cell block wasn't called yet. I could see the anticipation in Amir's eyes when his father came out. As soon as he walked through the doors he walked over to us and gave us both hugs and sat down. He and Amir talked for a while, and then he and I talked for a while. After that we went over to get a few pictures taken for Amir to take home. The visit was only allowed for one hour, so we stayed our full time and then left.

Rico wanted me to bring Amir up to the prison every week and his visits could only be scheduled on Mondays and Thursdays. I could only make Mondays because that was my day off. We started to do that, and on our third visit he asked us if we could switch our days because his girlfriend who was the mother of his youngest two boys wanted to start coming again and she needed that day. They were broken up for a while at that time because she was tired of him being in jail so she hadn't been there in some time. But when she found out that Amir and I were going to visit, she didn't like that. She wanted everything to cease. All I could say was, "Here we go again." I told him that he knew this was the only day we could come and if he didn't mind putting something or someone else in between him and his son again, then so be it. I didn't put up a fight at all. I went right along with the program, and explained to Amir that we had to stop for a while.

After that, Rico stopped calling, and then a year later, he called to tell us he was getting out. It really did not matter to me because it wasn't like Amir was going to see him on a regular basis anyway, if at all. So I continued to go on with our daily routine as usual. One day I was in the house and I heard a knock at the door; it was him. I was completely shocked and taken aback because he was the last person I expected to be standing face to face with. I was on my way out to pick up Amir from school, so I told him if he wanted to come back he was more than welcomed. Fear instantly took over me because it felt like an intruder trying to invade our space, and enter my son's life as if he was never missing. Later on that night he came back, but

CHAPTER 9 – PRAYERFUL

not by himself. He had his two younger sons and his girlfriend with him. It was her car he was driving and she did not want him coming alone. I cordially invited everyone in, knowing she didn't care for me. But that didn't bother me – it was about Amir.

Once they got in the house Rico and one of their sons went upstairs to Amir's room. The other son and his mother stayed downstairs with me, which was very awkward. I offered them both a seat and something to drink. She declined the drink and sat down on the edge of my couch in 'ready to go position' with keys in hand, and pocket book clenched. It was very silent for a moment and then she started talking. She said that all of this was new for her and that she never had to deal with other women concerning her man. While she was talking I was thinking "What other women?" All we have is a son together. I let her go on and I then shared my story of how Amir was looking forward for the day when his father would actually be in his house face to face with him sitting in his room. She then said that she tried telling Rico that he should make a relationship with Amir, and see him more. He told her that I never let him see him. After that the conversation started getting sensible, but I could see that she was a little uncomfortable and ready to go. A little while later she called for Rico and their other son to come downstairs and they left. We didn't hear from Rico again for years.

It baffled my mind because as badly as he said he wanted to see his son, he allowed the communication to fall into nothing again. All I could think was, his girlfriend either didn't want him to come over any more, because she was afraid of letting us into their world, or he was intimidated by seeing that Amir was well taken care of without him. After he disappeared again, Amir shut down a little. I saw it coming because he didn't talk about it or ask any questions. He just continued to act as if nothing ever happened. He began to withdraw more and more and would live inside his video games. It got really intense; I believe that was his escape.

When Amir turned thirteen it became a little challenging because he was going through the transformation of puberty. He didn't have a man to talk to about it and it was hard for him. He kept a lot

IN MY MIND

inside. He didn't want to talk to me sometimes because he said that I was a woman and also his mom. He said that he rather talk to his father about certain things. Some kids could do it, but not him. As a mother, I worried deeply for him. I tried to create things for him to do outside of his sports. I searched all over for help. I would ask men at my church if they could be a mentor and because they had their own families and responsibilities they didn't have time. I ended up finding a church in New Jersey that had mentoring programs. I would drive Amir over every Thursday for their rights of passage meetings. I sat in the parking lot in the car for two hours and read or slept while he was inside. I just wanted to keep his mind occupied.

I watched how his behavior started to decline again, right when I thought it was getting better. Here came the letters, the detentions, and suspensions. The middle school he attended at the time had a love-hate relationship with him. They loved him because he had a loveable personality, but when his uncooperative behavior came out, they were very displeased and frustrated. He would shut down, fall asleep, and not listen. If he had to be scolded he got really upset and tried to defend his case without listening to anyone else's. He had a very strong will and a determined spirit about him. But being the sweet gentle soul he was, he couldn't stand to be upset long, and he hated when there were any issues that weren't settled by the end of the day. He always ended up coming back and apologizing, especially when he was wrong.

My approach with him had to change as he started getting older. He wasn't a little seven year old boy anymore. I remember asking God to help me when he reached the teen stages. I dreaded it, but I knew it had to happen. I definitely did not want to handle it alone. So I had a strategic talk with God and asked Him to please step in and be his father and continue to take over. I also asked Him to show me what to do when it came to training up a teenage boy.

Because it was just him and I, and no one else intervening, I was left with God alone to help. Even when it came time for scolding and punishment, I asked God to guide me toward the right decision. I would tell Amir "God is watching you and even if I don't

CHAPTER 9 – PRAYERFUL

see what you're doing He does, and will eventually show me, so be careful." I loved it, because it was so true. I remember this time when my brother bought him a three hundred dollar mp3 player. I kept telling him not to spend that much, because it will either get lost or broken. But he got it anyway. One month after Amir had it; a teacher called me from his school, and asked to speak with me concerning his mp3 player that she found on the school yard ground. She told me that she found it the day before, and asked around whose it was, but no one knew. So she said on her break she decided to listen to it and see what was on it. Not too long after that, someone came to her and told her that it was Amir's. Well by that time she had already heard what was on it. She left it in her desk and didn't tell Amir because she wanted to talk to me first. When we talked, she told me some of the music on there had a lot of curse words. She said that she just wanted me to be aware. Amir never told me that it was lost because he knew that it was not supposed to go to school with him. A couple of days had gone by and he was going on like business as usual. I decided to pick it up from the school and not tell him. That day when he got home, I asked him how his day was, and fed him dinner, and then asked in a very Joan Clever-ish voice, "Where is your mp3 player?" He said, "Why?" I said, "Ohhh, just wondering." He got a lost look on his face, and told me that he left it in school. Here came the big one: "Well how could it be in school when it's right here?" I then pulled it out of my pocketbook. It looked as if he saw a ghost or something because he turned pale. He asked me how I got it, and I told him the story. I didn't give it back to him for three weeks after we had a long talk about what was on it. He told me once he got it back he would take the songs off. So when the three weeks were up I gave it back to him and trusted him to do that. Two days later I asked him if he took the music off yet, and he said, "Oooh! Mom I'm sorry I forgot, I'll do it tonight." I said, "Okay!" In this situation I wasn't going to hound him because I wanted to prove a point that God and I were working as a team. Then about a week later, we were in the bathroom at the time and I asked him again if he took the music off. He was brushing his teeth while I was straightening up, and before he could answer me, he turned around and his mp3 player fell out of his pocket into the sink right under the running faucet. It was damaged and could not be replaced because my brother never got insurance on it. So that was the end of that. As much as he cherished that thing, he couldn't get upset because he already knew that it was not my doing, but God performing his role in our parenting relationship.

As God started to work in that manner, Amir understood me more. He then started to understand that I wasn't just nitpicking, or being mean at times, but just being a caring and concerned parent. Through all of that we still had a close mother and son relationship. God continued to help me raise him, which was a huge blessing, because he became a real gentleman. He would open car doors for me, and when we were out, he opened doors for other ladies if we were coming out of a store or something. I was so proud of him. He came to me one day, and said, "Mom, I am changing, I am starting to open doors now!" I told him that I noticed and to keep up the good work. I could tell he looked for my approval with things, and I tried to make sure I paid attention. He would teach himself how to do a lot of things on his own. Much of that came from his self-determination and God's grace. He taught himself how to ride a bike, swim, and fix things. He could fix almost anything that was broken. Adults actually called on him for help when things were broken. Every time he accomplished a new thing he was so proud.

I hustled to keep him in environments that were good for him. I also wanted him to stay busy with activities. It felt good knowing that he had positive outlets beyond home and school. I wanted him to be in surroundings that were conducive for his growth and development, especially when it came to his schooling. It was a great sacrifice for me to keep him in private school, but I never missed a payment. Every year when it was time to register him for school again, I would say, "Okay Lord I don't know about this year, but help a sista' out." He would then bring peace to my spirit, even though it didn't make sense financially to me. Then determination

CHAPTER 9 – PRAYERFUL

kicked in, and I knew there was no other way but to go forward.

Because we had such a tough year, I wasn't sure if certain high schools would accept Amir. He had two suspensions on his record and quite a bit of detentions. He didn't fight or cuss out a teacher or anything, but those disciplinary actions came from him being obstinate at times with the rules.

The end of that particular school year was over and it was very difficult for me because I wanted to find a good high school for him. I researched different charter schools and well known schools that were better than average. There was a new school that had modern technology not too far from where we lived. I applied for that one as well as all of the rest that I researched. Not one of them came through. A few of them had lottery drawings, and the rest did not accept even one 'C.' I became a little discouraged and fearful because time was getting short and I had to find something soon. I knew about a few private schools that were recommended to me but I did not give them a second thought because they were a little pricey, and out of my range. They were extremely good schools that had great curriculums, and the atmosphere I was looking for.

But again, I couldn't see how they would be affordable for me. It was very intimidating. I felt backed into the corner. After my few moments of intimidation I toured three of them that were recommended. Only one of them stood out. My faith kicked in really strong and I had no other choice but to make an attempt to try this school. A few teachers, along with some of Amir's friends' parents' and I were talking about high schools one day in the school office. The school that I was going to apply to came up in our conversation, and when I mentioned to them that I heard about the school and I wanted a little more info, they made sly gestures and expressions that kind of hinted " Amir get in there, ha!" They didn't outright say that, but I could tell by their body language and silence afterwards. I did not let that defeat me; I went on and started the process. By this point my faith had kicked into super charge and nothing was stopping me. As far as I knew he was getting in there, even with his suspensions and not so good progress reports. The

IN MY MIND

process we had to go through was very long. First he had to spend the day at the school, to see if he liked it, and if it was a good fit for him as well as him being a good fit for the school. He absolutely loved it. It looked like a mini college campus. It had big green fields for sports, and well manicured landscaping, along with some very nice people. The area that it was centered in was perfect. The entire area was beautiful and peaceful. One week after Amir's one day visit, I had to meet with a few parents that were assigned to interview me and give their opinion, to see if my personality meshed with the school. Then, he and I had to come back and sit in front of a board, and be questioned. After that they made their decision for us to make the next step. Amir won them over by his mild-mannered and charming disposition. We finally made it to the last interview that day, which was with the principal and vice principal. While we were sitting there at the round table in one of the offices, they pulled out Amir's records from his previous school, and asked him what happened, and why he got suspended. He told them the truth, and then expressed to them why he wanted to attend the school. They were quiet and let him talk, and then said nothing but, "we will be right back" and left the room. My heart sank and all I could think was "Lord, you said to take dominion, and I take dominion right now in the name of Jesus. I speak favor right now, and they will accept him, please touch their hearts." When they came back into the room they said, "Amir get those books ready, because you are accepted!" The biggest coolest smile came on his face, with such a sigh of relief. All I could do was thank God, because I knew how big of a step this was for us.

The interview process was completed, but that was only the first part. The second part was the finances. I had to go to the business office to deal with tuition. I previously filled out the paperwork for financial aid. It took about two weeks to get back. When I went into the office, I sat down with one of the school's financial directors, and he said because I applied so late, other parents got first priority on the money they had to give. Then he said, "I am sorry, this is all we can do" and handed me the paper. When I looked at the paper,

CHAPTER 9 – PRAYERFUL

I smiled so hard within myself that I could have done cart wheels. I was expecting it to be an outrageous amount, and it was not. It was only seventy five dollars more than what I was already paying the last three years of junior high. I didn't worry at all because I knew it was God's favor that got him in there, so I knew that He would take care of it. It was all in the plan.

Now we had something else to be thankful for, and it was written all over our faces. He was accepted to a school that would help him for the next four years. All I could think was "Wow! My little boy is growing up." It seemed to come so fast. That meant I was getting older as well, because in a month and a half I would be thirty years old. Those good old twenties, with a junior high child were going to be in the past.

5-31-05

Dear Daddy, I am so looking forward to becoming thirty, if it's your will. I am riding those last bits of twenties out. I want my latter to be greater than my former. "Out with the old and in with the new." Please teach me how to mother a teenage high school boy. Help us to dedicate ourselves to a new life.

Love your daughter.

I shared the good news with everyone that I had intimate relationship with, even Amir's aunt on his father's side. We may not have talked every day but we kept up on things. She was happy to hear the news. In the midst of our brief conversation, she invited us to another one of their family reunions. Only this time it was her mother's side. Of course I said yes, despite what happened at the last one, because I wanted Amir to know and see his family and to get a feel of who they were.

I worked early that morning so I could get off around noon, in order to get there at a decent time. When we got to the park I allowed my expectations to be a little high again, because I just knew they were going to receive him with hugs, kisses, and joy, but was I wrong. They were very nonchalant as if they saw him all of the time. Thank God he didn't pay that much attention to it. He could brush things off so fast, that he wouldn't have known what hit him. What I think was more relevant to him was his father's greeting. He hadn't come yet, but I heard he was on his way. When he finally pulled up in the parking lot, he got out off the car with his two younger sons. I thought the president was there or something because his family praised him. This was their first time seeing him in a while since he was out of jail that time. It got a little sickening hearing them say "oh here comes my handsome nephew, here comes my big cousin! Look at him." All I could think was "Wow if they only knew, he doesn't even see or talk to his son who longs for his love and attention."

    The whole time while we were there Amir was trying to get Rico's attention, but he was so engrossed with his family that he didn't even notice. As the day started to wear down, Amir asked him if he wanted to play a game of chess with him. So they played about two games and after that Rico's attention started getting divided by his other boys, and he got up. All I could remember was my eyes following Amir to see where his feelings were, if they were hurt, or if he even noticed. I never badmouthed his father to him; I wanted him to notice things for himself. Finally we all ended up sitting at the same table: Amir, his father, his other sons, and a couple of aunts and cousins. Amir kept trying to talk to his father but his attention was still getting divided. I looked over at Amir, and he let out a big sigh, rolled his eyes up in his head, looked down and slumped back in the chair. I just prayed for him, and asked God to hug him. After a while it was getting dark, so they started packing up. When we left, Amir was quiet the entire ride home. That was the last time he heard or saw his father again for years.

    Whatever God's will was for that situation, it was definitely for Amir's good, even through all of his hurt, pain, and internal questions. A few weeks later his father was back in prison. God already knew the outcome before it happened, we were just catching up.

10
Enjoyment

"Surprise!" Everybody screamed as soon as my blindfolds were taken off. My mother gave me a thirtieth birthday party, and I was totally surprised. I had no idea what was going on while she planned it with the cooperation of my friends for an entire year.

The night before the surprise party, I told my girlfriends that I wanted to go salsa dancing, so they told me they would find the place, and to be ready when they arrived. That Saturday, early evening, I finished work and got myself together. I had the perfect black frilly salsa dress with little beads on it, so when I danced it would shimmy. By the time I finishing getting ready, my girlfriends began walking in. About ten minutes later, the other two showed up. We were in my living room clowning around and laughing at each other, and then decided to leave. As I was walking out, my friends told me I had to be blindfolded, or else we weren't going anywhere. Then they stuck a tiara with a big number 30 on my head. They informed me that the place they chose for salsa was really fancy, so they wanted me to be surprised, and it took a little while to get there so I had to be patient. We must have driven for at least a half an hour before we got there. All I knew was that I was getting car sick because my equilibrium was off every time we swerved or made a turn because I had blindfolds on and couldn't see.

IN MY MIND

We finally stopped after my adventurous ride, and they helped me out of the car. One girlfriend held my arm on one side and another held the other arm. As we were walking I felt like I was on the red carpet or something because all of a sudden I heard a man's voice say in a very distinguished voice with a deep pitch, "Good evening, Ms. Ward." It caught me off guard, so I jumped, and was trying to see out of my blindfolds from the bottom, but I couldn't. Then about fifteen seconds later, after walking down a long hallway, and only hearing the sounds of our heels clicking on the floor, I heard a different man's voice saying the same thing, "Good evening Ms. Ward." By that time I said, "Okay where am I, at a strip club or something?"

We finally stopped walking and I heard doors open that sounded like they were huge. They reminded me of those doors in The Wiz when Diana Ross, Michael Jackson, and the rest of the gang went to the palace. After the doors were completely open, I still didn't hear anything. So I started fussing at them, and asking them "Where do you have me? I am calling the cops for kidnapping." They paid me absolutely no mind, and started taking my blindfolds off. Whatever and whoever was on the other side of those doors were extremely quiet. I couldn't even hear breathing. As soon as I could see, everyone yelled 'Surprise!' There were at least a hundred and twenty people there. I was taken aback because that was the least of my suspicions. I didn't think anyone was doing anything for me, so I had already planned my own party for that following weekend. It was funny because I already retrieved names and numbers, and mailed out invitations.

One of my girlfriends who was in on the surprise party with my mother saw me going around church collecting data from people. She waited until I wasn't looking, and went behind me and told them not to pay me any mind. She gave them the real invitation to the main party and told them that it was a surprise and that I didn't know about it. Then one day she asked me for my clipboard and said, "I'll finish that up for

CHAPTER 10 – ENJOYMENT

you so you don't have to do all the work for your own party." She backtracked and went down my list and told everyone on it not to rsvp. Some people almost called, because I confused them. One guy thought I knew about the main party, and was wondering why I was giving out invitations when it was supposed to be a surprise, so he asked me something, but thank God I didn't catch on.

My mother and everyone else were geniuses at hiding and keeping quiet for that entire year. Even my employee was giving out invitations behind my back to my clients while I was in the shop. Because we worked so close together, I don't know how she pulled it off. I felt something fishy was going on regarding her quietness and sneaky look at times; I just thought she was trying something malicious, like persuading my clients to come to her or something. There was this one incident that happened with one of my girlfriends. She came in to get her hair done, and had never met my employee, and all of a sudden they became best buddies that day. I thought that was awful strange, especially when I saw my girlfriend slide her phone number to her out of the corner of my eye. I became angry; then I was hot for the rest of the day. I checked out, and didn't say anything to her because I didn't have a full case of evidence. I called my girlfriend that night and expressed my concerns, and she made up something real quick to sooth my curiosity, and I was cool. Little did I know, my employee was trying to get her address so she could send her an invitation, Ha, ha, jokes were on me.

They got me good. After they yelled surprise, I walked in with my hand over my mouth. Thoughts of joy and happiness were running through my head. A lump started to swell up in my throat and I almost cried. There were church family, my family, and friends from the past, along with a lot of my mom's friends, Amir, and even my dad and stepfather were there. It was perfectly decorated with my mother's touch. My initials were on everything: the plates, cups, napkins and favors. There was a vocalist that sang to me at my table and made me shed a tear while I was trying to be stoic. Certain people got up and grabbed the microphone to share their favorite memories about me which were both funny and terrifying at the same time. I had never had a party before, let alone experienced anything of that magnitude. It was really special.

After we ate, and all of the preliminaries were over, it was time to party. We made a soul train line, which was the funniest thing, because everyone went down the line, old and young. Some of my mom's girlfriends went down together doing the robot, then my stepfather went down on his cane and made it a dance, then my mom went down doing some kind of smooth hip hop bop, popping her collar, then my dad went down doing some old moves, where he did a split and bounced back up like he was on dance fever or something. Then after that a girlfriend and I went down doing the Kid and Play.

There was so much food left that I had to take most of it home. I ended up giving a lot of it away, along with half of the cake. It was big enough to feed two hundred people or more. My mom also created a memory book for people to sign, and write notes in. She had pictures of me on every page from when I was younger. She made it so one day I could look through it and reminisce and smile. After everything was over, they said to me in a joking way "Are you still going to have your own party?" I couldn't say no because my client had already extended her house and pool to me, and blocked her schedule out for that day. Even though she knew about the main party, she still wanted me to have something because entertaining is what she liked to do. I was willing to cancel, but I didn't want to mess her weekend up. So instead of making it a party, we down sized it to a get-together.

When I pulled up to her house, she had a big happy birthday poster on the door with two balloons on the mailbox. I had a big cheesy smile on my face because all I could think was "Wow! She and her family did all of this for me?" I rang

CHAPTER 10 – ENJOYMENT

the bell, while slowly turning the doorknob, and as soon as I got inside there were more decorations. She had all kinds of food laid out. The smell of the ribs and chicken was out of this world. As I walked by the beautiful cake sitting on the table with my name on it, I greeted everyone with a hug and expressed my gratitude. There was about ten of us total, five of my friends and five of her family members. We had so much fun. We played games in the pool, then had a soul train line, and just sat around and ate our hearts merry. After it was over, I drove home thinking what a wonderful thirtieth birthday I had for an entire week.

Now all I had to do was finish the last part of the summer with my second and last vacation for the year. I went to Hilton Head South Carolina for a week; it was great. One of my girlfriends, and a young lady who I mentored, and has also worked for me, came along. I wanted this vacation to be relaxing. I just wanted to sit back and chill. That is why I chose them to accompany me. My girlfriend was very laid back and I knew she wouldn't be high maintenance, and the young lady was not a bother, so I didn't mind. She had never been on a plane before, so I wanted her to see what it was like outside of the neighborhood, and her environment. She was well deserving of it. She was a very smart, respectful, mature, and sweet fifteen-year-old. I met her at one of the neighborhood schools in my area where she attended, and where I also taught. The school had a teen pregnancy class during their fourth period, and I went a few times to teach the girls life skills. She was not pregnant, but came for extra credit. We exchanged information after one of the classes because I was impressed by her motivation and desire to learn more and do better for herself. The classes were almost identical to what I taught at the young mothers' group at my church. I showed them how to manage their money, how to get motivated about the things they wanted to do in life, and what choices and decisions were best for their children.

IN MY MIND

Hilton Head Island was a very relaxing place. We did quite a bit of beaching and eating. I especially enjoyed the eating because I loved tasting new things; it was one of my favorite hobbies. Along with the island being gorgeous, it was a breath of fresh air. As we were driving along the roads, we took in all of the colorful scenery. Everywhere we turned there were flowers of different colors and smells. The buildings were lined up uniformly with matching pastel and khaki colors. Hilton Head became a tourist island less than sixty years ago. It later became a retirement place, somewhere to go when you were tired of the fast paced city life with all of the hustle and bustle. The atmosphere was very peaceful, and calm.

We tried to eat at a different restaurant each night. To our surprise, the food was phenomenal. I heard the Island was known for their seafood, and every bit of that was true. I cooked breakfast every morning, so we could save our money for dinner. After breakfast, our day was planned. Some mornings we just relaxed, and on others we took tours. My girlfriend went to the beach every morning to watch the sun rise. I tried to catch her, but before I could open my eyes she was gone. A couple of mornings the young lady and I rented bikes and rode some of the bike paths. Those paths were breathtaking. We rode through botanical gardens and well-manicured estates that were gated communities. The air was fresh, with mild winds blowing across our faces. We were so caught up in our beautiful escapade that we started to ride a little too far from our development. By the time we reached back it was almost the afternoon.

The next day we scheduled a tour to see and learn the history of the island. I developed a great appreciation as the bus took us through some of the neighborhoods. The geechy people were the natives on the island, and it was not always in good condition. Some of the original structures and houses were still there, and people still resided in them. Most of the people were related, or knew each other. Another day we drove

CHAPTER 10 – ENJOYMENT

about forty minutes off of the island to Savannah. Beautiful wasn't a word until we got there. I felt like putting on a dress from the 1940's and with flowers in my hand, go barefoot and skip through the grass. That's how quaint and southern the town was. We visited quite a few mansions, and saw some of the original architecture, and learned the history behind them. We also visited one of the oldest churches that were still being used for services. We strolled downtown, which still had some of the original cobblestone roads and buildings. There were horses and buggies sitting around waiting, in case someone wanted an old fashioned ride through town. Because I loved horses so much, I had to stop to pet and feed them. After spending time with the horses we walked through the stores and smelled the chocolate from the candy factories, which made us extremely hungry. We walked to one of the stops to catch a bus that took us around town, and within five minutes it came. We hopped on and asked the driver to let us off in the central part of town which was amazing. As we were walking, we passed the bench that Tom Hanks sat on when he filmed *Forrest Gump*.

We had a hard time deciding between the restaurants that were recommended to us. So we chose the one that had the most positive reviews. This restaurant was well known and very busy, especially for lunch. We cranked up our walking speed so our wait wouldn't be too long. When we got close by, we smelled the aroma of home-style soul food a block away. Once we reached inside, we were greeted with such warm southern hospitality. It looked like a house that had been converted into a restaurant. There was a living room and a dining room, and off to the side was the kitchen. It was very homey, and comfortable. The smell of those buttered biscuits and fried chicken almost knocked us off of our feet. I'm sure we looked really hungry and desperate, like we hadn't eaten in weeks. The older man at the register took our money with such a warm smile, and welcomed us with kindness. The waitress then came

IN MY MIND

over and asked us to follow her. She took us to the dining room area and sat us down at a long family sized table with other people sitting around it. That was different for me because I had never eaten family style before at a restaurant. There were no menus because everyone paid a flat fee for everything: the meal, drink, and dessert. Each person sitting at the table received the same thing. The main course consisted of four meats, four styles of vegetables, and four starches. Once the food was placed down, you were able to reach for whatever you liked. There was an option between three different types of drinks, and three desserts. There were three pitchers of juice on the table, so you had to pour and pass. Our table was interesting because there were four sets of people all from different places. There was a couple with their children from New Jersey. Then there was a true southern bell from Savannah who was a real estate broker. There was a guy from Boston who was there by himself looking for real estate to open up a few bed and breakfast spots. He told us that he and his girlfriend were supposed to come together, but she had to stay behind. We talked with him the majority of the time, because he was by himself. By the time we were finished eating, we did not want to move. The food was magnificent.

We wanted to get back before it got too dark, so we didn't spend too much time in one place. We left the restaurant, visited a couple more sites, and then worked our way back to the car. It was about five o' clock, which was a good time to drive back and still catch the sunset on the beach. By the end of our trip, I felt rejuvenated and relaxed. I just had one regret: I didn't get a chance to write or to read any material that I brought with me. I guess I was busier than I thought.

That vacation was just as good as my trip two months prior to Jamaica. The only difference was Jamaica was strictly for fun and enjoyment. Out of all my travels, I rated it as one of my favorites. There were four of us total: my son, one of his friends, his friend's mother, and me. It was a vacation of appreciation, because we were catered to on a very unselfish

CHAPTER 10 – ENJOYMENT

level by all of the staff and natives that we encountered. I heard so many things and opinions about the island from several people who had been there. I needed to form my own opinion, and I am glad I did. The most interesting thing about it all was that I was going to be in a wedding while I was there, and didn't find out until a couple of weeks before my arrival. A friend of mine that I worked with in a salon some years back, called me and asked me if I would be interested in being in her wedding because her sister backed out at the last minute. I told her thanks for thinking of me, and thanks for the offer, but I couldn't afford it because I was on my way to Jamaica in a few weeks. She started laughing, and said, "Oh my goodness, that is where my wedding is." She said, "That was going to be my next question. I was going to see if you could come to Jamaica to be in it."

When I told her the dates I was going to be there, she just burst out laughing again and said, "I don't believe it; you're going to be there the same time as the wedding." Then she said, "And guess what! If you can fit my sister's dress, you don't have to pay for anything, not even the jewelry." She told me that her sister and I were about the same height and weight, and then asked if I could come over her house to try the dress on. So I did go and try it on, and it fit perfectly, as if it was tailor-made for me.

As soon as we got off the plane, we had to go through customs. After waiting a little more than two hours, we left without half of our luggage, because it didn't make it on the plane when we switched in Fort Lauderdale. It sucked because no more planes were flying in for the rest of the day. We had no other choice but to walk outside and get a taxi. Because we had so many drivers to choose from, we just chose one that looked like he took extra special care of his vehicle. He loaded our things in the back of the van, and off we went on our two hour ride to our hotel. Our excitement and adrenaline made it seem like forty five minutes. The only thing that I did not particularly care for was the fact that our driver drove like a bat out of hell. He was doing about a hundred miles per hour. I had to ask him if he could slow down several times. He must have thought I was stupid or something, because he had the nerve to tell me that he really wasn't doing a hundred, it just seemed like it because something was wrong with his speedometer. So he would slow down for five minutes, and then speed back up. By then I had an attitude, and I figured out why he was going so fast, because time was money and he needed to get back because it was such a long drive. At least he was courteous during our ride to let us stop and get jerk chicken from a hut on the side of the road.

We finally pulled up in front of our hotel which was very pretty sitting up on a hill overlooking the city. By the time we got there it was dark. We were welcomed at our car doors by one of the hotel staff. The gentleman opened our doors, and took our bags for us. I checked us in and got the keys. By the time we turned around and paid our taxi driver, our bags were already taken to our rooms and sitting in front of the door. The walk that we had to take to our room was beautiful. It was a pathway filled with pretty rose bushes, and all sorts of flowers. When we got to the room, we settled our things down and toured the living space that we would be residing in for the next seven days. Our balcony's view was centered perfectly right over the pool. The pool had a swim up bar in the middle. We had a full kitchen with a pullout couch in the living room, and one bedroom.

The next morning we got up early for breakfast, and also to see if our bags had come. They didn't. There was a man standing on the side of the hotel at the front desk, and he started walking towards us, and asked if we needed a taxi. I know he was waiting there to pick up business so we decided to give him a try. It was so amazing to me, because he was a full blood Indian with a Jamaican accent. I really liked his personality, and felt comfortable with him. He told us after we

CHAPTER 10 – ENJOYMENT

ate breakfast he would take us in town to get some things to hold us over until our bags arrived. We ended up having him for a full day. He took us to a department store, and then to the straw market. After we left the market, he took us through the hood, as well as the high class areas. Once we were done with our mini tour, we went back to our hotel so we could get showered and dressed, because we were going out to eat that night. He waited around until we were ready and dropped us off at a nice seafood restaurant, and then picked us back up. After that night I decided to keep him for our entire stay. His price was right, he was on time, and he was patient. He agreed, and we set a weekly rate.

The next day we did the Bob Marley tour, which was a Tuesday. That was amazing in itself because those mountains were the skinniest two lane roads I had ever seen. They had no railings or side walls. One sudden move or sneeze, and we would be over the cliff. We made it up to the museum which had to be on the peak of the mountain, because when I looked down, the houses looked like little action figures. The museum was an addition to Bob Marley's original home where he and his mother lived, where he was born and raised. The house was extremely compact; the bathroom and kitchen were outside. Our tour guide took us around on the grounds and gave us a little history about Bob Marley's life and family. He told us how Marley had to walk his donkey down that big mountain on trips that may have taken days, just to go into town to get food for him and his family. All of the tour guides had their Rastafarian colors on, with long dreads, and straight white teeth. I had never seen anything like it. Their teeth were so white. While we were walking the grounds we stopped by a wall to look at a few things. Out of nowhere, this hand appeared from underneath the wall with marijuana wrapped up in white paper. It was strategically placed in between each finger. I was startled and jumped back. Our tour guide said, "Oh just ignore them, they are from the outside and just trying to make some money." After the tour was over and we were ready to get back into our van, two guys that were in a little hut behind some windows, tried to get my son and his friend's attention so they could sell them some weed. I was in shock that they were so bold. I told our driver "Okay I enjoyed the tour, but it is now time to go."

After we left we went straight to one of the beaches our taxi driver recommended. He dropped us off, and we stayed for a few hours. The boys got in the water while us ladies stayed in our beach chairs and took turns drifting in and out of sleep. When he came back to pick us up, we stopped at a curry chicken and oxtail shack on the side of the road for dinner. When we got back to the hotel, our bags had finally arrived.

On Wednesday we went horseback riding. This was different compared to what I was used to. On this tour, the horses would ride with us into the ocean. After the horse walked the path for about an hour, we made a pit stop at a place that had stables, rest rooms, and refreshments. The stop was for us to change in to our bathing suits. For those of us who couldn't swim, we had to put on waist life belts because the ocean could get a little deep at certain points. With a little fear, I tried not to think anything of it because I wanted to do it. We switched horses, I guess so the ones we rode up on could eat. When I got on my horse, she was a little antsy, and couldn't wait to get in the water. So our guides led the horses in single file. As they were trotting, they started picking up speed. The next thing I knew, the tour guides let them go free, and they took off. They thought it was play time when they felt that water. At that moment I sure didn't think it was play time; nor did I think it was cute. I started to freak out, because I couldn't swim. I held on to those reigns with the grip of death. By this time the water was getting deeper, and all you could see was the horse's neck. As I looked around for one of the guides to come and rescue me, I heard one say from across the water, "Relax, girl, it's going to be alright, don't worry man." But my butt and leg

CHAPTER 10 – ENJOYMENT

muscles were being challenged from me trying to keep myself from sliding off of the side of the horse. I started yelling, "I want to go back to land!" People were looking at me like I was crazy. Everybody else was having a good time prancing around through the water, but I was acting like a fool, and I didn't care. All I knew was I couldn't hold myself up too much longer and I was scared to death. My son kept saying, "Mom, calm down, its only water, and you have a life belt on." I yelled back "I don't care, I want to go back to land!" When the guide came over to me he was truly relaxed, and he said in a calm, seductive voice "Don't worry man, I got you." I kept yelling "I don't care! I want to go back to land now!" My heart was pumping out of my chest. He finally took me back and I sighed with relief, and watched the rest of them, while I stood right behind the rail, looking at my horse with an evil eye. Some of the people were in the middle of the ocean standing on the back of their horses jumping off, and doing summer salts into the water. I still enjoyed my ride, but laughed at myself later. I needed to de-stress after all of that so later on that evening we went out to dinner at one of the famous local restaurants.

Thursday morning we got up super early to go to Dunn's River Falls. It was only about twenty minutes from our hotel. I wanted us to go early because my girlfriend who was getting married wanted me to come over to their hotel and meet the rest of the wedding party. It was like a comedy show watching us climb those rocks. The boys did fine, but we were holding on with the grip of death. It was a little challenging but we made it to the top. Those rocks were so slippery that if one false move was made, you were down.

After we were done with the falls, we went to the beach area for a while, and then dried off, so when our driver got there we would be ready. He was standing there at the entrance on time as usual, and took us back to our hotel so we could get changed. He waited for us patiently so he could take us over to my girlfriend's resort. Once we got inside, we really did not have to leave. It was its own city within itself. She met us at the entrance, and took us back to her room. Then we went down to meet her fiancé, and her wedding party. Somehow she managed to get us in to eat dinner. The varieties that were there put our hotel restaurant food to shame. After eating we hung around for a little while. We let the boys go swimming, and we sat in the beach chairs and talked, and enjoyed the night island breeze. All that was missing was a "rent-a-boo" (a guy that I could rent for a couple of hours to hold my hand and whisper sweet nothings in my ear. Then I could give him back).

Friday was another fun filled and relaxed day. Once again our guy was out there early waiting for us. It was about seven o clock in the morning, and he brought his twenty-two year old son with him. He was a nice young man, and looked just like his father. We were on our way to Negril, and because it was a three hour drive, we had to leave early. The first thing we did once we got there was go to this place called Rick's Café. It was an outdoor café that had a couple of water sports for the boys to take advantage of. Out of anything they could have done, they chose to jump off of a cliff. There was this enormous cliff that seemed like the water was a thousand feet below. People were in line to do this crazy sport. They were doing flips, and splits in the air on their way down. I couldn't look, because I was a punk. After we guzzled down our fifth virgin pina colada, Amir's friend got permission from his mom to jump. I was hoping she wouldn't allow that because that meant Amir was next. Right after his friend jumped, Amir begged and pleaded for me to let him. As he reared up, and stepped closer to the edge, I prayed really hard. Meanwhile the crowd in the back was cheering him on. I wanted to go over and slap every single one of them. When they did a countdown and he jumped, I closed my eyes half way through. From what I saw, he did well. Fear was not in him. We stayed for some hours but had to leave because the wedding was the next day, and I didn't want

CHAPTER 10 – ENJOYMENT

to be too tired.

The big day was here for my girlfriend, and I had to be over to her place early so we could all meet up and practice. She made arrangements for her private taxi guy to pick me up, and my taxi guy would bring my other three a little later. Beautiful didn't describe what I saw before me when we pulled up to the villa. It was nothing short of heaven. It had amazing gardens, trees, and a beautiful view of the ocean. The villa was quaint with strong details. It had pretty cream columns holding it up, and it sat on a hill that overlooked the ocean. There were two tall trees that were on the side of the structure that swayed over the top of the roof like fans as the breeze blew. To the side of that, the wedding coordinator had tables set up on the grass with expensive white table cloths, and the chairs were wrapped in white with bows on the back of them. They were the same color as our dresses, and our dresses were the same color as the ocean, a bluish green. The weather was so perfect, it almost didn't seem real. The skies were crystal clear, and a slight breeze was blowing, which was just enough to cool us down from the sun.

There were eight of us total in the bridal party. The four of us women went inside to get our make-up on, fix each other's hair, and also help the bride get herself together. We were all in uniform and looked beautiful, but my girlfriend looked stunning. Her dress was embroidered in pearls, and was very form-fitting and flattering. From the waist down, it abundantly flowed with the same pattern as the top; it had a train that was the same length as her veil.

It was almost time to walk out, and hearts were racing as we were snapping pictures of each other along with the camera man. The villa had two large French doors that swung outward. As they were being opened by two of the male hosts, we looked out and all of her guests were sitting in anticipation, while soft music played. In order for us to get to the main level, we had to walk down these long skinny slopes of steps. It was an art that had to be mastered, without tripping on the bottom of our dresses. I was number three in line to go out. My heart was racing so fast because I could be clumsy at times, so my main focus was to watch every step carefully, and my objective was not to fall. All I envisioned was me looking up smiling, missing a step and starting to roll downwards and fall flat on my face in the grass. Thank God that didn't happen. The only challenge I had was with my heels. They kept getting stuck in the dirt with every step. Trying to look elegant and ripping heels out of the grass was a task, especially when I had to stay in tune with the music. The guy I walked down with didn't make it any easier. He kept whispering jokes as we were walking and I had to hold my laugh in.

When my girlfriend came down, the sun started to set, and all you could hear was the waves in the ocean flow along with the music. As she walked, her train and veil flowed so far behind her. Her husband to be was looking at her as if he had never seen her before. He had tears in his eyes that showed his love for her. After we saw him tearing, then we started tearing. While she was walking, the sheer fabric that was on the chairs and trees were blowing and waving in unison. Her veil picked up off the ground into the air and started synchronizing in the same exact wave pattern behind her. She had to walk to the gazebo where the preacher and her soon-to-be husband were waiting for her. It sat on a rock that extended out into the ocean, so when you looked over, all you saw was water.

After the ceremony, pictures, and dinner, it was time to party. We changed our clothes, and came back out, by this time it was completely dark outside. We had lighting from the villa, and whatever the coordinator put around the tables and trees. We danced and talked for hours. Out of nowhere my driver appeared in the crowd. He reminded me of the butler that was in one of Adam Sandler's movies. He always popped up when you least expected. That happened the entire trip. He just mingled his way into the crowd and enjoyed himself.

CHAPTER 10 – ENJOYMENT

We had to leave for the airport that next morning so we needed to get back and get our things together. Our flight was scheduled to depart at eight, so we had to leave the hotel by four thirty am. The wedding was a fabulous way to end our vacation. We had so much fun, and it seemed like a fairy tale.

When we got off the plane we were walking lopsided from tiredness, but still had smiles on our faces from the trip. One thing I can say is that was a memorable vacation because it allowed me to get away from the everyday hustle and bustle. It also enriched my faith in knowing that this life was also made to enjoy.

Me at 3 months old

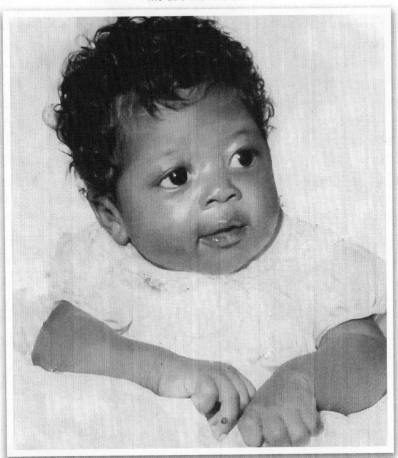

My godmother and me

My stepfather, my brother McKee, my mother, and me

My mom and me at an amusement park

My mother and stepfather's wedding day

Delivery day

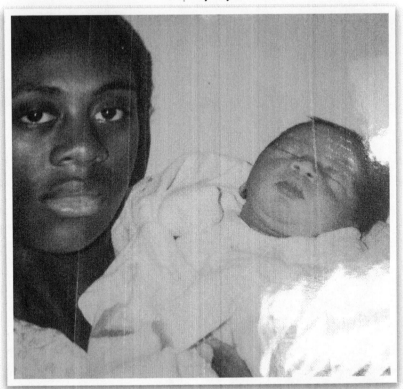

Amir at one year old

Me at 14 years old

Just leaving the club

Amir and me

Amir and me at my father's house

My brother McKee, Amir, my mom, and me at our old house in Southwest Philly while brother was home on a visit from the Marines

Amir and me at our first apartment

Trying to be grown at a club intoxicated

My mom and Amir

Amir and me on our first cruise

My grand opening at the salon

Enjoying the Pacific Ocean while visiting my brother

My mom, my aunt Candra, and me at a high noon tea with my church

My sister Vinny and me on my birthday

Me, Amir, mom

Amir at two years old

Amir's prom day  Amir's graduation day

11
Challenging

I experienced a few emotionally challenging things in the coming year including Amir starting ninth grade. The time came so fast, that I couldn't believe it. I had a son going to high school. I still felt like a little helpless kid myself. Ninth grade was both exciting and worrisome all at the same time. It was exciting because he was moving on to another chapter in his life, but it was worrisome because moving on in life also meant triple the peer pressure that was already being dished out in junior high. I understood that it was a part of life and maturity but as a single mother of a young black male who could easily be labeled in society I grew more than a little concerned. In his new surroundings he would once again be a minority. He experienced being in the minority at previous schools, so he knew how to adjust pretty much. His personality which was semi laid back but very engaging at the same time allowed him to have a delicate balance in any circumstance he was in. People gravitated to him and he made friends wherever he went. The unfortunate thing was it was hard for me sometimes because some of those friends were not always the best influence for him. He was a smart kid and knew his boundaries but in the town where he went to school the police were known to be prejudiced. Whenever he hung out with some friends I had a small piece of concern in the back of my mind for his safety. Sometimes I obsessed about his safety, which was not good. During those times every kid seemed to like wearing hoodies, so I had to talk to Amir about the dangers of misidentification and wrong assessments from other people. I told him when he walked in stores to take his hoodie off and hands out of his pocket because he didn't want to look suspect and gain the attention of people who were paranoid. I know it sounded unfair but that was the reality we were living in. To him with his nonchalant attitude, it didn't matter - he didn't see the big deal.

    Having to go through those things with Amir, I had to be sensitive. I didn't want to baby him, and I didn't want to scare him. I just wanted him to be aware and to use wisdom when he was out. Whenever he had concerns I had to take time to listen, and hear what he was saying both verbally and nonverbally. It could be a little difficult. When I felt his pain it was as if it was happening to me. I just wanted to jump in and save him from the world. I struggled very hard with not being too overprotective of him. There were times when people would tell me to loosen the reins on him and let him be free. All I could think was "they are not in my shoes." I had a son who was very independent and not scared of anything, so he would take risks because he was also daring. He was so cavalier that many times I didn't think he was paying attention to his surroundings; I felt like I had to do it for him. I allowed the enemy to increase my fear and worry over him to the point where it became unbearable for me some nights when I knew he was out and he didn't answer his phone. I wasn't trusting God. I had an embedded fear of danger and I was thinking like a pessimist. I could even remember being afraid of my emotions when Amir was born. I loved him so deeply that I didn't know if I would be able to handle it if anything bad happened. Those thoughts haunted me for years. I had many nights of praying and pacing the floor with tears and anxiety. Even in knowing that Amir belonged to God and he could do whatever He wanted with him- my faith still lacked in believing that Amir would be taken care of and safe. I learned that he had to go through whatever came his way and that I could not prevent the process that was necessary to build his character. God was slowly moving him from beneath my wings, and taking him under His.

    Going through ups and downs in my emotions, along with Amir going through his, was a big challenge, because I was trying

CHAPTER 11 – CHALLENGING

to play the roles of both mom and dad, which was very hard. I could only teach from a woman's perspective. I was never a man, so I couldn't teach him how to be one. He had to learn some things by trial and error which was painful for me but good for him. I had to be strong for both of us but there were those times when I felt like I was at the bottom of the barrel, or when I just wanted to crawl underneath a rock. A big one! There were days when all I could do was write. I was in a place of loneliness that I struggled with from time to time, and my heart was in anguish.

9-06

Kind of speechless, don't have many words. Daddy right now, help my emotions; keep my mind stayed on you. A little frustrated today, I yelled at Amir. I am crying because I feel a little lonely. I wish I had a little adult company.

Let your perfect will be done. Please let Amir do well at his new school. Help him with his attitude problem, because they won't stand for it.

I am in the midst of procrastination, and not knowing what to do next, not settled in my mind and spirit. I want to go somewhere.

I am getting antsy, I am ready to move, I feel stuck in one place. I keep trying to jump over that rock, but every time I get to the edge, I slide back down. I feel like my feet are glued to the floor. I keep reaching out to grab hold, but can't quite grasp it.

Amir sat in the house all summer long, because I had to work. There were no camps or jobs this year. Food has been my friend lately. It has been helping me to pass time. There aren't that many Rita's water ice trips in the world that's gonna keep fulfilling time. As you know, I sat in Wendy's parking lot and ate in the car by myself so I could get out and enjoy the weather. I love and enjoy doing things by myself, but not all of the time. No phone ringing. I feel pressure because I worry about Amir.

I don't want average, I am crying because it hurts, it hurts because I think that I am trying my best, but it seems not to be good enough.

I know my son's potential, and I want the best for him. No one seems to understand when I try to explain my situation because they are not in it. Lord I am mentally drained. Please help me to hear clearly.

10-06

God my father, my heavenly father, I love you, and I know that you love me. Keep me please. Help me up off my knees, wipe my tears. My arms are outstretched to you wanting to have a pure heart. My soul longs for you daily, but in a selfish way. A way that is still trying to do its thing, sleep, eat, TV, business. I want to be submissive, but my soul is stronger than my spirit. So I don't pray, study your word, worship, and help others the way I should. Peace is yearning for an outlet. So is joy.

Time alone with you is the most important thing there could ever be in this life. It's just a shame that it's not pursued. The cares of this world and the business of this life seem to take first place, and leave you hanging in the balance.

My focus is off, please help me to redirect it, and please help my son to become an awesome man of God.

Most of the time, I picked up from my prayer time and kept it moving, but somehow throughout the rest of the day, those negative thoughts would try and fight their way back in. When I

CHAPTER 11 – CHALLENGING

found myself dwelling there, I spoke to those thoughts and they would leave. Some days were easier than others. There were those times when it didn't matter how much I tried to think on the good things and tell the bad ones to leave; they wouldn't leave right away. They were those stubborn ones that I had to work at. Going to bed and starting a fresh new day would seem like the only option at times. Once the morning came I was okay.

By this stage in the game, my spiritual life was really being challenged, and had been for a while. The faith that I walked with so mightily had seemed to dissipate over time. It got to the point where I started feeling numb. I was in a battle. I was strong one moment, weak the next. There were times when I stopped trying to be strong because I knew weakness was right around the corner. Of course I was being deceived in my thoughts, but I kept allowing the enemy to chip away at me through recurring circumstances.

I wouldn't write as frequently, I didn't even pray with Amir as much anymore. I gave up on emotions. I had a "whatever" attitude which was my response to everything. I allowed things to really take a toll on me. I saw it coming every time. I would regain consciousness and get back on track. Then I'd fall again. It felt like I was waving my faith goodbye. This started to become an engraved routine in my mind. That's where the battle was, because the enemy knew that's where I was the strongest. He knew that he would never get to me fully, but enough to sidetrack me. Just thinking about how I allowed him in my space to distract me with his fiery darts was frustrating. I would let my guard down when things were going well in my life and that created an open door to allow the devil to harass my soul. By that happening my spirit would become weak and I didn't have enough strength to fight off the mental attacks. I knew that things started in the mind and manifested in the physical, but the busyness in my life and my lack of pursuing God took the forefront. There were those times when I really did buckle down and get into my word and pray on a daily basis and things would be great, but because I got comfortable in knowing that I was doing the right thing, a persistent attack would be waiting around the corner for me to catch me off guard. Sometimes the attacks succeeded, and sometimes they didn't. The ones that succeeded were those I had

IN MY MIND

to really overcome fast and seek God extremely hard to get a breakthrough. In desperation I would write:

> *Lord, I love and believe you. I cherish your word, and honor you.*
>
> *I speak these things into existence with authority. I want a closer walk with you.*
>
> *You hold my hand and walk with me. You love on me, and think about me. You kiss me goodnight, and tuck me in.*
>
> *I am special to you, Thank you.*
>
> *Give me all I ever need in you. Your agape love. Your joy is all I ever need. You tell me that I am never alone, and that you are always with me. Thank you.*
>
> *I need your peace, joy, patience, long suffering, endurance, and perseverance.*
>
> *You tell me to never give up, even when it seems impossible. I know the best is yet to come.*
>
> *You said to believe in you, and to believe in your promises.*
>
> *You know everything, and nothing is hidden from you. You are the almighty, and my strong tower, in the time of trouble.*
>
> *No hurt or danger shall come near me. You told me to believe always, have faith, and never give up. I won't cast my confidence away. I believe great things will come to pass, and that happiness is a choice, so I choose to be joyful.*

My struggle for peace was so intense at times that I felt like I was going crazy. I definitely did not want to portray that image to my son, even though I believe he picked it up on several occasions. Sometimes, depending on how my morning

CHAPTER 11 – CHALLENGING

went, it altered his, whether it was negative or positive. Most of my mornings, I woke up singing, dancing, and exercising, and some mornings I woke up without my peace intact. Those mornings I brought him in involuntarily because he would pick up on my downcast energy. I felt really bad by the time I dropped him off at school. I would apologize, and he readily accepted every time. He had enough troubles to deal with in school and his personal life, from homework and sports, to his father's absence; he definitely did not need any extra drama from home. My main prayer for him was that he would find a dependable, consistent male to talk and vent to. Because of his let-downs in the past, it was hard for him to trust. I would pray to God and ask him to take over.

As the school year continued, Amir asked if he could go to some of the parties he was invited to. I didn't have a problem with it as long as I drove him and picked him up. I had to allow him to start venturing out and enjoying the things of high school. He attended one party at the house of his classmate who didn't live too far from the school. I drove him and another boy there. I was petrified because I had no idea the house was so difficult to find. First off, it was raining hard, and I could hardly see, even with the windshield wipers on full speed. The house was located in the woods and it was extremely foggy.

The only way to get there was through narrow winding roads, going uphill with wet leaves on the ground. To top it off, the only lights I had to guide me were my headlights, and maybe a couple of lanterns on people's property alongside the road. It seemed to be a never ending journey. We were lost for at least a half hour because it was pitch black so we couldn't see addresses. Amir and the other boy were so excited to go that they could care less if I was horrified or not. All they had was one mission on their mind, fun! The party started at seven and was over at eleven. By the time I got them there it was eight thirty. There was no need for me to go all the way back

IN MY MIND

home and come back. Plus, I was not going to torture myself in that darkness and rain, and risk the chance of getting lost again by myself. So I sat in my car, under a tree in the dark with the heat and radio on and my chair leaned back. The next day, at school, one of the kids who were at the party snitched on another kid that was caught drinking, and he got expelled. Apparently the young ladies' parents didn't lock up their liquor. One thing I was proud to say was my son's name was never mixed up in anything concerning group behavioral actions. He always removed himself from anything that seemed like trouble, when it came to other people.

Some parents from the school were a little too free with their children. They would allow them to speak any kind of way, and call it freedom of speech. They were allowed to say where they were going instead of asking. Amir knew that it was a different ballgame in our house. He did try it on several occasions, but he knew his limits. He also knew that if I could not reach him on his cell phone at any time, there would be a problem. I had super powers like wonder woman when it came to certain things. For example, one day after school Amir asked if he could walk over a friend's house with about four other boys. I was a little skeptical because I didn't know where the house was. He told me that it was up the road from the school, and that the boy's mother would bring them back by six o clock for their basketball game. The only thing that made me say okay was the fact that I had met the boy's father a few times, and he was pretty nice. He was actually one of Amir's golf teachers. So I told Amir to give me two of the boys' cell numbers that he would be walking with, and the phone number at the young man's house that he was going to. He gave me the numbers and I locked them in my phone while working on a client at the same time. I told him to call me when he got there, and gave him twenty minutes to do so. Well, he forgot because absentmindedness runs in my family. It didn't help that cell phone signals were very hard to come

CHAPTER 11 – CHALLENGING

by in that area. Sometimes you could get a call through and sometimes you couldn't. I knew it would be hard for him to use the phone on the road. I called his phone and it went straight to voicemail, then I called the other two boys and the same thing happened. I called the house number and the operator came on and said wrong number try again. I gave him a couple more minutes while trying not to panic, and finished my client at the same time. However, panic started to take over when he didn't call me and I couldn't reach him. I waited a couple more minutes, and redialed every number one more time, and nothing, no response. By now all logic went out the window, and wonder woman was on her mission. I sat my client under the dryer, explained to her what was going on, and what I was doing. I asked her to give me at least an hour. She understood, and off I went.

    I really don't remember stopping at any lights or stop signs, but if I didn't, the cops were gracious that day. I had no idea where the boy's house was, so I didn't know where to start. The only thing I could think to do was go to the school. So I pulled up in the parking lot, jumped out, and asked anyone if they knew where the boy lived, At least I did know his first name. No one knew the exact address, but they did know that it was nearby somewhere. I went into the office to ask staff, but it was empty, everyone had gone home for the day, except for the janitors and some kids who were there for sports practices. So when I got into the office, I saw the parents' directory on the front desk. I took the book and whisked back into the parking lot. I felt it was obvious that the oversized book wasn't mine, because I went in empty handed. I didn't have time to stand in the office and browse through it, and then write the address on a piece of paper. I had no idea what the last name was and what I was looking for. Once I got into the parking lot, there was a young lady sitting on the bench. By now there were only a few stragglers left on the campus. I asked the girl if she knew the boy's father's name, because he was one of the golf coaches. She did, and I pieced it together. Then I was able to look up the address because I had first and last names. I sat in my car and flipped through the pages, and found the correct number and called several times. I got no answer. From leaving the salon to that present moment an hour had passed, which seemed like four. I needed to talk to someone at the house, so they could tell me how to get there. The sun was setting fast and it was getting dark, and I had no idea of which way to turn. My final attempt was asking a boy that was getting in his car from leaving practice. I asked him if he knew the boy and if so where did he live. He didn't exactly know where, but he pointed up one road, and said I think it's up there somewhere. I put my foot to the gas, and off I went into the sunset. I had trouble with seeing in the dark especially when those huge houses on the hill were sitting way back.

I finally found it; it was a beautiful house. It sat back behind the trees and had a little stream running under a bridge that I had to drive over in order to get there. The surroundings were still and quiet. I could hear the leaves falling off the tree. The driveway was so narrow that you would have to back out after coming in, because there was nowhere to turn around. The main door was wide open, and there was a tall, clear storm door that was shut tight and allowed me to see right into the house. Everything inside was immaculate. It looked like a model home that no one lived in. I rang the bell, and out of nowhere this big oversized black Rottweiler came running like he was in a race. He slid up against the door and started barking and growling at me like I was a piece of meat. I kindly backed myself down the steps slowly so I could place my heart back into my chest. Then this cute little six or seven year old girl came to the door with long golden blond hair and a big bright smile, with a missing front tooth. I said, "Hi! Is Amir here?" She said, "yes" and opened the door and let me in. Then she called downstairs to the basement for him. I thought it was a little dangerous because I could have been a kidnapper

CHAPTER 11 – CHALLENGING

or something, and no adult was around. When Amir came up the steps and saw me, it was as if he saw a ghost. He looked puzzled. The expression on his face looked as if he was saying "How in the world did you get here?" The expression on my face read, "If you only knew how bad I want to hurt you right now." My eyebrow was raised and lips tight. I asked him why didn't he call me and he told me he forgot. So I told him to come on, because I was taking him back to the school early for his game. He answered me back by telling me that the boy's mother was going to take them back. I told him not tonight, and to go get his stuff and let's go. Then I asked him if the boys mother was there, and then before he could answer, the little girl blurted out, "My mommy isn't here, she went to the store and will be right back." Then he had the nerve to say "Well if she isn't back by the time we have to go, we were going to walk." I had to check my ears to make sure I heard him correctly, because I knew he heard me say let's go. He did his little pouting thing and went to get his book bag and coat. Even though they were only down there playing video games, the point had to be made. I needed him to know that when I tell him to call me, there can be no forgetting. I also needed him to know that if I wanted to find him, he would be found. I ended up taking two of the four boys back to the school along with him. They were sitting in the back of the car looking scared as if I scolded them too. After I dropped them off, I went back to business as usual and finished my client.

The drive back and forth from his school and our house did get tedious. Most of the time, Amir stayed after school because of sports. I juggled so much at one time, with the business, his school, and my personal well-being. Trying to keep everything afloat wasn't easy, but it did get done. My goal was to keep him active while I was busy. He did almost everything- golf, basketball, baseball, soccer, and lacrosse. Quite a bit of my work hours in the evening were cut because I had to leave and pick him up. There were no buses that went directly to his school, and most of the kids that got rides home, lived in the opposite direction. Some clients understood and some didn't, but I could not concern myself with that because I had to keep his energy channeled.

12

Protected

Christmas with my family was always fun when I was growing up. First, the only children in the house on Christmas were my brother and I. Then, by the time I turned twelve, our cousins started to come over. Years later, my son, and my brother's children came into the picture. Of course, they were now top priority. My pile of gifts started dwindling down to eventually nothing by the time I was around fifteen or sixteen years old.

Our family tradition was to meet over my grandmother's house by eleven p.m. on Christmas Eve. Once we arrived, half of my family would be down the street at my grandmother's church. They would go every Christmas Eve, around ten and normally get back to the house by twelve thirty in the morning. When they walked in, dinner would be ready with the exception of what my grandmother and everyone else fixed and brought over. My grandmother used to do most of the cooking, but as years went on, people chipped in to help. She still ended up doing a lot of the cooking.

Part of our tradition was to eat dinner between one and two in the morning. My grandmother would make a big pot of soup before dinner. That was our appetizer, along with the homemade cookies and cakes that were lying all around. She had all kinds of goodies: sugar cookies, oatmeal cookies, walnut cookies, sweet potato pies, and lemon and pound cakes. Her famous soups were split pea soup and shrimp gumbo. They would be piping hot on the stove along

IN MY MIND

with a big pot of rice. The house was full of people: great-aunts and uncles, cousins, and neighbors from the block. We would all gather around the table in a circle holding hands while someone prayed. This person always ended up being my mother. After about the tenth minute we started getting anxious, every time. There were some of us peeping out of one eye trying to catch someone else, so we could give them that look, as if to say "come on lady, you asked God for everything already! Let's eat!" After years went by, her prayers were cut down to a minimum.

My immediate family was very old and small. We had eight children total. So from the time I was a young child, into adolescence, I was hardly around children, besides being in school. At one point I was constantly around adults. If it wasn't my family, it was my mother's friends. The older people in our family were blessed to enjoy long years of life, but eventually they started dying off. That had a ripple effect, which meant that our gatherings were becoming smaller and smaller, but the memories were everlasting.

After dinner was over, we lounged around and opened gifts. Everyone brought a bag that was filled with presents and at the appointed time we would take our bags and start to give out gifts. But there was only one stipulation, you had to leave an ample amount of gifts at your own house, especially for the children, so when they got home the next day, they had something under their own tree to open. While the gifts were being opened, there was always a card game going on somewhere in the house with the men, and my great-grandmother. They played cards for hours, with cigarettes lit, and glasses full. My great-grandmother's cigarette would be hanging out the side of her mouth, with a glass of liquor in her hand while she played her hand and challenged the men.

She was the smallest at five feet, but also the biggest, toughest one at the table. She would slam her cards down and shout over her wins. She started cussing if she lost.

There was always a group of people in the kitchen gathered around the table, laughing, joking, and sipping. Some were watching TV, while others were picking on left overs. Then there was the group that just couldn't hang. By now it was around four a.m. Bodies were

CHAPTER 12 – PROTECTED

lying wherever they could find a spot. Some were upstairs in the beds, some were on the couch, some would be in the chairs, and some on the floors.

By nine or ten o' clock in the morning it was time to get up and start making plates, and gathering up your things to get ready and go home. Whatever you found laying around was breakfast. By twelve, everyone was home, either in their beds, or getting ready to do other house visits.

Christmas was basically the only holiday our entire family spent together consistently. For other holidays like Thanksgiving or Easter, we either had our own personal dinners at home, or went to a friend's house. On Mother's Day my mom, grandmother, and my aunts would go to breakfast at my mom's church. For Valentine's Day, whether I was with someone or not, I always received a gift from my mother. It would be some sort of candy or jewelry. One thing I can honestly say about the women in my family, everyone had a giving heart. If anyone was in trouble, they would contribute money or their time.

My immediate family spent most of our Thanksgivings in Florida every year. My brother and his wife and children lived there. His wife and I were really close, she was like a sister. My stepfather, mom, my son and I would drive. As years went by, my son and I started flying. I couldn't take that fourteen hour drive any more. We rotated every other year between time shares. One year we would stay in Orlando. The next year we would stay in Kissimmee right down the street from Disney. We did the parks for a couple of days, and then spent the rest of the week eating out and relaxing. We always had a blast.

Everyone with us was a huge game player, except for my stepfather and me. I was always somewhere reading or writing, while my stepfather was watching sports. Every night no matter where we were, and no matter how late it was when we got back, my mother, my brother, or my son was pulling a game out. Those three were the biggest players of all and the other kids and my sister-in-law just followed along. Sometimes it became heated unnecessarily because my brother was the most competitive one. If they needed extra players they would try and grab my stepfather, or me, but I would dodge out before they could catch me, or hibernate in one of the rooms and write or read a book. Of course, I was called all kinds of names, like party pooper and boring, but that didn't bother me at all. I just did not like things that were long and drawn out. If they were playing charades or Uno, then I joined in. But if they were playing board games and trivia games I didn't want to be bothered. The only other times I joined them besides Uno and charades is when we played games that involved dancing. I definitely enjoyed that because we had a ball watching everyone make a fool out of themselves.

At each visit, my brother always had a surprise for us. Unfortunately his kids were used as his pawns. He made a dance or a rap group out of them every time. He would have them practice for a couple of days before we arrived. My brother made his own music and beats, and the kids made their own dance moves and lyrics. Their performances were very well put together. Creativity ran through our blood, we were all creative in our own individual ways.

Once I became thirty years old, I realized my flow was different. In the past things moved for me quickly. I don't know what happened along the journey. It seemed as if things became a little slower paced than what I would have liked. I remember one of my cousins and I would have lunch every couple of years at different ages and stages of our lives. We compared our lives and set goals for ourselves. We talked about our future and what we wanted to see happen at our next stage. When we were twenty-seven we went out and talked about looking forward to becoming thirty. Then when we turned thirty, we talked about our accomplishments and areas of stagnation. I did appreciate the accomplishments that were made, but I sometimes despised the stagnations because I felt that I would never get that wasted time back. I became too hard on myself for allowing some opportunities to whisk by, but then I had to stop and think that God may have allowed some

CHAPTER 12 – PROTECTED

of those road blocks because I simply wasn't ready yet. Progress was very important because I did not function too well with being stagnant. Boredom and frustration arose if I was stuck on something too long and not progressing. I had to keep it moving. However, I had a problem with working on too many things at one time because something would definitely get neglected. I had to learn how to have balance. It wasn't easy, it was a daily struggle. When it didn't happen the way I thought it should have, I felt like a failure. There were plenty of times where I had to encourage myself. People expected me to be the example, so it was weird when I felt like I failed. I didn't see myself the way others did. Little did I know, these experiences of failure were shaping and molding my character. They were my teachers and they showed me a lot about myself. They showed me how I handled and responded to certain things; I learned that my faith wasn't where I thought it was.

Sometimes my perceived failures turned into fears. Those fears would sometimes manifest in my dreams. Every time I was faced with a dilemma, a decision, or a matter I feared, I would dream about dogs. I actually did have a fear of dogs, so it made sense that dogs represented my fears in my dreams. I was always surprised that the dogs in my dreams never bit me. Every single dog that would chase me, transformed into having a demon face. It happened every time they caught up with me. They got right there in my face, but couldn't touch me. They would sometimes chase me until I got to a door or an opening. I would just make it in at the last second and shut the door before they could take that last leap. In some of the dreams they would run after me until I was cornered. Then I would say the name of Jesus several times, and they would disappear or stop barking ferociously, and just look at me. There was one dream when a dog actually did get a hold of me. He wrapped his teeth around my leg without biting and I felt nothing. I just called the name of Jesus and he let go.

After I woke up, I tried to identify the fears that were gripping me. Sometimes I knew instantly, and other times I had to really dig deep inside and ask God what they were.

IN MY MIND

There was this one dream that was much different from anything I ever had. It was weird because I wasn't one hundred percent asleep. I was in that in-between realm of sleep and consciousness. My eyes weren't open, and my body wasn't moving, but my mind was slightly awake. I was able to hear something like it was going on around me but not right next to me. Then all of a sudden Freddy Krueger appeared across the room. Now I haven't seen a scary movie in years, ever since I was a teenager, let alone a Freddy Krueger movie. While he was standing there, he had that crazy, funny, dumb look on his face. He had on his red and black striped sweater, big round hat, and had long-bladed fingernails. He never walked towards me, but had something in his hand. Then he raised one of his arms up and opened his hand like Spiderman does when he lets out a web. A white mask came from his hand and started flying across the room while getting bigger and bigger. It looked like the identical mask that was used in the movie Scream. It had a long stretched out appearance, with eyes and a hole for a mouth. Because I was still semi-asleep, I couldn't move. The mask suctioned itself right onto my face, and was trying to smother me. I do remember calling the name of Jesus in my mind because I couldn't open my mouth. After calling His name, I remember receiving some strength, lifting my arms and peeling the corners of the mask off of my face and ripping it off. I instantly woke up panting heavily and catching my breath while looking around my room. There was nothing there but I knew I experienced something. For the next couple of days, I was so afraid to fall back asleep. Reality came quick. I knew that nothing could hurt or harm me in any way because I was covered by the blood of Jesus Christ. I got back on my feet and stood against the spirit of fear that tried to creep back into my life from years prior when I was a little girl.

I will never forget the time I was around seven years old and I was getting ready for bed. I asked my mom for a snack first and she agreed. Afterwards I ran upstairs to brush my teeth and get in the bed. About ten minutes passed and I could not fall asleep so I started to whistle. Singing and whistling were two things I loved to do. I would do it so much that I learned how to harmonize and make tunes. I started whistling a tune I made up, and stopped to

CHAPTER 12 – PROTECTED

catch my breath when I got tired. About two seconds later the same tune was whistled with a clearer and more defined sound. It startled me because it sounded so close and I thought I was alone. I yelled out for my mother to see if it was her. Because she didn't answer, I called my stepfather to see if it was him, and he didn't answer. Instantly fear gripped me and I couldn't get out of the bed to see if they were downstairs. I started crying and pulled the covers over my head, curled up in a fetal position and put my fingers in my ear so I wouldn't hear anything. I laid there for about ten minutes frozen. It seemed like an eternity. I then heard the front door to the house open and close, and it was my mother and stepfather. When I heard my mother's voice, I yelled out for her in a panicky pitch. She yelled back with a voice of concern "what's the matter?" I told her that I was whistling and something whistled right after me, then I asked her where she was. She told me they went to the corner to see what happened because a house on the corner of our block was on fire. She then said the whistling I heard was probably my imagination, and I should try to go back to sleep. She kissed me on my cheek, turned off the light, and left the room. I turned over, pulled the covers back over my head, went back into a fetal position and shut my eyes really tight. My heart was pounding ferociously against my chest. That was the day when the spirit of fear entered my life.

I slept with the covers over my head well into adulthood. It didn't matter where I was; that was my ritual. Different levels and types of fears crept upon me over the years. That spirit had me so paralyzed at times; I would lose the sense of myself for a moment. I could never go into a basement by myself without being afraid. Because our laundry room was in the basement, if I had to wash clothes, I would turn on every light in the house, creep down the steps, and look around as if someone was watching me. Then I would throw my clothes in the washing machine, head for the steps and run for my life like I was being chased with an axe. By the time I got upstairs I would be panting and out of breath. The fear of feeling someone touch my shoulder was always present, along with seeing shadows on the wall, and feeling like a set of eyes was staring at me from a dark corner. My mind was out of control. They were just illusions. I would pray hard all of the time and ask God if he could take that fear from me. I felt like I was too old to still have those childlike disturbances residing within me. I didn't tell anyone about it because I was too afraid that if I said something it would get worse. I heard some people say that if you spoke certain things out loud, the devil would hear you and make it worse for you. The fear had me so tormented that I remained silent about it for years. I knew the devil couldn't physically hurt me, yet I was so afraid of being afraid that I just bowed down to it. I hated it.

Listening to other people's strange encounters didn't help me. They did nothing but feed the fear. I would project their happenings on myself thinking I was next. I had a friend who once told me when she was younger, she and her mother went over a friend's house and she used the bathroom. While passing one of the bedrooms there was a little old lady lying in the bed, and then the old lady sat straight up and looked at her. When she came out of the bathroom and walked by the room again, the old lady was gone. She just figured that she went downstairs or something. When my friend got downstairs she asked her mother's friend, who was the lady? Her mother's friend had no idea who she was talking about. She expressed to her that she was the only one living there. My friend said she was startled, and her mom just thought she was hallucinating. There were other incidents where people said they saw demons in their house, dishes being moved, and people walking up steps. I remember my mother telling me that when she was younger she and her girlfriends were coming home from somewhere and it was late. She said when she looked ahead she saw a little fog and an image in the middle of the road. It was a man standing there with overalls on and a pitch fork in his hand. He came out of nowhere. Before she knew it she had to swerve and ran right through him. Her and her girlfriends all turned back and saw nothing. He was gone. Because of hearing stories like that, I had to shut everything down: all scary movies, haunted houses at amusement parks, and listening to peoples' stories. It was very crippling for me. It got so bad that at one point

CHAPTER 12 – PROTECTED

I started obsessing by looking at my car's rear view mirror every five minutes to make sure I didn't see any images sitting in the back seat while I was driving, especially at night. It's funny now but back then it was horrifying. Here is one of the prayers I wrote one night to God in desperation about my stronghold.

> *Lord, I am not feeling your presence anymore. It is fear that keeps me from praying to you. I am scared. Wherever I seem to go I'm scared. This yoke has been haunting me for years and I want to be free from the terror of fear. Sometimes I don't want to get up and go to the bathroom for fear of seeing something. I don't want to see images or feel a false presence. Lord I always feel like something is watching me. Help! I need freedom so I can pray to you more effectively. I don't want to pass this on to my son.*

I always kept some sort of light or TV on while I slept. One morning I woke up and there was a pastor on one of the cable stations. Before I could even open my eyes I heard him saym, *"I pray for all of those who feel a demonic presence and suffer torture of the mind."* I opened my eyes and started receiving the prayer he prayed. Later on that same evening I became bold enough to speak out and tell someone. I called a friend and told her everything that was going on with me. She encouraged me and told me that satan was the father of illusions, and not to be afraid. After we hung up, I stood in the middle of my living room floor and yelled to the top of my lungs "Satan is a liar and the father of lies, and I speak out right now in the name of Jesus, I will not be afraid in my own home!" Then I said, "Today I will be delivered and not frightened anymore.

It's over!" That night as I went to bed I felt such a peace and calmness over me. There was no fear. I felt like I was in control of myself and it felt good. Of course the devil was mad because he tried to come back seven times stronger than before so he could elevate himself. He knew that I was serious and did not want to leave so easily. I did get sidelined every now and then, but I would remember the promises that God gave me in His word by telling me that He would never leave me or forsake me. One day I was standing in my kitchen cooking and a light bulb instantly came on in my head. I dropped the utensils that were in my hand, looked up towards the ceiling and stared into space dumbfounded for a moment. It hit me. A whole week went by and I had slept in the dark without a TV on and no covers over my head. I realized that I stopped focusing on the fear and it left without my knowing. I didn't even recognize the shift that took place that entire week. It left just like that, because I wasn't giving it life by feeding or focusing on it. All I could do was stand there and smile. My heart melted because all I heard was "I love you daughter."

The devices that satan would use for my distraction amazed me. Sometimes I took the bait easily, but other times I fought back hard. I had to learn that he couldn't hit a moving target. I realized that if my weaknesses weren't exposed at times, I would never know my strengths.

13
Swayed

My church and church family were very important to me. There were times when I didn't feel connected, but in my heart I knew I belonged. We had some great times together, especially when our services were held in a school auditorium before we got our building. I was really serious about my spiritual relationship with God. I made sure I was in church at all times when I needed to be. My pastor was great! He was our spiritual father and helped us to grow and gain more knowledge in our walk with Jesus. He was like a real father to me, from the pulpit. His heart was made of gold, love, and compassion. The thing that I admired the most about him was that his name was never heard in gossip around town, because he walked what he talked. There were no mistresses on the side, and no swindling of money. He had a heart pure before God, and would have given his life for his congregation if he had to.

To see that much consistency in a man and actually see the good in his heart was a big deal for me. The sermons that he delivered were always straight to the point. He said things that other pastors would have been too afraid to say, in fear of losing their congregation. My pastor was more concerned with what God thought of him than what people thought.

I met quite a bit of good friends at church. Some of them I bonded with instantly and our friendship remained, while some were just seasonal. For the most part, people seemed to just be there for a particular time. Learning a person's purpose in my life was one of the hardest things I had to deal with. I held special places in my heart for those who entered and I would beat up on myself because I thought I was doing something to make them leave. It was hard for me to accept the fact that their time may have been up in my life. Because I struggled with a heavy spirit of rejection, that brought on those feelings of self-condemnation. All kinds of things would run through my head but I believe God used those situations to teach me about myself as well. They taught me my strengths, insecurities, and abilities to depend on Him and not man. I worried myself so much that it was sometimes hard to see myself as God saw me. My self-image was so distorted. Some people had no idea that I struggled with those things because I would dress it up. I didn't walk around with my shoulders slumped, head down, and sorrowful looks on my face. I walked straight up and strong with an appearance of confidence.

My outer appearance caught much attention, but internally, I was still trying to find my place in society. I didn't know how to receive compliments, especially from men. I enjoyed the stares, but I couldn't handle the attention. I tried not to make eye contact so I wouldn't have to say hello and engage in conversation. The men probably believed that I wasn't interested, but the entire time it was a self-image issue presenting itself. If a guy was bold enough to say something to me, I would start to reason with myself as to why he should not talk to me. My reasoning would have me thinking my breath was too tart, the pimple on my face was too big, my face looked too old that day, my stomach wasn't flat enough, or I wasn't dressed right. These types of things would help me to remain disconnected. Compliments came a dime a dozen, but they still could not penetrate my self-image. When they came, I said, "thank you" quickly, then turned the attention on something else to get the focus off of me. I would fake myself out with false humility and

CHAPTER 13 – SWAYED

convince myself that I didn't want to bask in the compliments for fear of becoming self-righteous, or conceited.

Even in the midst of my self-esteem issues, my personality had many facets to it. I was very upfront and bold at times, and very withdrawn and timid during others times. When I was defending my loved ones, getting a point across, or engrossed in a group conversation or debate, my bold side appeared. During some of these moments, I would try to pull in the reins because I feared offending someone. That boldness played a major part in me being able to express my creativity, especially when I got a chance to help and serve people. This brought me great enjoyment. There was no better feeling than knowing I boosted someone else's self-esteem even though I was struggling with mine most of the time. I remember doing a hair and fashion show just for that reason. I really wanted to help the younger and older women to not be ashamed of their looks. I had all shapes and sizes of women which gave them an opportunity to express and feel good about themselves. They needed to be seen as naturally talented as well as beautiful. Their ages ranged from four years old to thirty eight. It turned out to be a great success. It was so good that people were asking me to have another one. They were so enamored in how well it was put together.

For the first event, there were a total of thirty models including men, women, and children. I had caterers, sound technicians, hostesses, decorators, dancers, and singers. My hat went off to them, because they were willing to make the show a huge success by contributing their time and talent. My gratitude was full.

The show was truly a blessing to me because I was able to exhibit other parts of my gifts, talents, and abilities. I had so much more to offer than what people saw. It only took me two months to put it all together. I stayed completely focused during the planning stage and even during the event.

Attendance was wonderful. We had a turnout of at least three hundred people. The setup inside the building was perfect

IN MY MIND

for what I wanted to achieve. It was a nice-sized round two story dance studio with large bay windows surrounding the entire upstairs portion. The owner was nice enough to let me utilize both upstairs and downstairs for the price of one floor.

Our rehearsals weren't too intense. There were three separate practices held each week for a month at my house. The dedication was unbelievable. Mostly everyone came after work or school. The men didn't practice as much as the women because it was a little harder getting them all together at one time. Since they had this challenge, I asked one of the guys if he could put a few scenes together for me. They really pulled it off well at the last minute.

Every day I ran home and fixed my son's dinner, then headed straight to my stereo for hours. I listened to so many songs trying to match them up with the scenes that my brain was fried. I almost became a little discouraged but I had to keep going because I knew I had a deadline to meet.

I allowed the two soloists to choose their own music. The first soloist sang a Yolanda Adams song, and the second one sang two of her original songs from her then upcoming CD. They both were amazing and truly gifted. I also allowed the MC to do her own thing. I trusted the fact that she was a natural because of her profession being an author and speaker. She knew how to keep a crowd entertained. I chose the music for the dancers. I wanted a certain message to come across through the dances; although they were able to bring their own creativity. I had five dancers total; three women, and two men. One of the dances that really stood out was a very innocent, but intimate dance. It was about a couple that was together for a while, but the woman realized she couldn't see the man anymore. She expressed to him that God came first, and that she needed to seek Him. The man didn't want to hear that. He kept chasing after her and she kept pulling away gently. They received a standing ovation because it was enacted so realistically.

The caterers also did a fantastic job and the food was

CHAPTER 13 – SWAYED

delicious. The presentation was very pretty. There were all kinds of salads, and any kind of wrap that could be thought of, along with chicken and different types of rice dishes. There were also all sorts of desserts and punches that were served. After the show was over, so much food was left that it had to be given away or thrown out.

Every scene was sharp. All of the models' hair was gorgeous, their clothes were fun and elegant, and they all looked great. The guys were handsome, clean shaven, and in suits. The women in the crowd went crazy over the men when they walked down the runway. They stood up and gave them huge applauses. This boosted the men's egos and made them stroll even harder. After three hours, the guys ended the show with a beautiful scene, from a song titled, "A Changed Man." It was expressing how this guy used to be involved in the wrong activities, and now wanted to change his life around. When the song began, one of the guys walked out without his suit jacket and tie, and his shirt was hanging out of his pants. He walked to the end of the runway and stood on the side, appearing thugged out, and about the wrong business. Then a few seconds later, another guy came out and started modeling his suit. When he got to where the thugged out guy was, he motioned with his hands as if to say "no way, I'm clean, and I am a changed man, I don't do that anymore." He walked up to the camera, opened his suit jacket to show off his shirt, belt, and tie, did a little spin and turn, and walked back. The same was repeated by each of the male models. After they all declined the thug's temptations, he started thinking and humbling himself, wanting to change. As he started to walk back off the stage, the rest of the guys came and grabbed him and huddled him in a circle. They cleaned him up, put his suit jacket and tie back on, and shocked everyone. As they opened the circle, a bride wearing a beautiful wedding gown was standing by his side. She slid in from the side door. One model had a bible in his hand as if he was performing a ceremony. After that they hugged and he walked his bride down the aisle spinning her and showing off her dress. There were so many ooh's and aah's from the crowd.

Throughout the entire show, I was in the background running up and down the stairs with my clip board in my hand and instructing everyone to be ready. When the wedding scene was over, the grand finale was next. The dancers came out from everywhere to a popular Kirk Franklin song. They were grabbing some of the people in the audience by the hand instructing them to stand up and participate. Following the dancers, the models came out dancing one by one. They then formed two lines across from each other to make a center aisle in between them. Now it was my turn. I really did not want to go out but I had to greet my guests. I walked down the aisle with my knees buckling. I was so shy when it came to speaking in front of people that it was pathetic. Everyone was clapping and shouting my name, while shouting chants and pumping their fists in the air. I glided so fast across that aisle, I didn't even blink. The MC introduced the behind the scenes people first, then the models, and then gave the microphone to me. I thanked everyone for supporting me and coming out. I then gave the microphone back to the MC along with an exhale, thanking God that was over. She prayed, then the finale music was turned back up as we were dismissing. A lot of people strayed behind, mingling and talking with each other, while all of the tech crew and models were cleaning up and getting themselves together. After I got home that night, I thanked God for another successful event that He allowed me to accomplish. No one could have even tried to peel the smile off of my face, or rip the joy out of my heart. This show was a great accomplishment for me because it took my faith to another level in trusting God. Even through all of my insecurities and esteem issues, the one thing that I was strong in was knowing that God would always take care of me. I never really worried about money, because it was always available when needed, and because of my go getter nature that whatever I put my mind to I did it with God's grace. It was

CHAPTER 13 – SWAYED

always something that naturally resided within me.

A couple of weeks after the show, I came down off my high and started battling with my thoughts. Defeat was waiting patiently for me. As much as I tried to fight it off, it continued to distract me more and more. It felt like my prayers weren't being answered and that my faith was basically shot. The inconsistency of my thoughts was very frustrating and I couldn't understand why I kept allowing them to take control of me. I knew that I was trying to live my best for God. As much as I fought it the harder it came.

Daddy, I feel like a stranger in my surroundings. And I can't blame anyone. Your love is better than life.

Please make me over again. Make me responsible for my feelings.

I want to work and be satisfied, knowing that I am in the right place.

I want to excel and be a good mother, Christian, worker, leader, businesswoman, and friend.

I want to remain confident in myself like a bold soldier. Not intimidated, or inferior, not afraid or fearful. And I want to stay out of victim mode, and be a conqueror.

Daddy, help me to see me the way you see me. Help me to walk in my authority.

Help me to see you in everything that occurs with me. Also help me to discern if I am in the right place.

Search me Lord, I have been hiding. Depression tries to

IN MY MIND

*over whelm me. It pursues me like a man
pursuing a woman.*

*I fight it, then I get weak. I fight, then I get weak.
Sometimes I am like an unstable man in all his ways.*

*Focus for me is temporary, hiding is my best sport.
Not healthy, but I mastered it.*

*My mind is surrounded by thoughts of failure
and defeat, but I know that is not true.*

*A stranger in my own skin, hiding, wanting to relate,
oh, so badly, wanting to relate.*

*Wondering why I am a Christian, I love God,
but can't get it, after all this time.*

*I feel like an alien to my church body. It's hard to relate to
me because I don't come out; I don't even keep eye contact.
What happened with the connection of true consistent
deliverance, and me?*

*I am tired of me not holding my ground. I know
that my latter will be greater.*

*I don't want to keep a boring life. New is what
I desire, consistency is what I desire. My voids filled
by you is also what I desire.*

*Please don't let the crops and harvest of bad
decisions eat me alive. Spare me Daddy; tears
have been my food consistently.*

CHAPTER 13 – SWAYED

I am just a shadow right now to most.

I want to come out, but I really don't know how.
Please teach me, I want to come back alive.

Lord I do love you, I do.

I feel stuck in time. I lost track of time.
Help me to reach my destination.

Inconsistency and forgetfulness is my flow.

Life must move!

I get numb and my faith is shallow. I get weak.

Consistency is key, help me!

Through the rain, storm, pain, and sickness; protection, security, love and assuredness, all come from you.

Why can't I just seem to get it? Why can't the light bulb come on for me?

Hold me; hold me, only you fill my voids. If I love you, why do I struggle with these emotions so deeply? Teach me how to allow you to have full control over them. I am not a loner! I am not a failure! A new season of life has arrived for me.

Sometimes I wonder why my friends still want to be friends with me, I am too emotional. I will give everything up for the sake of peace. Lord give me your perfect will.

IN MY MIND

"I am your husband, peace be still And know that I am God"

Thank you, Daddy, for your peace last night. The God of love, and full of compassion.

You are always there with me in my time of need.

I say to myself "Who could ever love me with their whole heart without getting tired of me. Who could ever stay by my side through every tear, and when I am done, say "My beloved, I am still here?"

My God! My God! Awesome is he, brilliant, majestic, he reigns in majesty.

I have never experienced a love so unique. Unique to the point where I ask, why me? Amen.

Those prayers came from a place deep down within. I was looking for peace, but being bewildered in my thoughts at the same time. After the huge accomplishment of the show was when everything emotionally started to overwhelm me. That was around the time when my relationship with the older guy started to get crazy and my focus was deterred. When that happened it left room for a flood of other things to follow. I would get bombarded with not feeling good enough, feeling like a failure, and suffering with a perceived heavy load of rejection. I realized that part of my problem was trying to look for approval and validation from people. During the production of the show, I felt great because I was helping people and feeling a sense of accomplishment and receiving admiration from my attendees. I had no time to stop and remember that underneath all of that business the roots of those issues were not cut. They were still alive and breathing just waiting for me to sit down and take a break.

14
Heartbroken

At age thirty-one, some things started to clearly come together for me. It was slightly noticeable before, but one of my light bulbs clicked on. I could finally see and understand some of the patterns that were swirling around in my life, especially when it came to men. At one point, men were indispensable. I had no problem getting one, and no problem letting one go. I knew how the pattern started, but I wasn't able to comprehend how to break the cycle. I felt wonderful when there wasn't anyone in my life, and would pride myself if I made it at least eight months alone. The problem was, when I did get back into a relationship, after a while, I changed. When I was younger, it really didn't matter, because if the guys didn't act right, or I got bored with them, I kept it moving to the next, and wouldn't think twice about it. But the older I became especially after my life started changing for the better, I noticed a difference in my selections. I spent time in thought and did not make any sudden moves. Even so, some of those choices still weren't good for me. During those relationships I was in denial. I truly believed that I didn't need men the way other women did, especially because I knew how to handle everything on my own. When I heard some women talking about other women they knew, saying things like, "I just don't know why she won't leave that man alone; she needs to learn how to be by herself. She doesn't always have to have a man around. Can she even function without one?"

IN MY MIND

I would come along and say "Yeah, I know, if they would just learn how to be content, and not depend on men, they wouldn't have to keep putting themselves through all of that drama." I didn't realize I was doing the same thing in my own life, depending on relationships with men and holding onto them even if they were no good for me.

I never really understood how a woman should be properly treated, and I didn't have a clear understanding of men and their thought processes and actions. Therefore, I chose men blindly even when I thought I was being cautious. It became a part of my dysfunction. I had no idea how to relate to men socially or at all for that matter. That particular area for me just seemed to stay in lack of wisdom. I let my heart get in the way of plain old common sense. My pastor would pick up on things that were going on around me. He would constantly say to me, "Keep going Cee, and don't give up. Continue to be the dynamic woman that you are. You're doing a great job!" That meant so much to me because it wasn't something that I was used to hearing. When he would say those things, it made me feel warm and fuzzy. It felt like a big bear hugging me. I didn't realize until years later that when he said those things to me he was speaking directly to me about my relationships. He could always tell when my focus was being thrown off because of a relationship. When I wasn't in one, my life would flourish in all areas: business, personal, spiritual, and mental. Something happened every time I entertained improper male company. I kept getting sidetracked because I was reasoning with myself by saying that I didn't need men financially, and I didn't need to see them on a daily basis. I believed that I only needed them when I wanted to catch a movie, grab a bite to eat, or go for a long drive. I just wanted a part time companion in a sense.

I heard people say that having several male friends was best because then you won't get so emotionally attached to just one. But that was so difficult for me. I couldn't seem to fathom that in my mind. I didn't know how to date more than one person at a time and not feel guilty. That is also what would trip me up. I

CHAPTER 14 – HEARTBROKEN

would put all of my eggs in one basket. I thought that hanging out with one guy would be okay, and wouldn't be anything serious. My motto was, "let's just take a day trip, or get something to eat, and after that, I will see you when I see you." That one outing turned into many, and after that we were in a relationship. All of my time would be spent with that one person, and then subconsciously, I started depending on them emotionally because I was searching for intimacy and love.

I remember one day going to talk to my pastor's wife at her house. When I got there I was in such bad shape mentally and emotionally. I had just broken up from a three and a half year relationship with a very nice guy, right before I met the older guy. We walked in the same faith and shared similar hearts, but there was one thing that was standing in our way. I didn't have the grace for his lifestyle, as well as him not having the grace for mine. Our personalities were truly different. I had a very determined, go getter personality, where I always took the lead and he didn't. He was more settled in a sense but I also felt he was too comfortable. He did not seem to have any interest in forward progression when it came to his career and living situations. After a while it started to become unbearable. When we were together I felt bad at times because I knew that I was just hanging on because of familiarity. I knew it needed to be over, but I also knew that it would be hard emotionally. We were best friends and told each other everything, but the attraction was just not there. I was sitting at my pastor and his wife's table crying my heart out, 'snotting,' with my hair undone, eyes blood shot red, and mouth dry, just thinking that I would never get over that hurt and be the same again. My pastor's wife listened to my woes, and when I was done my pastor stepped in and said to me, "Baby, I believe in my heart that you were supposed to go through this. The type of man that God has for you is someone strong; you need a strong man." That resonated in my spirit so deeply, and after that, they both hugged me and made me feel a whole lot better than the way I entered. Then my pastor's wife made lunch, and she and I watched a little TV before it was time for me to pick Amir up from school.

My heart hurt for a while, but it eventually subsided. Shortly after I thought that I was over everything, that's when I allowed the older guy that I mentioned before to enter my life. I wasn't even looking for a relationship. I was just looking for a buddy and someone to talk to. However, because I wasn't fully over the hurt of my recent break-up with my ex, I really wasn't strong enough to just have a buddy. That backfired on me. Right after my ex I forgot how happiness felt. I went from having a little cushion and regaining a sense of stability and peace back into my life for a couple of months, to jumping right in to another relationship with the older guy which changed my life for the worse at that time. My thinking was muddy, my perceptions were off, and I was imbalanced. My mind was boggled because I was trying to understand how I could allow myself to get into another relationship and let it affect me with such magnitude. In the midst of me trying to figure myself out, my passion and drive were being swallowed up in grief. It was during this time that I started to see my emotions spiral out of control. The strength that I depended on started to disappear. I saw myself reaching for it, but couldn't quite grasp it. Doubt would come and pull my arms down with resistance. I spent more time being frustrated with myself, than fighting doubt. I knew it wasn't good for me, but since my strength left, I just kept giving in. That deep rooted spirit of rejection that I carried snuck its way back into the forefront of my mind. I sat there and listened to those thoughts that told me that nobody wanted me, and that I couldn't do anything right. Battling frustration and rejection at the same time, led me right back to that walkway of solitude. I internally viewed myself as less than. I looked at myself as a failure again. While I was thinking all of this about myself, there was always this little voice trying to be heard. It kept telling me that I wasn't a failure, and not to believe it. But because what I viewed as evidence was haunting me, I believed the lie. It was torture and very unhealthy. I had no idea who I was, and neither did anyone else.

After everything was over, I thanked God every day because the

CHAPTER 14 – HEARTBROKEN

experience was irreplaceable. I truly learned so much about myself. There were things that were lying dormant inside of me that I had no clue were there. I experienced many disturbing emotions I felt toward myself and others. I lost my trust in people and I started becoming the rejecter in fear of rejection. My wall kept getting higher and higher. Throughout that time, God was chiseling away all of my old stuff. Explanations started coming forth as to why I would react the way I did, and why I allowed rejection to attack me so hard. The one thing that I did learn was that everyone developed differently. Some people overcame quickly, and some didn't. I wanted to overcome, but I couldn't' seem to pull that deeply planted root out of the ground. I would beat myself up constantly for repeating the same vicious cycle over and over again. I compared myself to others and I felt worse once I saw how fantastic they seemed to be doing on the outside.

It was sometimes hard to talk to people about my weaknesses, because I couldn't provide a clear explanation. Then there were times when I felt so desperate to talk that I would talk to anyone. Afterwards I felt stupid for opening up because some people that I shared with turned my vulnerability against me, and started to distance themselves. I guess I seemed like a basket case and they didn't want to be bothered. This strengthened me more because it helped me to understand people, and learn how to forgive even more. I had to thank God so much in the midst of my pain, because that is the only way I knew how to get out of it. It may have taken a while, but the wait built endurance within me. When I couldn't speak, I wrote:

Thank you so much for your love. Thank you for your peace.

Even when I fail you, and when I lose my way, and when I don't know how to put the pieces together, and I give up and throw in the towel. You are right there.

IN MY MIND

Cover me, love me, rejection tries to creep in like a thief.

I know I am not alone because you are right there by my side.

*I want no regrets. Please heal my wounded heart,
it feels beyond repair.*

It feels used, dumped, and rejected.

*You are amazing. You are the Almighty God,
you are I am, and there is no one like you.*

You are an original. Your love is better than life.

*Help me!!! I am drowning with a down cast spirit.
No speech, drained eyes, wondering why?*

Please pump life into me.

It could either kill me or I can fight it.

*But help me because I don't know how to
stop it from coming back.*

When I finally came back to reality, I was happy but disappointed at the same time. It seemed like precious time was wasted that could have been used helping someone else. I was baffled. On one hand I felt like maybe I had to go through that in order to help someone else, but on the other hand, it seemed as if it was taking forever, and I should have been over everything quickly. I felt that the people who were put in my path at that time weren't getting what they needed because I was so despondent, and had nothing to give. I had made up in my mind to roll with it because the fight to get over it was too hard and it would come right back again anyway.

15
Family

"Surprise!" Everybody screamed as my mother came through the doors. All two hundred and seventy-five of us got her really good. She retired from working for the state of Pennsylvania after thirty six years, so my brother and I decided to give her a retirement party. He called me one day and asked me what should we buy or do for her, and we came up with the idea. He lived in California, so I had to do most of the planning and leg work and he supplied some of the money as needed.

Immediately, I started writing a list of names because my mother knew a tremendous amount of people. The list kept growing larger by the day. I wanted it to be very special for her, so I invited people from all eras of her life: childhood to present. There were people on that list that she hadn't seen in twenty five years or so. I spent countless nights on the internet looking up phone numbers and addresses. I assigned one of her friends from her job to gather up everyone's information for me that would be attending. I also asked my stepfather if he could get all of their church members' information that she was close with. It was exciting during the planning stages, but also fast paced. We only had two months to get everything together between work and sleep.

It was an awesome day. My mother had no idea, not even a clue. We set the date, which was on my brother's birthday. We also planned for his children to come up from Florida with my sister-in-law. He flew into Philadelphia two days before the party and stayed at my house. The kids and my sister-in-law got in the next day.

Everyone started arriving, and the room was getting filled quickly. My mom thought she was coming to a function that was being held by her church members. When my stepfather pulled the truck up, the lookout person told the DJ to announce her arrival, and to let everyone know to settle down and get ready to yell surprise. In the meantime my brother and his children were standing behind the door, so they could pop out and be the second big surprise. They would be the last people that she would suspect to be there because we only saw them once a year. As my mother and stepfather got out of the truck, they started to walk towards the door. As they were walking, we were frozen in anticipation with our hearts racing. A feather could have been heard in that dead of silence. Within moments, she opened the door, and was stunned to see all of those people shouting surprise. My brother being a jokester was standing behind her the whole time mocking her while she was taking it all in. Someone finally pointed and told her to look behind her. When she turned around and saw my brother, she screamed and jumped up and down and started hugging him. He had just recently returned from the war in Afghanistan. When she thought that was it, the kids jumped out from behind and tapped her. When she turned around and saw them, she lost it. She was crying and rejoicing at the same time, and couldn't seem to comprehend how they all got there.

Because there were so many people, and we were on a time schedule, we asked everyone if they could hold their hugs and conversations for later - we needed to get the program started. We escorted my mom and stepfather to the front of the room so they could be seated. Once everything was settled down, the dancers came out. I had six praise dancers from my church come and kick the afternoon off with an awesome routine. Another highlight of the event was a DVD that I had made for her. I

CHAPTER 15 – FAMILY

went to her house and took all of the pictures that were stored away in boxes in her garage without her knowing. I also went to my grandmother's house to borrow a few from her. A gentleman who was referred to me by one of my clients created a beautiful montage of the pictures along with songs I chose to fit every part of the DVD. It was a journey of her life and experiences which made it very memorable. After everything was over, my brother, his family, me, my son, and my aunt, all went to New Jersey and spent the night at my mom and stepfather's house. We stayed up, watched TV, and counted all of the money she received. She received over a few thousand dollars plus gifts.

Her guests really showed their love and appreciation for all she had done for people over the years. I sat on the couch next to her after we opened her gifts and thought to myself how proud I was of her, and also proud to say that she was my mother.

Throughout my life, no one could ever compare to her. I almost had an obsession to get her approval. I had always wanted to dress like her, smell like her, and wear her jewelry, (which I sometimes did). Communication was the only thing that was missing between us, but over the years our prayers to have a deeper relationship with each other were definitely being answered. We always loved each other, but as I mentioned earlier, we did not always know how to relate to each other.

There were times when I wanted to go to my mother with my deep problems, but I knew she would shy away from me because her heart was very sensitive. She did not like to see me hurt or in pain so it was hard for her to deal with my problems in order to avoid grief. When I was maturing, especially in relationship with God, I started to understand the deception that the enemy was using to keep the women in our family separate. As far as I knew, it started with my great, great, grandmother, and it trickled down. Some of the mothers were not emotionally bonded with their daughters.

My mother's personality was strong and bold but yet gentle and reserved. My personality was strong, bold and to the point.

IN MY MIND

Even with the similarities in our personalities, our seemingly lack of understanding of each other was very frustrating and kept us from communicating properly. When we did try, it would not go so well and would end up with both of us agitated and shutting down. I kept a lot inside or wrote in a journal; that is how I would get my release. At one point in my youth she thought that I didn't like her because I didn't talk to her much. The real reason I didn't talk much was because my stepfather and I clashed and I knew that was her husband who she wanted me to respect. Both my stepfather and I had very strong and commanding personalities and were competing for my mother's attention, while she was stuck in the middle. I knew she loved me with her whole heart, but there was only one of her to share. I looked forward to those moments alone with her when my stepfather would go on his weekend fishing trips. Those were the weekends I stayed home and hung out around the house. I enjoyed experiencing the freedom and not walking around on eggshells.

My communication with my mother would be through letters expressing my feelings, because I didn't know how to express them verbally or physically. Her communication would be through gifts, and hugs. On the other end of my family spectrum, my communication with my father was very limited because I only saw him once or sometimes twice a year for a day or so. I knew he loved me, but it was hard to feel because of the distance. When I did see him he would make the day special because we would hang out and he would buy me anything I wanted. I thought of him as a super hero who could do no wrong. Whenever he came to town, I was in heaven. He lived in California for a while during my younger years. So, when I did see him, it was time he planned for a couple of days that were split up between his family, friends, my siblings and me. It was a long time before I even knew that I had siblings and other family besides him. Unfortunately I never got a chance to get close with my siblings and the rest of my father's family growing up. I didn't meet them

CHAPTER 15 – FAMILY

until I turned twelve. It was the same with my mother. She didn't meet her father's side of the family until she was also twelve.

While my father was living in California he planned a big two week vacation for some friends and family. There were at least ten of us who flew out. He had something planned for us to do every day. I had a great time, but it was an adjustment because I wasn't very accepted by some of my siblings. I didn't understand at the time, but later on realized that it was because we never got a chance to bond. One of my male cousins who went on the trip was an angel. I had just met him upon my arrival and he took me under his wing and made me feel comfortable.

My father had six children total and I fell next to last. When I went to California, I grew attached to my little sister. She was this cute little girl with slanted eyes and short pigtails. Her mother and my father were married. I adored her. She would be with me all of the time when her, my father and my stepmother moved back to Philadelphia. I would have her with me all of the time along with my little cousins and Amir. I was well known for having other people1's children and treating them to *Chucky E. Cheese*, amusement parks or movies. It was a deep passion of mine to see children have a good time and enjoy themselves. There were very few weekends where I did not have someone else's child with me. I would gather everyone up in the car and just drive. Sometimes we would end up at the park around the corner, or two hours away in Baltimore Harbor. Having my little sister along brought me comfort. It felt good to have some kind of connection with my father's side, even if it was with one person. My father was a bold and fun person. He knew how to have a good time, but he also wasn't someone you wanted to mess with either. He was a protector even if it came down to fighting – and he was good at it. I wish that I would have gotten a chance to meet his parents. As I got older I would hear everyone talk about them. I remember one of my older sisters talking about how much fun they had when they spent time with them. I felt a little isolated because I had nothing to relate to. They all called my grandfather, grand-dad. My sister said he would make his rounds and pick everyone up on some weekends and take them places. She also said they would spend the summers over at our grandmother's house. It really hurt when I would hear those stories because I felt like a stranger. They all had a bond that I never felt a part of. The remaining of my father's side of the family besides my siblings were very mature in age. He had a few aunts, but a lot of uncles, that would have gatherings and parties at their houses, along with my dad hosting his own. Every time I attended one of the gatherings, it was weird for me because some of them couldn't remember my name. There was one time when I was at a cousin's wedding with my sister and dad, and some of the relatives, including one of the uncles didn't even know who I was, and that hurt. They were asking my dad about my other siblings and how they were doing and I tried not to get jealous but most of the time I did. I really struggled with jealousy for years when it came to those issues. I never really felt like I had my entire dad. I harbored so much hurt because I wanted to feel like he was all mine. It took a long time for my siblings to start coming around and being a part of my life. I remember one time when I was about fifteen and I was on my way to work one morning at a salon where I assisted and I got off the train and I saw one of my sisters walking to get on the train. I got excited and I spoke to her and she just said, "hello" and kept on walking. My spirit was crushed. That moment just added on to the other feelings of rejection that I was experiencing. I thank God that time created healing in those situations. It wasn't easy and it was definitely a process. As I reflected on my past, I dug deep to get to the root of some of my behaviors without casting blame on anyone. I knew later on that things were already predestined, and had to go a particular way in order to get certain results. I understood that I suppressed a lot of things subconsciously. I honestly thought that I was fine until feelings and emotions started surfacing against my will. My problem was, no matter how physically close I was to anyone, I always felt a sense of disconnection. I never really

CHAPTER 15 – FAMILY

felt first in anyone's life. At that time I didn't understand that God had a plan for me. He would sometimes secretly and calmly speak to my heart and say, "I am your number one, and you are first in my eyes."

I fought Him hard because I wanted to hear those same words from a human. So basically it was hard for me to believe that God was enough. I spent several years fighting Him on that, and he still had patience and didn't give up on me.

It seemed like whenever I experienced a gush of emotions from rejection, I went through different stages. Some stages were times when I may have felt a sting of it and brushed it right off. Then there were other times when I may have felt that same sting and called a couple of friends, vented, got comfort, felt better, and moved on. But then there were times when something would just come over me and I felt like I was out of sorts with my emotions. I felt like I could not control the pain of that rejection. I felt like the whole world would be closing in on me, and I was standing isolated, while everyone else was living life. It got so bad that I couldn't even pick up the phone for encouragement. I just wanted to sleep for a week and forget everything when I woke up. The only strength I had, which was barely there was to cry out to God. I wanted to scream to the top of my lungs, but never wanted Amir to hear me. I didn't want to upset his world and put him into panic, or suppress his spirit. So I held it in until I could get to my bedroom, get on my knees, and put my head in a pillow and let it out. Then I would cry silently and uncontrollably to God. I would plead for His help and tell Him how much I loved Him and that He was all I had. When those episodes started to happen, I begged and pleaded for Him to allow someone to call and comfort me. Someone would call right in the midst of my despair. I knew He preferred to talk to me instead, but He was being gracious, and giving me what I desired at the time. It was funny because I may not have talked to that person for a while, and they would tell me that I just ran across their minds so they decided to call. Then as time went on, and

IN MY MIND

I started to mature, those pleas didn't work any more. God had shut all phone communication down. I guess He said, "Okay, you're mature enough to handle this without crutches, now talk to me and tell me what's on your heart. Let's work through this together." I had no choice but to suck it up and take it like a big girl. I would get my pen and paper and start to write:

Daddy, I long to hear from you, speak to me clearly. I don't want to do any extra theatrical so called spiritual things to try and get you to speak to me. I want you to myself. My spirit calls out to you in anticipation. I need to get to the point where you are my first love. I enjoy being thought of, loved and cared for by a human, but nobody can compare to you. So help me! I cannot allow my flesh to over power my spirit.

Daddy, you come first in my life, regardless. I know that my faith has been tested on several occasions and I failed. Thank you for being merciful, and giving me another chance.

Please help me to focus on your word; I know that you won't force me. Protect my heart, and help me to do the same. Help me to keep moving forward. You have so many things in the future for me, and Amir. You never give us more than we can bear, and you know what we need. Continue to keep me strong with your unconditional love. Thank you for hugging me, and loving me when I feel forgotten, even though, I know I am not. It just feels like a desert sometimes, but you always supply the water. Speak to my heart, and help me to hear closely from you. You have a specific time carved out for me. That's just the type of God you are. "Thanks." Even when it hurts or stings a little, you put the salve on it. Lord its all about you, and not me. Thank you for your presence. You are so awesome.

Please make me smile when I am feeling sad. I know that I was

CHAPTER 15 – FAMILY

created in the image of you, and am fearfully and wonderfully made.

Thank you in advance for teaching me how to deal with rejection a little better.

Help me to be content with you. Thanks for the supply of real friends. I know more are coming. Help me in my mind. I come against every negative and demonic thought, in Jesus name. Help me not to feel left out. I always find myself wanting to fit in, but for some reason I never do. Thank you for teaching me certain things through your lessons. I can't exactly see all of my future, but I will continue to trust in you. I will keep believing in you, and knowing that you are God. Again, please help me to control my inner thoughts. Help me to know that you have everything under control. In Jesus name, amen.

16

Loved

Finally, it felt so good to hear consistent praise for my son. His complete turnaround was a long-term prayer answered. He was in a process of trying to find himself without any male guidance. I could have imagined it being like a blind man trying to cross the street without his stick. I would try and find every opportunity to compliment him on his achievements, and he would respond by telling me that I trained him well. That put such a warm feeling in my heart and encouraged me, because sometimes I felt like I failed or did something wrong.

I was very grateful that he acknowledged the hard work that I put in. There were times when I would sacrifice my social life, work, and quiet time, in order to keep him busy, and out of the footsteps of his father's mistakes. I had him involved in everything that could have been thought of, from sports to academic programs. The mentoring group was another great outlet for him. The classes were taught by extremely well-trained men that had a heart for the well-being of those boys. They would take them on a weekend trip once a year to a camping ground for free. They went whitewater rafting, wall climbing, potato sack racing, and played all kinds of games. Each night before they went to bed, they came together and had group sessions. It gave the boys a chance to relate to each other in a positive setting, and to also see that there are men out there who care. Because technology was always his natural talent, I inquired about a cyber-camp that I thought was ridiculously over priced, but I knew that it was a good one. I showed him the brochure, and he fell in love with it. The camp itself, without lunch and sleeping over, was eight hundred dollars for five days. I didn't even have that in the bank at the time. I did some research and found out they had a financial assistance program. All I had to do was provide an essay as to why I wanted my child to attend the camp. I jumped right on it and typed one up. I proofread it twice, and was confident that my letter would be chosen. Well about a week later, I received a letter saying that we were not chosen for the grant. Discouragement set in for a moment, but tenacity kicked in. I was not a quitter, if I wanted something; I was going to get it. I didn't want to have that mindset of being at the bottom of the barrel. I prayed to God and asked if it was His will could he make a way for Amir to be able to attend the camp. Needless to say, he enjoyed his five days, and a mini graduation on the last day because business for me was extremely busy that week, and I made enough money to pay for the camp as well as pay some bills. A few years after the camp, he started a little business fixing computers. He had a name and business cards, but became discouraged after a few weeks because it wasn't picking up fast enough. I expressed to him that it takes time to build clientele, and he had to have patience. But his age and lack of drive at the time took over and got the best of him.

    He went through different stages that just were not appropriate in my eyes. The baggy pants syndrome with the hoodie pulled over his head was a definite no. We fussed all of the time like an old married couple. Yet, he never got out of line, and knew his boundaries; he just could not understand why I was not in agreement with his attire. I thought that phase would never end. I noticed that certain behaviors came along with that style and I found myself at times wanting to jump on him from across the room and grip him up by his collar. But God would tell me no. I had to handle it differently. It was a strict training course that I was on and it wasn't pretty. Once again, I had to take my hands off and be taught how to continue raising him. I needed to be shown how to act, and what to say without yelling to get my point across. I had to learn how to adjust with him while he was growing into manhood. I remember watching a pastor on TV who was talking about the male gender.

CHAPTER 16 – LOVED

The one thing that stood out from his whole message was, "You have to learn how to lean in on the curves of life with the males in your life." Then he gave a demonstration of being on the back of a motorcycle behind the driver, and when a turn is ahead you have to get ready to lean in together or else the cycle would be off balance, and the both of you will fall. That really stuck with me, and helped me to have a better perspective on how I needed to be with him while he was going through his transitions. As I started leaning with him, it changed for the both of us, because his ears were opening, and so were my eyes.

I used to talk to him about being a black male in society, and watching his surroundings. I also taught him how to conduct himself. The one thing that I appreciated about him was he listened. Even if he accomplished something that I told him, but gave credit to someone else, I didn't get upset. I was just happy that he got it.

We still continued to have date nights. They were less frequent than before because he had his own social life, but I still enjoyed the fact that he wasn't too grown to still catch a movie here and there with me. When we went out, I was surprised at what he knew. He showed me things that he learned over his friends' houses. He would watch how their families did things together. There was this one Italian family whose house was a second home to him. His friend's mother was one of his favorite cooks. They made fresh pasta almost every night, and when he was over there, they would show him how to correctly roll it with his utensils so it could be eaten properly. He taught me how to do it when we were at an Italian restaurant one night.

God always held up his part of the bargain. He allowed him to be exposed to different cultures and environments. He experienced different genres of life and was able to relate to almost anyone. Parents would come up to me and tell me how well mannered and sweet he was. They raved about how they just loved him, and how he could come over any time. I even had some parents say that they wanted him to be around their children because he was a good influence. It brought tears to my eyes when I heard these things. I remember there being a time when I could not leave him different places for long when he was younger because he did not know how to act. I remembered crying and thinking that phase would never end. To hear accolades brought joy to my heart. I kept a smile inside because I knew those nights on my knees, and pacing the floor for him weren't in vain. Instant gratification may not have come at that time, but when it came it was good. It was most gratifying because he was not the only one being changed; I was too.

It may have sounded weird to some, but in the midst of my changes, God would draw hearts for me to keep me encouraged, or just to say I love you. I knew that I wasn't crazy from what I was seeing, so I tried convincing myself that I was making something out of nothing. The very first time it happened I got a little freaked out. I didn't tell anyone at first because they may not have believed me. One night it snowed and in the morning I went out to get the snow off of my car, but it had turned to ice. I needed to get Amir off to school and my little ice scraper wasn't doing anything. I went back in the house and boiled three big pots of water. I had to do about six rounds in order for everything on the car to melt because the ice was so thick.

By the last round, everything was pretty clear. The pot still had a little bit of water left in it and was almost enough to cover the bottom. So I came in and sat the pot on the floor and stood back to give the car one last look. As I bent down to pick the pot up, the water had separated and left a big, perfectly shaped heart in the middle. I looked at it, rubbed my eyes, and looked at it again. I couldn't fathom in my mind how that happened, so I tried to convince myself that it was a coincidence. But the more I stared at it, I knew that it wasn't. The second time it happened was when I was washing dishes. I wanted to wash the sugar bowl. And in order to get to the inside of the bowl, I had to pour the sugar out onto a plate. I happened to look down at the plate to make sure I didn't spill anything and there it was, a perfectly shaped heart sitting in the middle of the plate where the sugar had separated. I started telling myself to stop tripping. The whole time I was reasoning with myself,

CHAPTER 16 – LOVED

I felt warm and fuzzy inside because deep down I really knew what it was. I called my son downstairs just to confirm that I wasn't crazy, and I asked him what it looked like. He in a nonchalant tone stated, "A heart" and then asked if he could go back upstairs to finish his game. Whenever it happened after that, I embraced it and enjoyed the moment.

Love showed up for me in every area. My pastor's wife's sister, Mrs. Pat definitely had a heart for me. The wisdom that she shared would always be right on time. She was the one who reminded me of things that I either said, or were spoken into my life that I may have forgotten. It was amazing to me how she had time for anyone who called her on the phone or stopped by her home. She never made anyone feel rushed or pushed to the side when it came to any situation that was brought to her. It didn't matter who you were, she had time. She told you what you needed to hear, not what you wanted to hear. When I would leave from talking with her about anything, I felt unstoppable. There were times when I was down and I would call her and share what was on my heart. She even remembered conversations we had together from years prior that I had no idea we even talked about. I don't know if she had a tape recorder built in her head but she definitely could remember. She really helped me to grow spiritually as well as confidently. The greatest confidence that she instilled in me was, knowing that I would be taken care of by God no matter what. I knew that by the end of the day, my needs would be met. There were times when something was due to be paid, and I had no idea how it would get done. Then the next day or a few days later it was taken care of. I remember times when I had to shop at inexpensive neighborhood markets for Amir and I to get all of our necessities and canned goods. The food I could afford wasn't really healthy; it was just survival food, because tuition and rent was due. I would tell myself that a day was coming when I would not have to shop at those places anymore, and we would upgrade to better, more quality foods. I also remember a time when my electric bill increased and became extremely high because I was doing hair at my home in New Jersey. I had one day left to pay the bill before it was going to be shut off.

I prayed and asked God if he could please perform a miracle. Later on that night I decided to switch my winter and summer clothes because it was starting to get warm. I pulled out a bag of summer clothes from two years prior. When I took a pair of shorts out to wash them, three hundred dollars fell out. It was the exact amount I needed to pay the electric bill. I was in amazement; I couldn't believe that I didn't realize the money was missing. God never failed me; he was always there to make sure we were taken care of.

Moving forward, God continued to make sure that we were taken care of by continuing to supply the energy, gifts, and talents that I had when it came to working and providing for Amir and I. During my years of employment I worked in numerous salons. It was no big deal to start in a new salon at any time. I definitely learned different things from each one, but my motivation to work for myself always stayed in the forefront of my mind. I knew I had to become completely independent, therefore when I made that move, it felt natural.

The thing that set my salon apart from a lot of my competitors was the service and the comfort. I didn't have anything extra special like wine and cheese, but I allowed whoever came into the salon to have freedom and not feel restricted or stuffy. The family style atmosphere was so welcoming that some people came in and felt relaxed enough to fall asleep. It was movie day on Saturdays, and the clients could choose what they wanted to watch. I had doughnuts and bagels for them in the mornings, until they decided to watch their weight, so I switched to fruit.

My clients were true blessings to me. Over the years, I had the opportunity to meet some great people. It really helped me to learn about different personalities and deal with people on different levels. It also helped me to develop my people skills. I made sure that my clients received my full attention. They didn't have to experience me on the phone, eating, or taking long shopping breaks. They definitely did not have to worry about gossip! In addition to catering to their

CHAPTER 16 – LOVED

needs I wanted to see them achieve their dreams, so I allowed my clients to advertise their inventions and products in the salon. As I watched them get their hustle on, and saw the responses from the consumers, I decided to sell a few things myself. Every two weeks I would get a couple of hundred dollars and either drive or catch the train to New York. I sold silver jewelry which flew off of my shelves. I made sure I purchased unique pieces that weren't seen everywhere. I didn't have to do much selling because the jewelry was already shined and glistening from across the room on the shelf; ready to be bought. I enjoyed it for a while, but I had to stop because of the distance and my son's schedule. Overall, Relax Your Mind Hair Studio brought me great joy. It also brought some hilarious moments.

One Saturday afternoon when our work day was almost over, there were five of us left. This little old man knocked on the door and I let him in. He looked to be around seventy five or eighty. He was a nice looking man, and I could tell that he was handsome in his youth. He was short, and had grey wavy hair. I asked him if I could help him, and he whispered to me that he wanted to talk to me about something. He said that he would just come in and have a seat. He didn't seem like he wanted to talk to me around people, so I told him that I had two clients that I was trying to get out, and asked him if he could wait. He told me no and insisted on me stopping to talk. I explained to him that he would have to wait. He seemed to understand and made himself comfortable. He went back to the water fountain to get a drink and then he sat back down, crossed his legs, and leaned back quietly staring at all of us, waiting for me to talk with him. By now I began wondering what this man wanted. After he sat for a couple of minutes he finally said in a low voice, not wanting anyone else to hear: "I want to see if you can fix something for me." While he was talking, he pulled this little box out of a plastic bag. He started taking the lid off of the box in slow motion. No one was really paying attention but me because they were busy watching TV and talking. All of a sudden he pulled this thing out, and I had no idea what it was. It looked like a ball of grey fur. It looked like someone took a razor and cut the fur off of a sheep's back. When he held it up, everything stopped. Everyone stopped talking and grew silent. The way he held it up, he looked so helpless, and he had those puppy dog eyes with this thing hanging off the tip of his fingers. After I examined it for a minute, I realized that it was a toupee. He started turning it around in his hand so I could see it. Because I had never seen a toupee quite like that one, it was a little shocking. So I put my comb down and walked over to him and tried to look at it without laughing. He then wanted to try it on for me, and bent down to put it on but then the one he had on his head fell off. We thought that the grey wavy hair was his. By that time I looked up and made a mistake of making eye contact with someone in the shop. I could not open my mouth because a burst of laughter would have flown out. I had to keep putting my head down because by this time my eyes were getting watery, and that tickle in my stomach kept trying to come up to my throat. I picked it up for him while he was trying on the new one, and when he lifted his head up, it got worse. He was looking at me with that same puppy dog face with the toupee cocked to the side of his head. I could not take it anymore. I excused myself by putting my finger up, and I walked to the back of the salon in the laundry room and let my laughter flow. I put my face in a towel so I wouldn't be heard. I had one of those uncontrollable laughs for about three minutes straight. My eyes were watery and my nose was running. I could not stop. All I kept telling myself was "you're going to hell." I felt so horrible laughing at that little old man, but I could not stop. I finally got myself together and went back to the front of the salon. I was still barely able to speak. I said, "Sir, I am sorry but I will not be able to service you, because I never worked with that type of toupee and I don't want you to be my guinea pig." He insisted that he still wanted me to do it. I kept telling him no, but he was not trying to hear me. Then I tried another tactic, I told him that I was done for the day and did not open up again until Wednesday. He then tried to put the toupee in my hand and inform me that he would pick it up on Wednesday. By this time I had to get a little stern and

CHAPTER 16 – LOVED

tell him no because he was not getting the hint. He got an attitude and left. After he left, everybody in the shop laughed for at least ten minutes. We felt so bad because we were chuckling over the elderly. At that point I was waiting for Ashton Kutcher to walk in, because I thought that I had been punked.

Along with the funny moments, I also had some unfortunate ones as well. The problem with owning a business was people thinking that you as the owner qualified as a national bank. There were all kinds of sob stories that people were conjuring up. I remember this one guy coming by and trying to sell me dirty stuffed animals and said that his church was having a fundraiser. Then there was an incident where an old lady who was known to be on drugs came by and asked if I could give her money to buy milk for her grandchildren because they had not eaten. Then to top it off, one day a guy kept walking the neighborhood with a red hoodie on. He had blond hair, blue eyes, and was fully bearded. He looked very grungy and disoriented. One of my neighbors across the street warned me about him a few days prior. He knocked on the salon window while looking right at me through it and asked me if I could help him with something and if I could open the door. Because I said no, he proceeded to ask me if he could have some money to get home. In a gentle tone, I told him no and that I didn't have it. He then started to become very persistent and asked why. I started to get a little scared, so I walked over to the phone to dial 911. He started mumbling obscenities and walked off.

About two days later I was about to take my son to school and noticed the entire side of my car was deeply keyed to the metal from front to back. It must have been done that morning because the dust was still fresh. A few days later, I found out by someone in the neighborhood that the guy with the red hoodie did it. After that, he never showed up again.

Being an owner and the new kid on the block I also had my challenges with territorial people as well. One day this guy was randomly sitting on the salon stoop. I kindly asked him if he could please move. I did not like guys just standing or sitting in front of the salon because it made the clients feel uncomfortable. He told me, "no!" He also informed me that I did not own the block and he can sit where ever he wanted to sit. By now my horns were raising, but I also had to remember that he was still a man, with possible man strength. I went back in to gather my thoughts as he still continued to sit there. I walked backed to the door and started talking to him through the glass. I asked him again, with a nice tone, if he could please move before I called the cops. This still didn't work. Then something came over me, and my fear left. I swung open the door and stood straight and tall with this calm but crazy look on my face. I told him that he was being very rude and disrespectful. He stood up in anger flying off at the mouth with profanity. While standing face to face I became very quiet and stared him down real hard with the stare of death directly into his eyes and said nothing. That shut him right up. Then I told him that I was going to pray for him. He responded with a real calm voice staring right back at me and said, "The devil knows the word too." Then with a slight roll of my neck I said, "I know he does." All of a sudden, out of nowhere, he snapped out of whatever trance he was in and asked me what church did I belong to as if we were buddies. I was still in my stern mode, and answered him back by saying "Freedom, why?" I wanted to catch his angle to see where he was coming from. I was not letting my guard down. He then told me how he had heard of my church before, and that he used to go to the church down the street from the salon. He carried on a conversation that was just as normal, as if he wasn't cursing and raising hell a few minutes earlier. That issue was settled, and he never sat there again. God kept a hedge of protection over me and my business. There were several robberies all around me throughout the years, and probably plots for mine, but it was not allowed to happen.

17
Conviction

Sex for me was so overrated. It was such a consistent part of my life as a young teen that it just became habitual. It was just something you did when you were in a relationship. Most of the people I knew had the same mentality. If you got pregnant, you just got rid of it. If you caught a disease, you just went down the avenue to the clinic to get some pills. After you were better, you just "strapped up" again for awhile. You went back to your normal routine if you felt you could trust that person again.

I never had a problem with being an open book, unless I felt a little reserved about a person. It did not matter to me if they knew my present or past. I had already resolved things within myself and with God. I was not ashamed because I knew that my old history was not me anymore. I also knew that I did not experience what I went through in vain; it was for me to help someone else overcome. Most of the time when my conversations ended up being about relationships and sex, people would be shocked. They seemed to be amazed when I told them things that I encountered, especially that I was able to remain celibate since the age of twenty one. It was hard for them to comprehend how a young vibrant woman that could easily get her freak on did not allow herself to indulge every now and then. I first told them that it was by the grace of God. I explained that I didn't allow myself to be in certain environments, or watch and listen to things of a sexual nature. When I watched a

IN MY MIND

movie I made sure it was clean. And I definitely would not listen to music that I knew would start a mood that didn't need to be started. It may have seemed silly to some, but I knew what I needed to do for myself. A lot of people's responses were aroused out of pity. A few told me that they were not able to do that. I totally understood because certain things weren't as easy for other people. I had clients that believed and loved God just as much as I did, but abstinence wasn't easy for them at all. One of them was molested by men and women when she was younger, so that perverted spirit gravitated to her. I remember her sharing with me that when she used to work for a certain company, an older married man would always flirt with her and make her feel good. On their lunch breaks, they would go into his office and have sex. That went on for a long time. His wife even came up to the job on occasions and my girlfriend would feel horrible. It was an addiction for her. In its deceptive ways, it made her feel good about herself and pretty for the moment.

I also had a girlfriend who was adopted. Her mother and father died before she turned seven. The system got a hold of her and her three brothers, and they were all separated and placed in different foster homes. Their own family members didn't even fight to keep them. As years passed, she moved from home to home. She never stayed anywhere for too long. She passed through so many foster homes that she stopped counting. She was molested in quite a few of them. Finally a married couple adopted her at thirteen, and she was stable for a moment. Her and her adopted mother would go downtown every Saturday after she did her chores. One particular Saturday she didn't finish her chores in time to go, so she was left at home with the husband. While they were home he asked her if she could grease his scalp. Because she was so short and he was extremely tall, a chair would not have worked so she had to sit on the edge of the bed while he sat on the floor in between her legs. The rest was history. After a few times, he told her that she better not say anything. Then he started buying her clothes to keep her quiet. She became so numb, that sex was just what she did without even thinking twice.

There was another girl that I knew through a friend of mine, and

CHAPTER 17 – CONVICTION

she had a different story. She wasn't touched as a child or anything, but she allowed the devil to steal her life away when it came to sex and rebellion. She was a very intelligent girl. Anything she put her mind to she did it. Her personality was very strong but she allowed that strength to turn into rebellion. She started hanging around the wrong people, getting high, drinking, and smoking at a young age. Her next course escalated into dealing with married men. That added all kinds of drama to her life. Outside of that, she would give you the shirt off of her back but she played hardcore for so long that it became a part of her persona. God tried to catch her attention all of the time. This girl knew the Bible with her eyes closed. She preached to other people about what they were doing, but wouldn't allow herself to receive it. She would even say to us that she knew she was running from God, but wasn't ready to surrender yet. She knew that she was playing with fire, but it was too good to give it up.

I knew that everyone's own conviction spoke to them loudly, and they knew the difference between right and wrong. But as the years went by, I watched so many people hit a ditch, I understood that some people just liked taking chances and living for the moment. As knowledge was imparted in me and I received clarity concerning people's motives, this gave me greater compassion and patience. By no means was I a perfect angel, or had I arrived, but I knew the severity of consequences that were waiting as a result of disobedience.

I understood because there were occasions when I came across some things that tried to hinder my abstinence while being in relationships. In the beginning I set my standards and rules, but dropped the ball after comfort set in. I never kissed right away and no company was allowed at my home past eleven in the evening. Strange things happened after that time, especially after a full stomach, and a movie. Before you knew it, there was heavy panting and shirts being unbuttoned. It was such a battle trying to figure out how a Christian relationship could be sustained and kept holy. I would indulge in those behaviors, and found myself being the aggressive one at times. At first there would be a lot of repentance, but as it kept happening my heart hardened. Then I found myself making excuses by saying that it wasn't sex at all, it was only kissing, touching, and a little groping. So while I was trying to convince myself and God, it didn't feel too bad. Then I found myself becoming distant from certain people and church. I was fearful in thinking that they could see right through me and know what I was doing. I had this standard to uphold, and I didn't want it to be marred. It got to the point where I forgot about how God must have felt, and was more concerned about what people were going to think. So I would stay away for awhile until I got myself together, in order to maintain a positive image.

I would allow myself to once again become sidetracked with distractions. I found myself always feeling bad, and not talking to young ladies anymore about purity. I felt like "Why should they listen to me?" All along it was a plot from the enemy to kill my testimony and to keep me from helping as many girls as possible. I put my guard down, got comfortable, and left the door open. I remember when I was coming out of my last relationship with the older guy and really hurting so badly that I didn't know if I was coming or going. My pastor called me up front one day during service and told me that I didn't need a man to validate me. I was a strong woman and I was special. It took me back for a moment to when I was six years old. I actually heard God say clearly, "You're Special." It was so soft it sounded like a whisper. At that time I had no idea where it came from. As my pastor was speaking I could feel the intensity of his words. "You are uniquely designed and so is the man he has for you." After a while I started getting the revelation that those words were not just for me. It was also helping other women in the congregation that were listening.

Outside of the sex realm, I still had an issue with intimacy. It was hard for me to say I love you. This applied to anyone. It wasn't because I didn't want to. I just did not know how to say it effectively. I froze up every time I had to respond back to someone who told me they loved me. It wasn't only with men; it was with women as well. I could be on the phone with someone, and right before they hung up they may have said, "I love you." I would clench up real

CHAPTER 17 – CONVICTION

tight and sometimes shut my eyes, and say it back quickly, and hang up. I could never say the whole thing. The shorter version "love you too" was better for me. It didn't seem as intimate. There were times when someone would look me in my eyes and tell me, and I would say "love you too." I would then look downward so I did not have to encounter the mushy response. It made me feel vulnerable. As bad as I wanted to share in those emotions with that person, it was hard for me to connect.

Going through all of that was very beneficial because it allowed me to share myself with others in the future. I had many opportunities to sit and talk with women from all walks of life throughout the years. They were young, old, rich, poor, educated, and uneducated. I was able to grab different perspectives from each of them, and understand why they did what they did and allowed what they allowed. I could relate to them when no one else at the time could. I easily picked up on things they carried. I could tell when they were covering something up because it was so close to home for me. I spotted insecurity through someone's smile, laughter, or quietness. I would be at a function or a social gathering and my radar would pick up loneliness and insecurity. It never seemed to be obvious to anyone else but me. I would tell myself to stop over-analyzing and looking so deeply into things. But by the end of the night or days later something was always revealed. Sometimes if the opportunity presented itself, I would ease my way over to the person and make small talk and befriend them, especially when they were sitting by themselves. I always knew from experience what could be learned by invading someone's world for a minute. Many times they were waiting for someone to enter in, even when it looked like they didn't want to be bothered. I remembered plenty of times when I wanted to talk to someone, but just did not know how to initiate.

It was very frustrating when I heard people say "Give it to God, He'll take care of it, allow Him in your heart and He will fix it." Well I'm standing on the side silently saying to myself "How? Is there a magic wand or something? Do I click my heels three times? Do I sit in the middle of the floor in peace and quiet for two days and wait to hear an audible voice?" I could never seem to comprehend how to get it right and just do it. I would see people in church with their hands lifted, and having certain looks on their faces like they just sucked on lemons. I heard loud prayers which sounded like they just finished reading the encyclopedia. Sometimes the choir would get up and sing, and people would fall out or start crying. After seeing all of that, I didn't want to feel like the oddball. So I would lift my hands, close my eyes, and hold my head upward as if I were looking towards heaven. I thought maybe some dew would fall or something. Or maybe if I positioned myself the right way, God would be ready to talk to me and tell me how to get out of my struggles. Then if I didn't feel anything, I spoke in tongues, thinking He would move a little faster. In my heart, I did none of that to impress the people around me, but I did it because I felt like I needed to do the right things in order for God to speak to me properly. I knew He loved me but I thought He needed my outward appearance to be positioned a certain way in order to receive from Him. I didn't realize it was my heart He needed positioned correctly.

After I got that revelation I found myself doing the extreme opposite of the church antics. I felt like if I just stood there without doing anything, I would hear much better because I wouldn't have all of the distractions from trying to make something happen. My heart and mind still felt confused. How were all of these people seemingly entering into the presence of God and I still feel like I'm on the outside? It felt like a game of double-dutch. I felt like I was rocking back and forth for a couple of seconds trying to wait for the rope to balance out in enough time for me to jump in. That is how it seemed for a while. God started enlightening me in my relationship with Him. He showed me that I was comparing Him with other people. He revealed to me how I thought I had to do certain things or be a particular way in order to get rewarded. I would always feel that He was upset with me when I didn't get something right. Every time I thought that I screwed up on something, He sent someone to come and compliment me. I would look at them cross-eyed afterwards, and try to down play it. I told myself that they were just trying to be

CHAPTER 17 – CONVICTION

nice, and that they knew I screwed up.

God showed me different parts of His personality. He allowed me to mess up at times, and didn't send anyone to compliment me. I had to figure it out on my own, and realize that it was okay to make mistakes; they were a part of life. He also helped me to learn that I was not perfect, and that I should not let pride and embarrassment get in the way. I had to have a sense of humor along with His, when those moments came. I remember one time when I first moved to New Jersey. In order to work as a cosmetologist I had to do one week of schooling to be able to take my state boards and get my license. The school was about an hour away, but it was worth it because I met new people and learned quite a bit in a short amount of time. One day, two other students and I walked to the store on our lunch break. Somehow out of nowhere, I fell. Nothing was in my pathway at all. I didn't even trip over my feet like I normally did. I just landed on the ground mysteriously. I fell so quietly that they kept walking and talking and did not even notice.

They finally realized that I wasn't talking anymore, turned around, and looked down. We all just burst out laughing.

I also had an embarrassing moment at church. After service was over, there would be a large crowd of people coming down the steps at one time. This one particular Sunday my son and I were walking down and he was in front of me. He suddenly stopped for no apparent reason, except for being a kid and not paying attention. I was very close behind him so I tried to avoid him and lost my balance and fell down a full flight of steps. When I landed at the bottom, my dress was up and one heel was broken off of my shoe. Despite all of those people trying to help me up, I bounced right up like a champion laughing and trying not to be embarrassed at the same time. I just started walking like nothing ever happened. Walking a block to my car with a broken heel was a challenge, but it had to be done. All I could say was, "God had jokes."

18
Together

Everything that I had planned for this year was coming together nicely. I became spiritually and emotionally healthier by making certain choices from trusting God more. I really started to understand His promises to me with more clarity when He said that He would never leave me or forsake me. I was also enjoying the blessing from tithing. I made sure that it was one of my first priorities. I never missed a tithe since the day I got saved. Even if I didn't have a lot of money I still gave my ten percent and even more. God blessed me with the money anyway so I figured why not give it to Him because that's what He requires of me. I had also visited some of the places I wanted to see. The year was really fulfilling and beneficial, and it allowed me to continue learning about myself and others. My eyes were opened to many more things that I did not see in the past. My senses were expanding and I was coming into my own.

It was definitely bittersweet during the process, because a lot of my distorted thinking was burning off. I had to go through a good deal of challenges for those thought patterns to die, especially with people. One thing that I appreciated was, those situations kept me humble and constantly asking God for help. I think the greatest thing that came out of the year was the fact that I could see the light of my emotional and mental healing. In addition to that I finally learned how to balance my friendships. I understood what friends were for, and not to put everyone in the same category. Everyone served a specific purpose in my life and I gave great honor to the ones who stuck it out with me. I knew that there were some days when I frazzled their nerves because of my flustered and bewildered self. Even if I did irritate them, they never showed it. They were true friends and they definitely had the grace to love me. It would have taken a lot for them to step away.

Another wonderful thing that flourished in me was a great sense of self-esteem. I no longer found myself trying to fit in. I always knew that I was an eagle, but it sometimes got very lonely up there. I remember times when I would have dreams of standing behind a large glass, with people on the other side, having a good time. All I could do was look in. At one point I had developed a dislike for my own personality. I condemned myself for not being this outgoing individual that everyone gravitated to. I never seemed to be the life of the party like others. I was so busy comparing myself to others; I didn't realize that some of those outgoing people had insecurities as well.

I never stopped to look at the fact that people gravitated to me also, just in a different way. People would come up to me and tell me how they admired my strength and capability to be able to handle so many responsibilities, and also be a good mother. They said watching me helped them to become better. My insecurities had gotten the best of me so much so that I could not even comprehend what they were saying at one point. I didn't realize the power and influence that God had put in my being.

The year was moving along with such a great flow that traveling was just an addition to make it even better. I needed a little getaway so I went to Miami with my sister and one of our cousins. My sister started growing up and we had a little separation time when she went off to college. Every now and then, we would find time to connect. There was one weekend we had an opportunity to go somewhere on one of her school breaks. We decided to go then because our cousin was graduating from nursing school at that very same time, so she wanted to reward herself.

When we got there, it felt good to be in a different place. Even if the weather was smoldering hot. Our hotel was right on

CHAPTER 18 – TOGETHER

the beach, so if we needed to run for cover from a sun attack, we could. Those big beach umbrellas didn't do it for me. They only created a partial shelter from the heat. I needed an industrial fan. The evenings were good, because the sun had set, and the air was clear. I also enjoyed the food, especially the sushi. I ate it every night, and had a back up platter in our refrigerator to hold me over. The trip was a good refresher, and I definitely took advantage of it so I could relax.

For some reason traveling had seemed to be my thing that year. Every couple of months, I was on a plane. A little over six months after the Miami trip, I went to Mexico with a group of women from my church. We had so much fun. We were there for five days and four nights. It was short but sweet, and in that time we got a chance to relax, relate, and eat a lot without feeling guilty. We went in mid April, so the weather was a little cool at night, and slightly breezy, but the days were warm and gorgeous. My pastor's wife and I were roommates, which was good, because we hadn't spent time together in a while. The trip was a part of our woman's ministry gatherings. What made it so special was that we had a variety of ages, ranging from the thirties on up to the late seventies, and we blended very well.

The atmosphere reminded me a little of Miami. It had that party feel, but was still laid back at the same time. I paired up with different groups of women every day and went out. One day four of us went in town to the marketplace and ended up getting lost until it got dark. Hardly anyone spoke English. Every time we asked for directions, we were sent the wrong way. At one point we were in the hood in back alleys. We ended up meeting a young lady in the midst of our travels and she led us to one of our destinations. While we were walking she was telling us that she was there helping her mother who had cancer. Prior to that she was living in California. She was a tough little thing but had a very gentle spirit.

Another outing we had was a bullfight. I had no idea what that entailed. At first they had a cute little show with horses prancing around with pretty draping on, and the riders made sure they were well synchronized and positioned. About a half hour later, they cleared the floor and out came this huge blind folded horse, with a man dressed in his bullfighting attire and his red flag. He had on big oversized metal boots with sharp blades the size of butcher knives on the side of them. Then out came a big bull charging out, looking mad and grunting. The Mexican men were standing on the side shouting "Olay!" Every time the bull missed the man and the horse, he got more furious. Then the horse led by the rider's instructions would start to gallop towards the bull. The rider would then side swipe the bull with the blade that was on his boot. It would slide clean across, and blood would squirt everywhere. We were all stunned because we had never been to a bull fight before, so we had no idea what to expect. We thought the bull had been accidentally injured, and we were wondering why no one was coming to his aid. The more he bled, the louder they cheered. Then a few seconds later, another man on a horse came out with a large stake, and stabbed the bull right in his back and left it there. By this time we all were sick at the stomach. Little did we know the purpose of the fight was to conquer and kill the bull so he could be dinner. That was their tradition. When the bull started to collapse, we got out of there.

The night before we left Mexico we took an evening boat ride to a secluded island where they had dinner and a show for everyone. Before we reached the island they had games and dancing. Of course as soon as the electric slide came on, everyone jumped up. Once we reached our destination, there were people standing everywhere greeting us with a warm welcome. We could smell the aroma from the food as soon as we stepped off the boat. After we ate we watched the show, and headed back to our resort. Once we got back, my pastor's wife wanted all of us to come together and have a game night. Because there were so many of us, we had to use one of the resort's lobbies. We had such a ball. Some went upstairs because they were tired, but the rest of us

CHAPTER 18 – TOGETHER

hung in there. The next morning we got up, had breakfast, and gathered our things so we could get to the airport on time. While we were on the plane, our next trip was already being planned. We knew that once the women that did not attend heard about how much fun we had, they would definitely want to make the next one.

My traveling for the year did not stop there. Two months after I got back from Mexico, I was headed to California for five days. My son and I went along with my mother. It was a necessary trip, but also a mini vacation. My mom had two brothers that lived there as well as my brother. I had a Godmother that lived there also, so she was definitely on the list for one of our visits. One of my uncles had cancer, and my mother wanted to see him. She had been talking to him over the phone for a couple of months, and his condition was worsening, so she wanted to make sure nothing happened before she could get out there. So I made all of the arrangements with my brother so he could take off of work for that week and be with us.

As soon as we stepped off the plane and came down the escalator, my brother was standing right there. It was a good feeling when we got a chance to see him; there were smiles on both ends. We all hugged and grinned and started walking to the car. There was an agenda planned for each day while we were there. We tried to fit in as much as possible.

Our first day was quite a surprise. We drove straight to my brother's place so we could drop our bags off and get something to eat. When we got there, he told us to sit down because he wanted to show us something. He turned his huge flat screen TV on that was almost as big as the wall, and he put a DVD in. It was another one of his DVDs that he put together of his children. But this time it was only my niece. So we watched the clips of her basketball and softball games, and right at the end there was a still shot of her, and we thought that the DVD froze. While we were looking at the TV, trying to figure out what went wrong; her head popped out from behind the wall and scared the crap out of us. We had no idea that she was there. She lived in Florida at the time, and I had just talked to her that week. She was spending the summer with my brother, and he wanted to surprise us. We were so happy to see her. It just made our trip better from the start.

After we got ourselves together, we went out, got something to eat, and did a little window shopping. It was absolutely gorgeous there. Our next day, we woke up bright and early to go and see my uncle who had cancer. As soon as we walked in the hospice center, it was so freaky because my uncle looked like the male version of my mother; they were almost identical, from the hair on down. I had never seen him before, not even in a picture. I had no idea of what he looked like. He was quite a character. He loved telling stories and jokes. His whole demeanor reminded me of my grandfather so much that it felt like we were sitting there talking to him. We stayed for a couple of hours and kept him company. We spent most of our time in the court yard, so he could get a little sunshine. There were these huge plum trees all around, so my niece and I started picking and eating them; just having a good time.

Right before we left it was like a movie. My mom told us to wait in the hallway while she went to talk to my uncle. She offered him Christ, prayed for him and gave him comfort. We don't know what was actually said, but knowing my mother, she made an impact. After she came out of the room, she looked at peace. I told her that this may be the last time we see him, and she looked back at the room and said, "I know." While we were walking down the hall, he came out of the room with his walker, and slowly walked with us to the front door. After our last goodbyes, hugs and pictures, we got in the car. All I could remember was his frail body standing in that big bay window, watching us pull off. His face looked like a mix of a little boy wanting his mother, and of appreciation for us coming that long way to see him. It was the first time in almost thirty years that he and my mother saw each other, and it was the last.

CHAPTER 18 – TOGETHER

That same day after we left the center, we wanted to see my other uncle, whom my mom hadn't seen in a long time as well. So she called him and asked him to meet us over a cousin's house that lived there. They moved there from Philadelphia, and had been residing in California for over twenty years. We were all happy to see each other because my brother and I were getting an opportunity to meet family that we never knew existed. It felt good to see an extension of family from my grandfather's side. So my uncle pulled up, while the rest of us were getting acquainted. I could see the smile on my mother's face when he walked in the door. Out of her two brothers, my mom was actually closer in relationship with him. We had a good time catching up and taking pictures. He was full of life and energy, and had changed his life for the better. He started going to church and raising his grandchildren. This was the first time I had ever met him. I did remember his face from seeing him in pictures, and every now and then my mom would mention him, but not enough for me to become overly familiar with him. It started to get a little late in the evening so we decided to leave because we had one more stop to make while we were on that end. We were about two hours away from my brother's house and wanted to knock everything out that night. We used our navigation system to find out where my godmother lived; she was waiting for us. She cooked a lot of food banking on our arrival; enough to last a week. My brother, my son, and my niece had a ball eating it. They did not want to get up from the table, especially after she brought out the homemade cake. It was funny because she didn't want us to leave, so she kept trying to bribe them with more food. She had moved there about twenty years ago because of her health. She suffered from multiple sclerosis, and the weather was good for her. I couldn't wait to get there to see my god-sisters and their children, which I hadn't seen in many years. I remembered when they were little. That meant I was getting old.

The next day was a big day, especially for my mother and my son. They wanted to get to Hollywood badly. They were both

IN MY MIND

hoping to run into someone famous. I had to laugh because every time my mother saw a limo, she would wonder who was in it. After being there for a while, we realized that it wasn't the stars' hangout. They only came when there was an awards show or something. So after that reality set in, we moved on. That was a really fun day. We felt like little kids. First we ate at a famous chicken and waffles restaurant, and then we walked the walk of fame. Right after that we stood in front of the Chinese Theatre and saw the handprints of famous people in the cement. When it became dark, things started to get a little livelier. My mother wanted to go to one of the museums on the strip, so she went and purchased five tickets. They had a special where we could get into three museums for the price of two, so we did. We had a ball, bouncing from place to place, and enjoying each others company. One of them was a wax museum. It was so amazing how real the figures looked. It was as if the images of the people were frozen in time. It also had a horror section that my mother, my niece, and I weren't too fond of. Jason, Michael Meyers, the *Chainsaw Massacre*, and many others were done in wax. It seemed as if we were the only ones in the museum because of the time of night; it was empty. There were a few stragglers, but not many. It was so funny; we got separated from my brother and son because of the many different sections inside. My niece, my mom and I got lost in the scary section. We were petrified, but laughing at the same time. We thought the guys disappeared on purpose so they could scare us, so we were tip-toeing around and yelling through the hall for them to come out. Little did we know that they were looking for us. While we walked slowly towards the entry of the hallway with our eyes half closed, scared to death and giggling all at the same time, the guys walked in the other entrance behind us, and asked us "Where have you been?" We all ran and screamed. All they could do was look at each other and shake their heads. Once we were done we headed back to my brother's house. By the time we reached, it was almost three in the morning, and we were tired. For the next two days we

CHAPTER 18 – TOGETHER

went to the San Diego Zoo, which was super huge, and to the beach, where we got to see the California surfers. While at the beach, we had lunch at a restaurant in the middle of the ocean. It sat right on the tip of the pier, which extended out into the water. The view was absolutely gorgeous. Every now and then we felt ourselves sway back and forth with the waves. But that didn't stop us from enjoying our food. We ended our last night at a county fair, and an outdoor Sinbad comedy show. When we finally got back home to Philly, we were exhausted but fulfilled.

It was about one month after we came back that my mother received a phone call. It was the mother of both of her brothers. She was out there taking care of the one who had cancer. But the phone call was not about him, it was about the other brother. She told my mom that he was diagnosed with terminal liver cancer, and only had a few months to live. That was very surprising because we were just sitting on the couch talking with him. Their mother was a strong woman. God gave her the grace to deal with her only two children having terminal cancer at the same time. Being in her late seventies and having to deal with something like that must have been difficult. She stayed strong and did what she had to do. The brother that was diagnosed with the liver cancer looked perfectly healthy when we saw him that month prior. The crazy part about it all was he died before the brother we went out there to see. The day he died, the family went to tell the other brother, and he ended up dying the very next day. My mother had to fly back out to California only four months after our vacation for both of their funerals. They were held one day apart. She was actually okay after a while. God gave her the grace to deal with death, because she experienced quite a bit of it in her life. There were times when I would look at her and wonder how in the world she stayed so strong. Watching her helped me build and shape parts of my character.

19
Journey

Wow! Time seemed to be moving at warp speed. Months were flying by. Everything was moving so fast, it felt like time was passing me by and I couldn't catch up. It felt as if every time I tried to grab a hold of the rope, it would get yanked back. I asked God what was going on, but I did not get an immediate answer. The only thing I would hear from Him was "Trust."

My feelings of obligation started to outweigh my enjoyment of standing behind the chair. I loved making people feel good about themselves and making them look beautiful. But something about it started to make me physically sick every time I worked. I was mentally drained because I wanted out for a while. I needed a break from my constant grind of doing the same thing for over 19 years straight. I felt like my passion was dwindling, and I was just existing. My perception was totally off. I woke up every morning thinking "another day of torture."

Knowing that doing hair was my only source of major income at the time, made me feel like a slave. My observation was twisted, and I could not see the bigger picture. The only thing I felt at the time was I needed to get out, and get out soon.

Hey Daddy, I know that I have been acting a little crazy lately, but I really want to fulfill my life. I know fulfillment only comes from you. I am going to be straight up; I want to know what is going on! Is it not the right timing? Why does it seem like I can't

IN MY MIND

get to where I need to be? I want to get focused! I have to get focused! I cannot stay on this path of defeat in my mind. Yes, I am grateful for what you have done for me, but I need to know more. My mind is jumping all over the place, and I know you are trying to get me on a steady pace for my own good. My skills and passion seem dead. They only come alive when I do complete makeovers on someone who is feeling down about themselves; I want them to see themselves in a whole new light. Daddy, please help my mind to stay stable and stayed on you, so I can seek you with my whole heart, by praying and reading your word. John 4:24 "God is Spirit and his worshippers must follow him in spirit and in truth." Lord I noticed that when I focus on you with my whole heart, I am at such peace. Once I get you; everything else will follow: ideas, dreams, love, money, people, and desires. Whenever I lose focus on you, it seems like depression sets in, or I feel a little crazy. You told me to seek you with my whole heart, and I will be able to overcome distractions. Thank you for listening.

My drive would come and go throughout the years. There were times when I was happy with my work, then times when it was just a paycheck. I started to lose clients because of my lack of interest. I just didn't care anymore. The only thing that kept me motivated to at least try and make a little money was my son's tuition. I did not want him to be affected by my carelessness. Bills were still being paid on time, and groceries were still filling the refrigerator. I guess God was saying, "Lord have mercy on this child, she is a little thrown off right now because of her lack of understanding, but she is still my daughter, and I love her."

Despite how I felt, I still needed to take care of my business. Knowing that God still provided for us during my inconsistency made my faith in Him even stronger. It told me two things; that He loved me, and that I had no time to waste. I needed to keep a steady pace in alignment with my destiny. I couldn't trust my feelings because they changed from moment to moment. He let me know that I was getting too comfortable and that He had to

CHAPTER 19 – JOURNEY

shake things up a bit to get me moving on to the next part of my journey. That is one of the reasons why those feelings kept coming. Whenever God was trying to bring something new in my life, my comfort zone was being tampered with. So things would become uncomfortable, but after a while I realized that it was for my good. I knew that it was sometimes the only way to get me moving with certain things. Ultimately it was for me to keep moving up the ladder with new experiences. He trusted me enough to know that once I caught on to my vision I would grab tight and run to make things happen.

My time of reconstruction was an extreme time of loneliness. God didn't allow anyone or anything to stick to me. All of my crutches were gone. I had no choice but to totally depend on Him. Because His plan for me was taking course, I didn't want to fight it and make it worse. He didn't even allow any possible dates to blow my way. There were times when I would be in Home Depot getting paint or house supplies, and men would see me walking up and down the aisles. They would strike up any conversation they could think of, just to have something to say. Some of them even offered to paint my house for me, while others just wanted to carry my things to the car. After all of the back and forth flirting, I knew deep down that I could only respond with a smile and a 'no thank you'. It was like God was saying "You can look but don't touch." The pressure was on. I couldn't go anywhere without running into old male friends that I either knew from school or from my past. I would randomly get phone calls from friends or clients who were trying to hook me up with guys. They were tired of seeing me alone all of the time, and felt sorry for me.

I tried to take matters into my own hands and figured that one little innocent outing with an old friend would not hurt. I reasoned with myself by saying that there was no way possible God really wanted me to sit around and not have a good time right now with a little male companionship. When the day came for us to hang out, he picked me up, and we went to an amusement park about an hour and a half from my house. We had the greatest conversation on the way there. We laughed, flirted, and enjoyed each other's company. As soon as we got there and pulled into the parking lot, his car battery died. He got a jump from a man that was about to leave the park with his family. After the jump he tested the car to see if it would start up again by turning it off, and then turning it back on, but it died again. He then called one of his father's friends that coincidently did not live too far from the amusement park where we were. He asked him if he could come and help him put in a spare battery that he had in his trunk. His father's friend could not come right away so we decided to enjoy the park for a couple of hours while we waited and not waste a perfectly good day. We had a great time. We rode a lot of rides, ate pizza, went to the water park, and caught up on some old times. A few hours later his father's friend called him and told him that he was outside of the gates, so we left the park a little early. After they changed the battery, we got on the road and were on our way back home. About forty five minutes into our ride, his car shut off. At the time we were doing 65 miles per hour on one of the busiest and darkest highways. We were all the way in the left lane away from the shoulder, so we had to drift our way over in the dark. I was petrified. It looked like freaky Jason could have jumped out of the woods. He called one of his friends to come and find us, because we weren't near any road signs to tell him our exact location. His friend was at the movies with his family and couldn't get to us until about an hour later. He was okay with that; I wasn't. I whipped my phone out of my bag so fast and started calling everybody. The car was rocking so badly because the trucks and cars were riding by us doing eighty to ninety miles per hour, and we were on a narrow shoulder. Any false moves and we could have been hit. I called my mom, dad, and one of my girlfriends. My mom called AAA, and my dad was on his way. By that time, my friend's friend called him back and told him that he was on his way. I called my dad

CHAPTER 19 – JOURNEY

back and told him not to come anymore because I already had a ride. While waiting for AAA and his friend, we stayed inside the car and started talking. In the midst of our conversation, he asked me if I could tell the cops that I was driving, just in case they stopped while we were sitting there. I said, "Uh! Why?" He told me that his license was suspended because of a legal matter. Now I'm scared and pissed off because he wanted me to lie. I wasn't going to jail for nobody. Before I got a word out, guess what pulled up - a police car. I knew that I wasn't going to lie, so I was preparing myself to be a disappointment. After we were being blinded by the cop's headlights, the officer started walking towards the car. As he was approaching I started to pray so hard that I could have busted a blood vessel. When he got to the car he asked if everything was okay. I thanked God that he didn't ask for license and registration. We explained to him what happened and that AAA was on their way. He walked back to his car and pulled some flares out to put down on the road for our safety. He told us to be careful because it was a dangerous highway. I could have told him that! I was so nervous, I couldn't think straight.

My friend started getting upset with me because the entire two hours of us sitting there, I was on and off the phone giving updates of my well-being. He expressed to me that he could not understand why I was so scared because I was with a man and a protector. I told him that he couldn't even protect me from a dangerous trip. He knew his battery was bad when he picked me up, and he also knew that his license was suspended. On top of all of that, he wanted me to lie for him so I could have possibly gotten in trouble with the law. His friend and AAA arrived around the same time. They were minutes apart from each other. He rode with the AAA guy, and I rode with his friend. His friend's wife and kids were in the car and I was so embarrassed because I really didn't know all of his personal business and I wasn't sure if this was normal thing for him or if he was a player and I was just another one of those girls that happened to be in a situation like that with him. My mind was racing because I was thinking to myself," I have a son waiting for me to reach home and I am getting in the car with strangers because I was stuck on the side of the road and could have possibly been in trouble with the law." After I got home, I didn't hear from him again.

I began directing my attention to other things. I had to keep it moving. My fear of falling and never rising again was always before me, so it didn't take much to snap me back to reality. Focus had to be in the forefront of my mind, and not loneliness. To keep myself occupied correctly, I continued to work on my house. I also ended up taking every Saturday off so I could attend more functions and enjoy other things outside of work. I had worked every Saturday since the age of fifteen.

God's reconstruction in my life really helped me in so many areas. I for once was comfortable in my own skin. At one point I allowed all of those negative spirits to control my mind: loneliness, fear, rejection, low self-esteem and inferiority. I had two choices: allow God to continue to build strength and character in me, or build up a resistance from pain, and become desensitized and act like I didn't need any connections. Both realities would war against each other and it was up to me to choose.

God wanted so much more for me, and because of His patient nature, He held my hand the entire way. I asked Him if the loneliness and the sting of rejection would always be a struggle for me because I felt like a repeat offender when it came to constantly dealing with the same issues. I kept running into these issues until enough courage was built up in me to deal with them. I wanted to get out of that self- created seclusion and be free. I wanted all walls to be knocked down. I knew that it was a natural thing to have a strong need for human connection. So why wasn't I experiencing it? I heard God speaking through messages that I heard at church on the wilderness experience. During the wilderness experience, discomfort manifests in each person's life in a distinct way. I asked God why I had to have these particular weaknesses, and why couldn't I have gotten something else, because it hurts. He responded by telling me that it was

CHAPTER 19 – JOURNEY

given to me because I had the grace to handle it, and I would be equipped to help someone else without grief attached.

As I started to understand and see the bigger picture, I learned to embrace my weaknesses and grow from them for my benefit, instead of groaning and complaining. I learned that I could recharge my spiritual battery without distractions. I could also clear my mind so I could hear God give directions about different ideas and moves I should be making.

During those times, my walls of seclusion were being chipped away one brick at a time. Consistent sunshine appeared and I could see things for what they were. I learned to live outside of myself again, and start giving more of me that I kept from other people. It still took time, and was not an overnight success, but the goal was being met. I learned to appreciate my personality, and understand and love how God made me. I knew that there were definitely more obstacles ahead, but in the end I knew God said I win! Philippians 4:6-8 would unfailingly pop up in my head.

> *"Be anxious for nothing but by prayer and supplication let your request be made known unto God and the peace of God which surpasses all understanding will guard your hearts and minds through Christ Jesus. Finally brothers, whatever things are true, whatever things are noble, and whatever things are just, whatever things are pure, whatever things are lovely, and whatever things are of good report. If there is anything praiseworthy- meditate on these things."*

As I started putting that scripture into practice, it taught me how to think properly. In the midst of my singleness, I became more comfortable. There were times when I would get a little lonely and want male companionship, but that would cease after a few minutes. I prayed, read the Bible, and stayed occupied with important things for my son and I. People would wonder how I continued to strive. I simply told them; it was by the grace of God.

I understood that marriage and singleness were both good. People would try and portray singleness as a disease that was terminal. I learned to enjoy and embrace it. Hope was definitely still alive, but I also kept a mindset that if God allowed me to be married or not, I would be okay with it. Whatever He had planned for my life, He knew best. He would also give me the grace for whatever route my life was headed in. I was at peace in my heart. People would always tell me that they are praying for me that I get a husband soon, or ask me why I wasn't married yet, or why am I not dating. I told them when the husband is supposed to come, he will come.

It wasn't hard for me to get a man; the challenge stepped in when it came to me upholding my standards. I would not compromise. I had three main standards. The first was the man had to love God more than he loved me. If he loved God more than me, he would treat me like God treated me. Of course I knew he could never compare to God, but at least I would know that his love would be pure. Secondly, he had to show interest in my son. If he did not accept my child then it was a 'no-no' for me. Lastly, he had to accept my abstinence before marriage. It had been over thirteen years and there was no need to break the chain for 3 minutes of pleasure and then feel guilty for weeks. I also didn't have time to train someone to keep their hands off of me, and respect me and my space. I was very comfortable with my choices and didn't budge.

When I did talk to men, my mindset was totally different than it was previously. I no longer took disinterest as rejection. I learned that some people will be interested in you, and some will not. Sometimes you will get as far as a phone call or two, or maybe even a date or two, then complete silence. It's not personal, its life. I remember being asked out by a super fine guy who did work on my house. Our first time on the phone, he

CHAPTER 19 – JOURNEY

told me that he was a little intimidated by me and did not know how to approach me, because it looked like I had it going on. He said that's what attracted him to me. After a few conversations, we went out. We had a wonderful time. He asked me to suggest the first part of the date, and he would choose the second half. I chose a really inexpensive Italian restaurant not too far from my home. Afterwards, he took me to a beautiful park. It had gazebos, ponds with ducks swimming around, swans wandering all around, and a fancy mansion sitting on a hill. We walked across a bridge to get to the benches that were overlooking the pond, and sat under a huge tree for shade. After talking for a while, we walked back across the bridge and walked towards the hill that had the mansion sitting on it. We ran up the hill towards the no trespassing sign, and were acting like little kids giggling, and peeking in the windows. After our time out, he drove me back to my car and I went home. I really didn't want it to end because I was having such a good time. He called me to make sure I got home safe, and that was that. He made no effort to hang out again. I asked him what the problem was, and he said that he remembered me saying in one of our conversations that I was abstinent, and he couldn't handle it. I respected him for his honesty and moved on.

One time I was with some women from my church at a hotel spa party. We were all sitting in the room trying on undergarments, eating, and talking. A janitor walked in to fix the sink in the bathroom. I didn't pay him any attention because I was engrossed in our fellowship. While we were all in the living room talking and laughing, one of the ladies looked sneaky as she was getting up going towards the bathroom door to talk to him. She told him to meet her in the hallway in five minutes because she had a nice young lady to introduce him to. She told me to meet her out there as well. She asked him about his relationship with God. Once he satisfied her question with the correct response, she was sold. When she had us both in the hallway, she made the introductions and walked off. We were standing there speechless, and then had a little small talk. He had this huge grin on his face. He was tall, had a beautiful smile with dimples, and a friendly disposition. We exchanged phone numbers and shook hands, and went our separate ways. When I got back to the room, everyone was laughing and grinning.

As soon as I got in the house that night, he called me. We talked for an hour. He seemed to be a very nice individual, but throughout the conversation I could tell that it probably wouldn't go anywhere. I was trying not to be biased. We talked again a couple days later and set up a lunch date. An hour before we were to meet, he called and said that he needed to go grocery shopping. He asked if I could pick him up at the market and take him home to drop his bags off first, because his car was down. I cringed with disappointment. Well, that was cut very short. I went back to church and told the lady who hooked us up, thank you but no thank you. I told her that I appreciated her effort and in a joking manner, to never do that again.

20

Freedom

Two months after my California visit, I went on a cruise. There were seven of us, my mother, my son, one of his friends, two of my mother's friends, one of their daughters, and myself. We really had a wonderful time. It was an eight day, seven night southern Caribbean cruise. I booked the trip because I wanted my mother to have a getaway that she could relax and enjoy without any worries. She never experienced a cruise to the islands before.

We flew into Puerto Rico to board our ship. We were all excited and looking forward to the rest of the week. After we settled in, we danced a little at the sailing away party. There was an air of anticipation for the next moment.

The sun was setting, and the scenery was breathtaking. As we sailed through the night, we all wanted to go to bed so we could wake up early the next morning and start our day. The ship docked each morning at an island between eight and nine.

The seven islands on our agenda were Puerto Rico, St. Thomas, Dominica, St. Lucia, Barbados, Antigua, and St. Kitts. We were able to get a little taste of each by spending nine hours visiting them each day. I had so many favorites, but if I had to choose one it was definitely Dominica where I was really able to enjoy nature, which I love. Most parts of the island were very poverty stricken, but there was something about it that captured my heart. Whenever I visited a place I was fascinated by its history. I also enjoyed watching how other people articulated themselves and lived differently from us.

The island was very intriguing with its warm hospitality and serene atmosphere. Its pristine wilderness captured my attention. They had the largest tropical rainforest I had ever seen. The views on the tour we took were absolutely gorgeous. We stopped on the top of a mountain where all I felt I had to do was reach up and grab God's hand. Our tour guide was very personable. She asked us to exit the van and follow her. She led us to this little shack on a section of the mountain. There was a man with a great big smile and a very bubbly personality standing there chopping something up. As we got closer, he introduced himself and started to name all of the foods on the table in sequential order. There were certain fruits he named that sounded foreign to me. Everything was chopped up neatly and put on the table into bowls. He carved designs into the fruit while throwing them in the air and catching them on the tip of a knife. After he finished he would offer us a taste. Some people were a little skeptical about eating the fruit because they were out of their comfort zones. I had no shame; I got a napkin and a fork and had a good time. After a while people started to dig in and clean the bowls. As we were standing there enjoying ourselves and watching him showcase his talent, a huge crack of lightning and a big bolt of thunder came out of nowhere, sounding like the mountain was exploding. After I finished shaking, I was in awe. It seemed so close because we were so high up. The amazing part to me was , as soon as that happened the natives stopped what they were doing, looked up and said, "I hear you God" and then went back to what they were doing. They respected nature and their habitat.

After we tipped the fruit man, we boarded our van and drove up the mountain, moving closer to the point. During our ride, our tour guide explained every type of plant life to us as we rode by slowly. A lot of the plants and flowers would have been a fortune to buy in the states. Their colors, shapes, and smells were

CHAPTER 20 – FREEDOM

amazing. Our next destination was a hiking tour. My mother had no idea of its intensity until we got there. Even though she had a bad knee, she handled it like a trooper. We climbed rocks, crossed manmade bridges, and walked trails, which made us have to pay attention with every movement. Fifteen minutes into the tour, we arrived at a lake called the Emerald pool. It was peaceful, had a waterfall, and was crowded with people. Our tour guide gave us an option to either get in, or just stand on the side and take pictures. Of course most of my group did not budge. I held on firmly and climbed my way down the slippery rocks. The water felt like a soothing warm tub bath. It wasn't a problem getting in; the problem came when it was time to get out. I had to really take my time and pay attention because I did not want the same thing to happen to me as did one lady there. As she was getting out of the lake, she slipped on a rock and ripped her entire big toenail completely off and had to walk all the way back to the entrance bleeding and in pain. Once we got back to our ship, everyone refreshed themselves for dinner. Each night was filled with nothing but entertainment. There was so much to choose from, between stage shows, karaoke, dancing, game shows, eating, and the list goes on.

    I was exhausted after a full week of vacationing. It would have been nice to take another week just to rest! When I got back to work, my answering machine was running over with appointments. At that time, I was without an assistant and had to tackle everything on my own. It was nothing for me to do that in the past. My friends would tease me and say that I needed Ritalin because I moved so fast and was always busy doing something. It was because I was a mother and I had to multi-task everything. My days would sometimes begin at five in the morning and end at eleven at night. At that time I had to do what I had to do. But this time was different. I don't think my body could keep up with everything that came my way. About a week after being back I started having slight heart palpitations. I did not get alarmed because I had them before, and I knew what to do to calm them down. But for some reason, this particular set of palpitations was not subsiding. By the second week, I had enough. I was in the middle of curling a client and my heart felt like it was going to pump out of my chest. When I saw my shirt moving up and down with the rhythm, I dropped the curlers and told my client that I was so sorry, and that I would not be able to finish her hair because I needed to go to the hospital. She was okay with it, and understood. I tried to stay calm so I would not upset Amir or myself. I tried to make him stay home and finish his homework, but he insisted on going with me.

When we got to the hospital, there were about ten people waiting in front of me. Once I signed in they took me right away. Anything dealing with the heart, they take it seriously and put everything else and everybody else on hold. My heart rate was high, and my blood pressure was rising due to my nervousness, so they took me back for more testing. They ran all kinds of test on me but didn't find anything major. After they gave me some fluid through an IV, my palpitations started to calm down a little. Basically I had a built-up condition of being overworked and dehydrated. After six hours of lying in the hospital bed with needles in my arm and being hooked up to heart monitors and machines, I was released. As Amir drove me home, I had a long talk with myself about cutting my work schedule in half. My life was too important, and I was not ready to leave the earth just yet. Things had to change. I needed other outlets outside of being busy. I had to start rearranging things in my life. Even though I was a healthy person and for the most part took care of myself, that did not make me invincible against anything.

As I started to retract, I had to cut a few more days and hours in the salon. I also had to get more help so I could alleviate some of the pressure that was on me. During my time of settling down and reflecting, I also realized that a part of my problem was separate from being overworked. I realized that I had internalized things and pushed them to the back of my mind. I was not even conscious that they were slowly eating away at me. I thought I

CHAPTER 20 – FREEDOM

was okay and clear of any strongholds from my past. As I learned from previous experiences, things will sneak back up on you when you thought you were over them, especially if the root was not cut and dealt with. One weight that was increasingly difficult to bear was my single parenthood. It was taking a toll on me and I ended up having a little breakdown. As those feelings of emptiness started surfacing, insecurities began to creep back in and try to convince me that I had lost it. My mental struggles started taking a toll on me physically.

I remember sitting in my car one evening waiting for Amir to come out of his basketball practice. I decided to call one of my friends who knew Rico's family and asked her if she heard anything about his status in prison, and how long he had left. She told me that he had been out for nine months already. I became extremely quiet. Normally that would have not bothered me; but this time it did. This news actually triggered something within me. All I could think was "He only lives fifteen minutes away from us by car and he couldn't think enough of his son to come and see what he even looks like now?" That thought instantly struck a chord within me and I broke down and started to weep. Amir's face popped up in my head at the time and my heart went out to him. My friend was trying to comfort and encourage me. She told me that I made it this far without him and that I needed to let it go. Honestly, I never thought I had to let anything go, because I didn't think I was holding anything in. Throughout all of those years, I never shed a tear over Rico or the situation. I actually felt sorry for him because I knew that his father wasn't in his life, so I gave him the benefit of the doubt. I figured that a generational curse was passed down to the men in his family and he had no clue about fatherhood, even though he was helping with him and his girlfriend's children. I prayed hard for him that one day his eyes would be opened and that he would recognize that his son needed him. I knew deep down in my heart that God would make a way one day.

Cutting those roots of bitterness and low self-esteem was a

process. God was repairing that last hidden piece of shattered confidence that I had resonating inside me about being a failure as a mother and not having any help for my son. God wanted me to love myself, and obtain my identity from Him, not from what other people thought of me. He didn't want my circumstances to continue to overpower my trust in Him. For a season, I stopped receiving compliments from other people. I began to feel really invisible so I would change my hair every two days and try different outfits on hoping that would help. It seemed as if nothing was working. I didn't like anything about myself. I started putting my head down when I talked to people because I didn't want them looking at me. I felt ugly and old. I knew that it was a lie from the devil, but it was hard for me to fight it. The entire time, God was working on me and taking away any shallowness that might have been lying dormant within me. He was molding me into a beautiful flower of permanent self-confidence. I knew that it would take some time because those old roots were deep. I just wanted to be transformed for good.

    I began to thank God every day. My confidence was soaring, and I felt good knowing that God always had my back. He would never leave me or forsake me as humans had the capability of doing. In addition to that, my son was doing well in school. No more detentions, suspensions, and disciplinary notes were being sent home. That was such a great feeling. He started to enjoy attending church a little more, and I didn't have to fight him. He knew that it was only God who was keeping him and helping him with school. I knew the time was coming when he would be off to college. It had been just the two of us for so long, reality started to hit when I realized it would be just me after he was gone. It was a little frightening, but yet exciting. I marveled at the strength God gave me to be able to handle a teenage boy; I had to trust Him for everything.

    During one of my legendary days in the park reading and relaxing in my car, I started thinking about how God did a three hundred and sixty degree turn around in my life, and also with

CHAPTER 20 – FREEDOM

the people in it. The moment that I prayed for had finally come. I was in church one day at an evening service and saw one of Rico's cousins. Rico and his cousin were extremely close. There was no separating them at one point. I was in total shock to see him because the last memory that I had of him had nothing to do with church. He said that he was there with his wife and they were just visiting. He then asked me if I had spoken with Amir's father. As soon as I told him no, he excused himself and went outside to call him. When he got him on the phone he came back in and asked me if I could come out and talk. While walking down the steps, he raised the phone to my ear. Rico was on the other end sounding hyper and cheerful as usual. He started asking me about Amir and his well-being, and then told me that he wanted to get in touch with him, and asked if he could have his phone number. I told him that he could actually get his number from Amir himself. By that time Amir was coming out of church with his friends because service was over. I said goodbye with gratefulness in my heart and then passed the phone to Amir. They talked for at least a half hour. It would have continued but his cousin had to leave, so he needed his phone back. Amir and his father exchanged numbers and started talking regularly. By now it was near the end of Amir's last year in high school. His father started coming to lacrosse games, basketball games, and even made his prom and graduation. My heart was full and I felt blessed. I held no record of wrong in my heart for him at all. I was just happy that he finally showed some consistent concern and care. I was proud of him for humbling himself and making that move and realizing that his son needed some kind of connection whether he showed it or not. Once again, God was faithful to his Word and my prayers.

 I also reached a turning point concerning my stepfather. As I expressed earlier He and I did not see eye to eye at all growing up. Our personalities clashed and we stayed out of each other's way. As time went on and he and I both got older, it was hard because I would see how he interacted with everyone else at his church. I felt like he knew how to relate to everyone else but me. As he matured and became an older man, I really started to see his heart for who he was. I believed that he loved me, but it was hard to tell. He wasn't the most affectionate, and neither was I. We had never even shared a hug. He and my brother were really close, especially since my brother's father was deceased. My stepfather and I never really communicated much, but I knew that he cared. Not once in our lifetimes did we say I love you to each other. It was hard for the both of us to say something that just seemed to be foreign for us. Of course it was awkward every time we were in each other's presence but as years passed we learned how to be tension free. Both of us were trying, and we got beyond surface level into a little more depth. We started to do little things for each other. A few times during my vacations I would buy him a souvenir. Because he liked fishing so much I brought him a nice carved wooden fish with his name engraved in it. There was also a time that I got a suite hotel room for him and my mother on his birthday. Another married couple that they always would hang out with came along also. They had a good time. My stepfather stayed in the pool where you could always find him. And they all went out to dinner and came home the next day.

What really touched my heart was when I came back from my seven day cruise with my mother, son, and her friends. After I was dropped off at my house from the airport, I walked in the door and was shocked. I had a beautiful chandelier hanging from the ceiling in my front hallway. My stepfather had bought it and put it in to surprise me. That melted my heart because he did that for me. What really made it special was that he was not in the best shape anymore. His walking was limited and he actually climbed that tall ladder by himself just for me. My hallway ceiling was really high and it took an extra-long ladder to reach it, but he did it.

My stepfather kept getting a pain in his bad leg where he had screws from one of his motorcycle accidents and my mother took

CHAPTER 20 – FREEDOM

him to the hospital to get checked out. After they ran the test they found a huge blood clot in his leg. They decided to do some more scans and tests, and then found cancer. It was in his colon. My mother being the calm person she was, even though I knew it was fear under control, told me he had cancer and that they were not sure of the stage yet. Around that same time my brother was scheduled to leave for Afghanistan in a couple of weeks. I had to think reasonably and be strong for my mother because I knew it was too much for her at one time. She had just gotten out of the hospital a few weeks prior. When she told me the news I instantly started praying for my brother not to go to war and for my stepfather to be healed. When I prayed for them I prayed nonstop. I believed in my heart that something was going to break through. I knew that God listened to me and that if it was His will it would be done. Two weeks later my brother found out that he did not have to go to war. It was a miracle because once you are scheduled you have to go. God knew that he needed to be around. The day after my stepfather went to the hospital, he and my mom were in the room and the doctor came in and said he was already at stage four and there was nothing they could do. He had less than a year to live. My mother was in shock, and my stepfather played it strong as he always did. He didn't have a quitter spirit so he hoped for the best, and kept saying that he was going to be healed, and he needed to leave the hospital and go on with his life.

    He was still very active at seventy four. He couldn't sit still for too long. As months were going by he was getting weaker from the chemotherapy that he had to take. We all watched him go from being a vibrant man to wanting to sleep all the time. Because he was so determined, when he wasn't asleep he was working on something around the house, still pulling weeds, lifting heavy boxes, you name it. He even did all the driving on a ten hour trip to North Carolina with my mother to see my brother and his children. At about the sixth month, my mother gave him a seventy fifth birthday party, and had all of their church family and friends over. A lot of people showed up, and it was standing room only. He really enjoyed himself but you could see the sadness on his face at the same time. He kept busy by making most of the food as he normally did.

Everybody kept telling him to sit down and rest but he wanted to do everything himself. About nine months in, I started spending the night at the house to help my mother. It was definitely tough for her, and because they lived an hour and twenty minutes from the city, it was hard for a lot of people to get to them. As he started weakening there were more emergency hospital visits. It was very unpredictable. During one of those visits when we thought we lost him because his sugar wouldn't go down, I was at the hospital with them. My mom had to leave the room to take care of some paperwork and it was just him and I. It was so awkward because we still had that hidden 'I love you' in our minds. So we would just talk casually at surface level. He asked me about Amir and what my plans were for the future. I told him and then he started getting very weak because his blood sugar kept rising. Then my mother and his ex-wife and daughter came into the room. That was the first time that I actually met the both of them. When he came to, our conversation was on hold. There were other opportunities to talk, but we didn't. Again we both understood how we felt. I do believe that he wasn't too sure how I felt at times because I wasn't verbal. I didn't know how to be, especially with him. The affection that he did show was when he referred to me as his daughter to others. He never called me step- daughter from day one. I remember being four years old and he got on his knees to come down to my height and asked me if I could call him dad. I said 'No' with a stern voice, and was adamant after that to call him by his first name.

During the last couple of days my mother wouldn't tell me what the doctors were telling her. She kept it inside like she always

CHAPTER 20 – FREEDOM

did. She was the type, if you don't ask, she won't tell. And even if you did ask she would change the subject. I figured it out that the doctors were giving her updates on his status as far as days he had left and that he should have been in hospice care. But because my stepfather was who he was, he was very adamant about being home and sitting in his Jacuzzi tub to soak and relax. So we brought him home, and had to end up calling emergency the same night. My mother kept getting these feelings about what was going to happen. Back at the hospital he kept getting these visitations from God. When he would be in his right mind from the medicine wearing off, he would share what happened. One time he said that he saw an image of Jesus sitting in the hospital chair across from his bed and they were talking. He then said that all of his diseased organs left his body and were sitting in the palm of God's hand. He said that God told him to speak over them. There were a few times when he would just randomly start talking about God on a regular basis, saying things like, God is infinite and He can do whatever he wants to do. But when he would say these things it was as if God was speaking through him, because it didn't sound like him.

My sister in law flew up from Florida to see him. She left my niece and one of my nephews because they both had school. My other two nephews were with my brother and were going to come with him. My sister in-law and my stepfather had a really tight bond from over the years of us traveling to Florida every year. He didn't know she was coming so when I brought her up to the hospital and she walked into the room, tears rolled down his face. He couldn't talk at the time because his voice would come and go. It was a special moment for the both of them. As time was moving forward we knew what was coming. Two days before he passed he had a room full of visitors that Sunday. He was being himself as usual cracking jokes on people and calling them names. He then said, "why is everybody coming to see me, am I dying or something?" While everyone was there he wanted to shave his beard. So the nurse gave him the razor kit and we held the mirror for him while he shaved in slow motion. After everyone left, my mother, my sister in-law, and I were still there. A couple hours later, I decided to leave and go back to the house to cook dinner so that when my mom and sister in-law came home they would have something to eat. As I was walking out, he asked me where I was going and I told him that I needed to go to the house and cook dinner, and that I would see him tomorrow. That was the last words we had with each other because he died the next morning.

I was at peace but it was hard to think about my mother's wellbeing. She was already going through some physical challenges of her own and I was concerned that my stepfather's death and their separation would be very heavy for her. Of course she had her moments because her husband of thirty years was gone, but she knew that he had made it to heaven so that gave her some solace. Her strength in God played a big part as well.

She was a tough cookie. She had been through so much in her lifetime and made it out okay so God knew He could trust her with more. I would look at her sometimes and wonder how she managed to deal with so many deaths and continue to keep going. I knew there were times when the devil would try and steal her joy because she would show signs of sadness quite a bit. It bothered me because I wanted to protect her. I did not like to see her sad or go through any internal anguish. I remember as a young child walking by her bedroom door on my way to the bathroom and I would see her sitting on the side of the bed looking sad, and that would hurt me. So I would try to come up with something to say that was totally off topic than what she may have been feeling at the time, just to get her to talk. I did the same thing even in my adult years when I saw that she was troubled. I would also come over her house and go to the supermarket and buy groceries and cook. Sometimes I bought a lot of food and would make a variety of choices and freeze them for her so she could just pull a container out whenever she got hungry - just like my grandmother showed me. It was a bit of an

CHAPTER 20 – FREEDOM

emotional ride for me because I knew that my mom had a long road ahead of her, but what gave me comfort was the fact that I knew she trusted God with her whole heart. She also knew how to pray so I realized that she would be okay. She was very well supported by her church family so that made me happy as well and gave me peace. The lesson I learned from the entire situation was to always trust God no matter what happens. People are not guaranteed to stay with you the rest of your life. And life still has to continue even after they are gone.

Even though my stepfather and I never hugged or said I love you, we knew. I was settled in my spirit that our time on this earth together was not in vain. God had a purpose for everything. It took me a long time to figure that out but I am glad I did. For the most part of my childhood and adult life me and my stepfather's relationship was empty and a blur but I am glad that we did have a few years to really bond in our own unexplainable way. Even as time passed I would sometimes sit quietly and reminisce on some of the good times we all had when our entire immediate family would get together on Thanksgiving in Florida. My stepfather was always the driver and the one arranging the trips. He made sure he booked those timeshare weeks a year in advance so there would be no problems. I realized that he is gone now and all of the kids are grown up and don't want to do Disney World anymore so that particular tradition was broken. But as I said in agreement along with my mother, brother, and sister in – law, the kids can still go when they get a little older and have their own families because the vacations are accessible to them for free. At that moment of me saying that I realized all things must come to an end but as soon as you open your eyes there is a new beginning. That thought resonated in my spirit so much because I did not want to take life for granted - I knew my life was just a vapor. I didn't want to wake up every morning and continue the same routine that always was. I wanted to live everyday as if it was my last. Just like the Bible says "no one knows the day or the hour." God in His infinite wisdom knew what was going to

IN MY MIND

happen in my life before I was even born so there was no surprise of how it turned out and what I went through. I didn't know why God did the things He did or allowed the things He allowed but I know that I tried my best to walk upright and trust Him. He knows my end before my beginning. He said in the end "I win." There are no losers on His team. It may sound weird but I would not take back any of the craziness that I experienced in my youth or the mental torture I experienced in my adulthood because it was all worth it. I get joy from being able to help someone else.

During those few months after my stepfather's passing I practically stayed at my mother's house every night. I would drive across the bridge almost every day after I closed the salon. It took me about an hour and twenty minutes but I didn't mind, I would get my favorite songs on, turn up the radio with loud bass, crack my windows to get a little fresh air, and enjoy the stillness of the night during my drive. Sometimes I would maneuver my clients around and have them all come on the same days so I could stay at my mom's house for four days in a row without having to leave. One good thing was Amir being away at college so I didn't have to worry about being home. I was free to get around without having to worry about taking him to any sport practices or getting him to school. All I had to do was send him money on his card, and he was taken care of. The only other responsibility that I had, outside of making sure that my mom and Amir were okay, was my grandma. She and I were very close. I had to make sure she got out of the house. So, almost everywhere I went, during the week, I would ask her to come along. She even rode with me to Amir's college which was two hours away if her arthritis would allow her to. Sometimes, she couldn't sit in one place without moving for too long or she would get stiff, so her long rides were determined by how she felt that day. We really enjoyed our time together because we had so much in common. We both enjoyed some of the same foods which allowed us to have a good time in the supermarkets and produce junctions. We also enjoyed some of the same stores and would get excited over the smallest things.

CHAPTER 20 - FREEDOM

She was my riding partner. Her walking started to become a little limited so we couldn't do some of the same things that we used to do. I remember she used to catch the bus over to my salon to get her hair done but within the last year it has been hard for her. Needless to say, she is doing well.

Things were settling in and life was moving forward. The sun was shining brighter and my heart was pumping love. Dreams were more vivid and my vision was attainable. I could see clearly what God was doing. My spirit was at such peace because I knew my future would be greater than my past. I knew God was preparing me for something because I could feel it. My life was taking a turn. I started reading more and going to classes to gain knowledge on programs and other businesses I wanted to start. I began practicing my teaching skills because I knew the opportunity would be coming soon. I was preparing myself for things to come. I did things ahead of time because I did not like to get left behind. I wanted to be ready when an opportunity presented itself. Of course the devil tried distracting me while I was in the process of reinvention, but I had to stay focused and fight. I couldn't allow the little menial things to get me off track anymore. There were definitely things that happened within my close and distant family that I could have allowed to make me quit but I had to show God that I trusted Him to take care of me. By no means am I perfect or have I arrived, but one thing I do know for sure- God has my back.

IN MY MIND

Words of Encouragement

You are beautiful

You are special

You are amazing

You are loved

You are fearfully and wonderfully made

You are courageous

You are number one

You are a winner

You are intelligent

You are important

You are a diamond

You are successful

You are strong

You are powerful

You are creative

IN MY MIND

You are blessed

You are worthy

You are not alone

You are not a mistake

You are not a loser

You are not a failure

You are not ugly

You are not stupid

You are not weak

You are not stuck

You are not your circumstance

You are created in God's own

image and His likeness!

Your Personal Prayer To God

Father,
*   Thank You so much for loving me the way that You do. I appreciate You being patient with me and giving me breath to breathe every morning.*
*   Please help me to know You personally, and I ask You to forgive me of my sins.*
*   I come to You in the name of Jesus. I acknowledge to You that I am a sinner, and I am sorry for my sins and the life that I have lived. You said in Your Holy Word, Romans 10:9, that if we confess the Lord our God and believe in our hearts that God raised Jesus from the dead, we shall be saved.*
*   I confess Jesus as my Lord and Savior, and I believe that He is Your Son and that He shed His blood for me so I would not perish but have eternal life. You raised Him from the dead.*
*   Come into my heart. Fill my soul. Change me. Mold me. Heal me.*
Deliver me. Transform my life and cleanse me. Give me a new mind, a new heart, and a new spirit. I surrender to Your will.
*   Thank You for saving me by grace through faith. All good gifts come from above and there is nothing we can do to earn our salvation.*

*   Romans 10:9-10*

IN MY MIND

Scriptures For Life

Anxiety:
Be anxious for nothing, but in everything by prayer and supplication, with thanksgiving, let your request be made known to God; and the peace of God which surpasses all understanding, will guard your hearts and minds through Christ Jesus.

Philippians 4:6-7

Confidence:
Have I not commanded you? Be strong and of good courage; do not be afraid, nor be dismayed, for the Lord your God is with you wherever you go.

Joshua 1:9

Depression:
Therefore humble yourselves under the mighty hand of God, that He may exalt you in due time, casting all your cares upon Him, because He cares for you.

1 Peter 5:6-7

IN MY MIND

Faith:
But without faith it is impossible to please Him, for he who comes to God must believe that He is, and that He is a rewarder of those who diligently seek Him.

Hebrews 11:6

Fear:
There is no fear in love; but perfect love cast out fear, because fear involves torment. But he who fears has not been made perfect in love. We love Him because He first loved us.

1 John 4:18

Peace:
You will keep him in perfect peace, whose mind is stayed on You, because he trusts in you.

Isaiah 26:3

Seeking God:
But from there you will seek the Lord your God, and you will find Him if you seek Him with all your heart and with all your soul.

Hebrews 4:29

Prayer:
Let us therefore come boldly to the throne of grace, that we may obtain mercy and find grace to help in time of need.

Hebrews 4:16

SCRIPTURES FOR LIFE

Rejection:
What then shall we say to these things? If God is for us, who can be against us?

Romans 8:31

The Mind:
And do not be conformed to this world, but be transformed by the renewing of your mind, that you may prove what is that good and acceptable and perfect will of God.

Romans 12:2

Worship: Therefore since we are receiving a kingdom which cannot be shaken, let us have grace, by which we may serve God acceptably with reverence and godly fear. For our God is a consuming fire.

Hebrews 12:28

About The Author

A former at-risk teen, turned youth/young adult advocate and entrepreneur, Candra Ward is on a purpose-driven mission to inspire and change the lives of every teen and young adult that crosses her path. Her volunteer work as mentor for at-risk teen girls and young mothers over the past 15 years was motivated by the dangerous and traumatic experiences she endured as a young girl herself.

Born and raised in Philadelphia, PA, Candra grew up in the inner city, but was afforded a decent upbringing. It was not always easy. At the tender age of 15 she became pregnant. After giving birth at 16 she was one of the best examples a young mother could be. Her struggles with self-esteem created obstacles in her life that caused her to make unwise decisions at times. However, as she matured, she had a greater perspective of life, and a full turnaround of victory.

IN MY MIND

Through all of her turmoil, Candra was a true fighter. She was very determined despite all of the physical, emotional, and mental abuse that she endured through her relationships with men. One of her goals was to be self-sufficient and successful. An entrepreneur at heart, Candra worked hard and made a good life for herself and her son.

Prior to reinventing herself, Candra moved to Florida, willingly leaving behind Relax Your Mind Hair Studio, the hair salon she owned and operated for nine years in Philadelphia. Her transition to Florida created an exciting phase of her life where she is taking on new challenges and blessings. Her desire to break the barriers of those who suffer in silence prompted her to publish the story of her life, *In My Mind*, and share her message all over the country and abroad as a speaker and life-coach.

Candra's primary goal is to help youth and young adults overcome obstacles and give them hope. With her strong yet gentle demeanor which commands attention when she speaks, Candra has dedicated herself to pouring wisdom and love into messages of self-esteem, goal setting, and beauty, accessible for all young people regardless of their background or culture. Her desire is to see them become who they were created to be.

For more information about Candra, her personal coaching services, special events, booking, and products, please visit her website:

www.CandraWard.com

Book Club Guide

About this Guide

The following guide is intended to help you obtain understanding and healing for yourself or someone else. I hope this book has been a source of enlightenment and a blessing to you.

In My Mind Book Club Guide

Discussion Questions:

1. How do you feel about Candra's promiscuity in the beginning of the book? Also share how you think she felt about her lifestyle.

2. Do you think Candra's relationships with her family: her mother, father and stepfather especially, influenced how she reacted to other relationships? Explain your answer.

3. Chapter Four describes Candra's wake-up call from God. What do you think made her surrender? Do you think it was a challenge for her to embrace her new life? Explain your answer.

4. How do you think Candra was able to sustain being a single mother? If you are a single parent, what helps you maintain balance? What resources do you rely on?

IN MY MIND

5. Throughout the book, Candra outwardly portrayed strength but many times she really felt weak on the inside. What do you think made her that way?

6. Candra's mind was continually bombarded with distorted thoughts about herself, and it sometimes made her reduce or limit who she really was. Do you think those thoughts were from the devil, or her past? Explain your reasoning.

7. In your opinion, why was the plague of inconsistency of staying on the right track mentally and relationally so strong in Candra's life?

8. Whatever Candra put her mind to she got it done. Do you credit her faith or tenacity for causing her to reach her goals? Explain.

9. How do you feel about Candra's desperate prayers to God?

10. Do you agree that Candra had to go through her tumultuous times in order for her to be able to help someone else, or do you think that those experiences could have been avoided? Candra is a naturally energized person and a go-getter. How can you relate? What have you accomplished?

11. Do you find yourself being someone different with other people than who you really are? If so, explain why and how it started.

12. Do you believe it is truly possible for someone to overcome their past and become a new person? Please explain your position.

13. In your opinion, when did Candra's final healing process start taking place? Discuss a healing process of yours and how God helped you, or is helping you.

BOOK CLUB GUIDE

14. What is your attitude about God in your life? How has He been or how could He be a Father to you?

What To Do Next?

- Go to CandraWard.com to post your comments, and blogs.

- Contact Candra for bookings:

- Read scriptures for life before you start your meetings and add them in with your discussions.

Made in the USA
Lexington, KY
07 February 2014